The Chávez Code

Cracking US Intervention in Venezuela

The Chávez Code
Cracking US Intervention in Venezuela

by Eva Golinger
foreword by Saul Landau

OLIVE
BRANCH
PRESS

An imprint of Interlink Publishing Group, Inc.
www.interlinkbooks.com

To the memory of Danilo Anderson,
who was assassinated in Caracas on November 18, 2004

First published in 2006 by

OLIVE BRANCH PRESS
An imprint of Interlink Publishing Group, Inc.
46 Crosby Street, Northampton, Massachusetts 01060
www.interlinkbooks.com

Library of Congress Cataloging-in-Publication Data
Golinger, Eva.
[Código Chávez. English]
The Chávez code : cracking US intervention in Venezuela / by Eva Golinger.—1st ed.
p. cm.
Includes bibliographical references and index.
ISBN 1-56656-647-9 (pbk.)
1. United States—Foreign relations—Venezuela. 2. Venezuela—Foreign
relations—United States. 3. Chávez Frías, Hugo. 4. Venezuela—Politics and
government—1999- 5. Venezuela—History—Attempted coup, 2002. I. Title.
E183.8.V3G6513 2006
327.7308709'0511—dc22
2005036054

ISBN 13: 978-1-56656-647-6

Printed and bound in the United States of America

CONTENTS

FOREWORD

∙∙∙

The Shape of Things to Come

When about-to-be Secretary of State Condoleezza Rice declared at her January 2005 confirmation hearings in the Senate that Venezuela belonged in the Latin American equivalent of the axis of evil (with Cuba, of course), every informed citizen should have heard warning bells. Rice's declarations added to the growing body of official and non-official clamor demanding "action" against President Hugo Chávez. But what terrible crime had he committed?

A *Washington Post* editorial found Chávez guilty of an "assault on private property." They referred to Chávez's "war on idle landed estates," and labeled taking over idle land as another step toward establishing dictatorship. The editorial omitted the fact that Venezuelans had reached consensus on the subject. Indeed, even some of Chávez's business enemies agreed that all Venezuelans would benefit from ridding themselves of the large idle *latifundios*. The editorial also failed to mention the huge number of landless people across Latin America, the shocking disparity of income between rich and poor, and the fact, emphasized by UN researchers, that the US-backed "free market" solution had contributed to the worsening conditions.

Rice also failed to mention any of Chávez's specific "crimes." But, backed by Castro-hating Senator Mel Martinez (R-FL), she raised the definition of verbal chutzpah to new levels by accusing Chávez of interfering in the affairs of other nations. Can any serious person imagine a high US official accusing *others* of interfering?

Did memory fail this Solonic body? Did Senators forget that in March 2003 President Bush invaded Iraq, without a trace of *casus belli*? Indeed, over the last century the United States has interfered in the affairs of almost every third world country.

The senators and the media also failed to confront Rice about her knowledge of US support for a coup in Venezuela in April 2002 and about ongoing efforts to undermine a government that received solid electoral support on three separate occasions.

Ignorance, denial, or avoidance? It doesn't matter. Citizens need to know what US operatives are doing around the world to alter the destiny of others. Venezuelans chose Chávez in democratic elections on three occasions. That's why Eva Golinger's book should hit the moral reader with a shock—of recognition, not surprise. She lays out a well-written, carefully researched history to show that the US government has made a concerted effort to destabilize and overthrow the elected government of Venezuela. She demonstrates that the threads of imperial history have far more strength than the republican principles that once served as foundation for US laws and treaties.

She allows the documents she obtained through the Freedom of Information Act (FOIA) to guide her fastidious reasoning on the US role in attempting to overthrow the Chávez government. All students of history know that the CIA overthrew the government of Iran in 1953, Guatemala in 1954, tried to or did assassinate Patrice Lumumba in the Congo in 1960, orchestrated an invasion of Cuba at the Bay of Pigs in 1961, knocked off the Goulart government in Brazil in 1964, and participated in the destabilization and coup in Chile from 1970 to 1973. The CIA operated the murderous Phoenix Program in Vietnam after the United States illegally invaded and occupied that country for more than a decade. Are you starting to yawn over this very partial list of interventions?

In each case, the CIA always emerges as the black hat, the agency ready and willing to take the rap. But the blame goes higher. The CIA functions as one the President's Praetorian Guard units that become activated every time people of a foreign nation elect a leader who plans to redistribute wealth to the poor. A veritable red alarm bell sounds in Washington's national security apparatus and, as if in a Pavlovian experiment, the CIA and the other attack dogs respond automatically to the stimulus. Occasionally, presidents and secretaries of state repent—years later of course—for the damage caused by "aberrant" CIA operations. Colin Powell apologized for Chile—30 years after the United States helped instigate the September 11, 1973 massacre there. Bill Clinton said he was sorry for what the CIA did in Guatemala—almost 40 years later. As many as 100,000 Guatemalans died as a result of the CIA's overthrow of their democratically elected government.

In the case of Venezuela, as this book makes clear, the US government added yet another stain to its national honor. Golinger shows the incontrovertible facts of Washington's attempt to overthrow the government of Hugo Chávez. She obtained the documents from national security sources—a vestige of older freedoms—and turns them into prosecutorial swords that generate moral outrage instead of wounds to the plotters and liars. I visualize high officials placing hands on Bibles and swearing to uphold the laws while holding images in their minds of crossed fingers.

Golinger's prose radiates a fierce sense of the law's moral importance. This young Venezuelan-American attorney uses her fact-filled pages almost like a legal brief, to show the jury—the reading public—that the defendant, the US government, acted in a premeditated conspiracy with the wealthy classes of Venezuela to undo a democratic process in that country: free and fair elections, a functioning legislative and legal system.

Worse, as the brief continues, we see that the US government worked with its Venezuelan (and Israeli) counterparts to involve the mass media in its efforts to mis- and dis-inform the world's public as to the nature of reality before, during, and after the April 2002 coup. During the

Presidential debates of 2004, John Kerry eagerly fed at the interventionist trough. He dutifully followed the Bush line—lie—that the democratically elected President of the Bolivarian Republic of Venezuela, Hugo Chávez, constitutes a threat to the United States. Kerry bought into the media portrayal of Chávez as an authoritarian villain who seeks to "Cubanize" his country.

When I met Eva Golinger in Caracas in December 2004, we both observed that, contrary to the US stereotype, Chávez was trying to redistribute wealth and power to the majority—the poor. Far from acting like a "terrorist threat," Chávez showed himself to be a well-educated, clear-thinking, and responsible political leader.

Washington never complained when a kleptocracy governed Venezuela for more than three decades, until the mid-1990s. We heard no complaints from Bush, Kerry, Rice, and the major media when in 1989 Venezuelan soldiers and police killed as many as 2,000 protestors (the *Caracazo*) who refused to tolerate more "structural adjustment" from the IMF.

The federally funded National Endowment for Democracy (NED) directors did not see a threat to democracy when Venezuelan presidents routinely kissed up to the US in international fora. They saw nothing wrong with shooting poor people when they protested. The very misnamed NED understands "promoting democracy" to consist of financing a small and wealthy minority who reject the ballot when they lose elections. Indeed, as Golinger makes clear in her book, NED funded some of the very people who backed the 2002 military coup.

The Chávez Code not only reveals and analyzes the nefarious plots, but sets a model for researchers. Students and professors alike should imitate Golinger's care in presenting and interpreting documents and drawing conclusions based on the facts.

—*Saul Landau*

PREFACE

···

Finally, *The Chávez Code* has found its way into the belly of the beast, and will make its way to audiences throughout the English-speaking world. I am thrilled with this edition of my book, published by Olive Branch Press, and honored to have the opportunity to reach new readers with this account of the latest US intervention attempts in revolutionary Venezuela.

It may be of use to know something of the book's history. The first edition was published in Spanish by the Editorial Ciencias Sociales in Cuba and released in the Fourth International Book Fair in Santiago de Cuba on March 5, 2005. I never expected such a magnificent international reaction to the publication of my very first book. The second edition was launched on March 21, 2005, published by the Fondo Editorial Question in Caracas, Venezuela. The 5,000 copies released were sold during the first week after publication. Immediately, 5,000 more were published and gone within two weeks. In Venezuela, they say that the measure of success of a book is when it is bootlegged and sold in the street. Well, *The Chávez Code* was bootlegged at the speed of light and sold by practically every street vendor. I don't support piracy, but I do want as many people as possible to have access to my book. And so, the third edition was published, again by the Editorial Ciencias Sociales in Cuba, but this time, more than 100,000 copies were released. I gave out more than 25,000 free copies in the streets of Venezuela. Within a few months, the remaining 75,000 were gone, consumed by hungry readers throughout Venezuela and Latin America. In November 2005, the fourth edition was published by Monte Avila Editores Latinoamericana and is presently in distribution throughout

Venezuela and the rest of the continent. The German version, *Kreuzzug Gegen Venezuela der Chávez Code,* was released in November 2005 by Zambon Verlag.

A lot has happened since I first wrote *The Chávez Code* at the end of 2004. I have received hundreds more declassified documents from distinct US government agencies, evidencing even more destabilizing actions against the Venezuelan government. We have witnessed an increase in aggressions toward Venezuela during 2005 and the beginning of 2006 from US government officials. There has been a growing regional presence of US military bases and soldiers in the continent, including a new military base in Paraguay and various visits by US warships to the Caribbean region, close to the Venezuelan border. The media campaign against Chávez has become more and more hostile, aggressive, and manipulative over the past year and the Pentagon even launched a new team of military experts in psychological operations (PSYOPS), the Joint Psychological Operations Support Element (JPSOE, or "gypsy") to initiate contra-propaganda campaigns in Venezuela and Bolivia.

The Reverend Pat Robertson called for the assassination of President Chávez in September 2005 and caused an international scandal. But Washington remained silent. They say that silence is complicity. Extremist anti-Chávez groups protected by the US have grown. Calls of violence toward Venezuela increase daily in local Miami media, and the US government awards their authors political asylum instead of questioning such anti-democratic behavior. The National Endowment for Democracy (NED) gave a new $100,000 grant to the opposition group Súmate, and President George W. Bush received its director, Maria Corina Machado, in the Oval Office in May 2005—it was a great photo-op. The US Congress authorized $9 million more to USAID and the NED to fund opposition groups in Venezuela during 2006, an election year. And the NED also launched an international movement to promote its interventionist model—The World Movement for Democracy. Súmate appears as a member of the movement, but that's no surprise to us anymore.

Officials of the Drug Enforcement Agency (DEA) were accused of espionage and sabotage in Venezuela and expelled from the country, along with a military attaché from the US embassy in Caracas, John Correa. And more revelations about the malicious Plan Balboa, a plan to invade Venezuela, have circulated over the last few months. In October 2005, a Doctrine for Asymmetric War against Venezuela was published by the Institute for Strategic Studies of the US Army and Venezuela was named in the 2006 Department of Defense's Quadrennial Defense Review as a "growing threat." As a prize for the success of my book in Latin America, I was named an "official troublemaker" by the Pentagon. What an honor!

And so, dear readers, enjoy this long-awaited edition of *The Chávez Code* and remain alert for my next report on US intervention in Venezuela. I am ever more committed to bringing to light the injustices caused at the hands of the US government and conducted in the name of the US people.

ACKNOWLEDGMENTS

··

Investigating United States intervention in Venezuela is not an easy task. There are risks and there are sacrifices. The overwhelming displays of love, solidarity, and support that I have received from people around the world, especially in Venezuela, have guided me and encouraged me to continue this difficult journey. The sincere and powerful embrace I have received from the determined people of Venezuela, and their heartfelt appreciation for the revelation of the information I have discovered, have made all the sacrifices and dangers encountered during this investigation worthwhile.

The risks have been many, the dangers always present. I have received many death threats from anonymous sources and my legal practice has diminished, due in part to client fears, political disagreements, and my own dedication to this investigation, which in many ways has taken over my life.

Otto Reich referred to me as "an agent of the Chávez government," unsure as to whether I was paid or unpaid for my work. For the record, this entire investigation has been conducted out of my own pocket and my bank records will verify. I even had to move from a beautiful duplex in Brooklyn, where I lived for three years, to an old family home out in Long Island because finances became so tight. So, Mr. Reich, if I am to be an "agent" of anyone, I am an agent of the people, a people struggling to achieve a more harmonious, just world.

This book would not have been possible without the love, support, and expertise of many brilliant people who have entered my life over the past few years and decades. I am indebted to Jeremy Bigwood for his master FOIA skills; Andrés for genius ideas; Roselena for focus and clear thinking;

Angel for encouragement and brainstorming; Wendys for incredible photography and solidarity; Balza for always believing in me; my mother, father, and brother Jon for amazing, unconditional support and love; my furry little Lola who gave me company, love, and warmth during late-night research and writing; and to my family in Mérida, my friends Piki, Ernesto, Celia, Gretchen, Sarah, Lely, Gilberto, Temir, Samuel Moncada, Mario Calderón, and other *compañeros*, without whom daily life would not be as pleasurable.

But most of all, I owe this book to the powerful, brave and *lindo pueblo venezolano* and their brilliant leader. I can only hope that the following pages aid true seekers of social justice.

All documents discussed in this book are available on my website, www.venezuelafoia.info.

INTRODUCTION

··

W hat message do you have for my country?" General Rafael Oropeza had no answer for the United States military officer standing before him in the Fort Tiuna military barracks in Caracas, Venezuela.

It was April 11, 2002, and before the day was over, a coup would take place against the democratically elected president of the country, Hugo Chávez Frías.

Colonel James Rodgers, a registered military attaché at the US embassy in Caracas, repeated the question. At the time of the coup d'etat, General Oropeza was in charge of the registry of all those entering and leaving Fort Tiuna, the base of Venezuela's Ministry of Defense and the nation's largest military fort. Photographs of Rodgers driving around the Fort during the days of the coup were later published in a national Venezuelan daily, *Ultimas Noticias*. But the US State Department has denied the existence of any James Rodgers, despite the fact that he was found inscribed as a military attaché in the Embassy in Caracas.

When Rodgers realized General Oropeza had no answer to his encrypted question, he asked instead for Efraín Vasquéz Velasco. Vasquéz Velasco, a member at the time of the high military command of Venezuela's armed forces, was one of the leaders of the coup against President Chávez. From just these few words, Rodgers made it clear that he was the US liaison with the Venezuelan military officials executing the coup.

But the most incriminating moment for the US military came on April 8, 2002, at an exclusive farewell gathering for a Chinese military attaché at the elite Hotel Meliá in Caracas. It was on that evening that US naval officer David Cazares mistook General Roberto González Cárdenas for

General Nestor González González. It was an easy mistake. Both men were bald, about the same height, and wore a military officer uniform, dressed with honors and a nametag that simply said "González."

Cazares sidled up to General González and accusatorily asked, "Why haven't you contacted the ships that we have on the coast and the submarine submerged in La Guaira? What has happened? Why has no one contacted me? What are you waiting for?"

General González had no idea what this US naval officer was talking about, but before he could respond, a military attaché from Brazil approached him at the party to say goodbye. Cazares took advantage of the distraction to ask Captain Moreno Leal, standing nearby, if that was the General González, "the one who had been stationed at the border." Moreno responded, "That is General González, but I don't know if he was stationed at the border."

Cazares then continued his interrogation of General González Cárdenas, insistently inquiring into why no one had yet contacted him or the three ships and the submarine standing by right off the Venezuelan coast. Prudently, González Cárdenas limited his response to a mere "I'll find out." The two met again in the elevator, leaving the gathering. "This has an operational cost. I await your answer," said Cazares firmly.

Venezuelan General Nestor González González was a key player in the April 2002 coup d'etat against President Chávez. On April 10, 2002, General Nestor González González went on national television demanding that Chávez step down, "or else." In a post-coup television broadcast on April 12, 2002, it was revealed that González González's statement was made purely for the purpose of keeping President Chávez from traveling to Costa Rica, where he was scheduled to participate in an Organization of American States (OAS) General Assembly meeting that very same day. The plot had been successful. Chávez remained in Venezuela and the coup was executed as planned. Yet the erroneous interaction between Cazares and González Cárdenas days before was overlooked and dismissed by Venezuelan investigators after the brief ouster of President Chávez, and the US just let it slide. Cazares' term in Venezuela was later cut short and he was shipped off to Chile once the *Ultimas Noticias* article began to raise some eyebrows.[1]

Other tidbits relating to movements of the US military during the days leading up to and during the coup that have been left hanging include a phone call from Colonel Donald F. MacCarty, US Air Force attaché, to the Intelligence Division of the Venezuelan Armed Forces on Friday April 12, 2002, requesting authorization for the flyover of a Hercules-130 that was transporting "diplomatic cargo," 5 kilograms of lithium battery, 5 kilograms of compressed oxygen class 2.2, 56 kilograms of ammunition, 40 kilograms of demolition cartridges, and 2 kilograms of detonators. The request for flyover authorization was cancelled by Colonel MacCarty via fax on April 15, 2002. It never took place.

On Saturday, April 13, 2002, while President Chávez was being held prisoner on La Orchila, a small island off the coast of Venezuela, a US ship was detected nearby facilitating small airplanes engaging in flyover exercises. No authorization had been given by Venezuelan authorities for such activities and the US government later stated the exercises were "unrelated" to the situation unfolding in Venezuela and were just normal practices. Witnesses also attest to several Black Hawk helicopters landing at the Maiquetia airport outside of Caracas on April 11–12, 2002. The US has denied such allegations.

US submarines, naval ships, Black Hawk helicopters, flyovers, coup plotting... while many of these facts and rumors are semi-substantiated and still controversial, the full story of US military involvement in the April 2002 coup d'etat against President Chávez remains a mystery. But what has been uncovered and deciphered through a meticulous and ongoing investigation of US involvement in the coup and other destabilization efforts in Venezuela is a very complex and sophisticated intervention crafted by a US government with decades of "regime change" experience.

This book reveals by far the US government's most advanced form of intervention. By penetrating all sectors of civil society, political parties, and the Venezuelan Armed Forces, the US has been able to facilitate several attempts to overthrow Venezuela's democratic government. Yet it has failed each time in these efforts despite multimillion-dollar investments and complex, well-studied operations. We must remember that it took a decade to remove the Sandinistas from power in Nicaragua—that tiny, poor nation in Central America. President Reagan risked his presidency to prevent a socialist-oriented revolution from expanding throughout the hemisphere. When Congress denied him the funding for CIA covert operations with the Contra armed forces, Reagan sold arms to Iran to raise the money. It was a scandal. But human beings have short memory spans, and Reagan successfully placed the blame on Colonel Oliver North, who withstood the wrath of congressional hearings and investigations. Though humiliated, North's willingness to play the responsible party left Reagan with all the terrain and resources needed to continue efforts to impede the success of the Sandinistas.

The creation of the National Endowment for Democracy (NED) began a new period in US intervention around the world, and it was in Nicaragua that this method of interfering in the internal affairs of sovereign nations first evolved. More than one billion dollars were invested in Nicaragua during the 1980s to destroy the Sandinista Revolution.

Venezuela presents a new and more threatening challenge for the United States. As the fourth largest supplier of petroleum in the world, Venezuela, the "port of South America," is a national security interest for the US. The Orinoco river region in southern Venezuela has substantial oil reserves, most of which have yet to be exploited. Until 1998, Venezuela was a submissive player to US policy, a collaborator of the most desired type. The US was on the verge of being the number one benefactor if the lucrative oil industry, which had been nationalized since the 1970s, were privatized. But then came Chávez.

President Hugo Rafael Chávez Frías was elected by

approximately 60 percent of the vote in 1998, defeating Venezuela's traditional two parties, Acción Democrática (AD) and COPEI (Christian socialist party), by a landslide. He appealed to a cross-section of Venezuelan society in that first election, primarily because he offered an alternative to the corruption of those parties, which had ruled the nation for 40 years and had managed to run the economy into the ground. But Chávez's immediate implementation of his campaign promises, including a restructuring of the state-owned oil company Petroleos de Venezuela (PDVSA) and a redrafting of Venezuela's young constitution, proved too radical and abrupt for many Venezuelans accustomed to political leaders who abandoned promises and spoke of, but never implemented, structural change.

Despite shock from some sectors at the swiftness of the Chávez administration's actions, more than 70 percent of the electorate participated in drafting and ratifying a new constitution in 1999 that would authorize sweeping changes in Venezuelan society. As a result of new constitutional terms, presidential elections were held again in 1999 and Chávez won with a similar 60 percent margin. With the authority of the 1999 Constitution behind him, Chávez was able to initiate a series of structural changes within PDVSA to enable a more equal distribution of the company's profits and, in turn, provide income for social programs intended to decrease poverty and ensure social services for Venezuela's vast low- and no-income population.

During the period of 1998–2000, Chávez encountered a relatively indifferent US policy toward Venezuela. It wasn't until George W. Bush arrived in the White House in 2001 that relations between Venezuela and the US took a turn for the worse. Chávez administration policies did not sit well with the Bush administration. The idea that a government in charge of one of the most important oil industries in the world might work closely and openly with Fidel Castro was a difficult pill to swallow for a Republican administration that had again tightened the noose around the Cuban economy with the 40-year-old goal of ousting Castro.

Furthermore, Chávez's revitalization of the Organization of Petroleum Exporting Countries (OPEC), an entity the US would have preferred muted, and his visits to fellow oil-producing countries such as Libya and Iraq, rubbed the Bush administration the wrong way. Not to mention the Venezuelan government's focus on policies to reduce poverty and promote a participatory democracy, ideas repulsed by diehard market economists. Add a very disgruntled and wealthy Venezuelan business elite with friends in high places in the US government and corporate world, and a clear dislike for the Chávez government was clinched.

The overt statements and declarations made by US government officials indicating the start of a break in relations with the Chávez administration began in early 2001. After President Chávez expressed his outrage at the US bombing of Afghanistan in response to 9/11, relations between the Bush and Chávez administrations quickly deteriorated. Chávez was not playing by the "with-us-or-with-the-terrorists" rules, and his country was too important to leave in the hands of such a disobedient actor.

The CIA in Venezuela

It may seem as though the CIA is not mentioned very much in this book, considering that when we think of US intervention in a foreign country, we think primarily of the CIA. Yet we know from the Senior Executive Intelligence Brief (SEIB) documents obtained through this investigation that the CIA had intimate, detailed knowledge of the coup plans. We know that the CIA was issuing Spot Commentaries on the days of the coup, which implies the Agency was operating in Venezuela. Without a doubt, as this book shows, the CIA maintains a presence in Venezuela. But apart from traditional covert operations, more important are the newer sophisticated forms of intervention that are applied today in Venezuela — and these may go by different names. (For help in understanding all these acronyms, see the Glossary at the back of this book). Penetration into civil society, participation in battles of ideas, psychological operations, and the financing of opposition movements that seek regime change are the modern forms of covert/overt CIA operations. The Venezuela case is the CIA's 21st-century experiment.

Ex-CIA officials confirm that 75 percent of employees in the political offices of US embassies are actually CIA operatives.[2] The majority work covertly, under the guise of embassy officials, and even carry out embassy duties as cover. The embassy in Venezuela is no different.

Look at the hundreds of cables from the US embassy in Caracas declassified under FOIA through this investigation. Ambassadors Maisto, Hrinak, Shapiro, and Brownfield, and other embassy employees—Cook, MacFarland, and Ellis, to name a few—were all sending multiple daily informative reports to Washington about every imaginable detail pertaining to Venezuela. These reports were compiled and analyzed by the CIA and used in determining how the intervention should proceed.

The National Endowment for Democracy (NED) and the US Agency for International Development (USAID) function as outlets for the CIA to penetrate civil society, funneling in millions of dollars legitimately and therefore avoiding Congressional scrutiny. As much as NED and USAID deny any connection to the CIA, no one can negate the fact that these agencies were established to overtly engage in activities once practiced by the CIA at a time when Congress was clamping down hard on the Agency's budget and past clandestine operations. Both USAID and NED employees have at times been CIA operatives, carrying out the Agency's agenda under the guise of "promoting democracy."

And there is no doubt that the CIA maintains hundreds, perhaps thousands, of paid agents in Venezuela, providing intelligence information, carrying out operations, and ensuring the success of the ongoing political crisis. These individuals live freely and anonymously in Venezuelan society, earning their salaries from the conflict they work to encourage.

The CIA also maintains non-official cover operations in Venezuela. Development Alternatives, Inc. (DAI), International Republican Institute (IRI), National Democratic Institute for

International Affairs (NDI), Science Applications International Corporation (SAIC), and numerous US corporations with offices throughout the country provide fronts for CIA activities. These entities also help the CIA launder funds for its Venezuela operations.

So, no need to think that the CIA is not active and alive in Venezuela. It most certainly is. Agency operatives in Venezuela were caught red-handed during the horrific bombing of a Cubana Airlines plane in flight from Barbados on October 6, 1976. CIA agent Luis Posada Carriles, an anti-Castro Cuban, had recruited two Venezuelans to carry out the terrorist act that killed all 73 people on board. Hernan Ricardo Lozano and Freddy Lugo were later caught by Venezuelan authorities for placing the fatal bombs aboard that flight and served 20 years in prison. Luis Posada Carriles was also caught. But with the help of the Cuban American National Foundation, he escaped from a maximum-security prison in Venezuela on August 18, 1995. After carrying out numerous other terrorist acts against Cuba, he was jailed in Panama in 2000, when Cuban President Fidel Castro announced the discovery of a plot to assassinate him, headed by Posada Carriles. As a final act, outgoing Panamanian President Mireya Moscoso pardoned Posada Carriles in 2004.

Posada Carriles worked hand-in-hand with Orlando Bosch, the infamous anti-Castro Cuban terrorist responsible for more than 100 terrorist attacks against Venezuela, Spain, England, Japan, Mexico, Poland, and other countries that traded with Cuba, even on US soil. Bosch was also known to be part of a CIA assassination squad, Operation 40, responsible for the political murders of Cubans and others associated with the Cuban Revolution.

Bosch was jailed for eleven years in a Venezuelan prison for his role in the Cubana airplane bombing in 1976, but he was released in 1987 with the help of his old friend Otto Reich. Reagan had just rewarded Reich with the ambassadorship in Venezuela after his good work in Nicaragua, and Reich sent numerous cables to the State Department requesting a visa for Bosch to enter the US.

Despite denial from the State Department, President George H.W. Bush pardoned Bosch after he was caught illegally entering the US in 1988 and imprisoned. Bosch resides freely in Miami today, along with a crew of self-exiled Venezuelans conspiring against Venezuela's democratic government.

Posada Carriles illegally entered the US in March 2005 and flaunted his exile in the "land of opportunity" to the press. As soon as the Venezuelan government learned of his presence on US soil, an extradition request was formally filed, in accordance with the extradition treaty signed by the US and Venezuelan governments in 1922. US authorities detained Posada Carriles several months later, on May 15, 2005, but not in compliance with the extradition request. Rather, immigration authorities captured Posada as he was making a very public escape (broadcast live on local television) and detained him on charges of "illegal entry" into the US—an accusation far more innocent than the homicide and conspiracy charges pending against him in the Venezuelan courts. On September 26, 2005, Judge William Abbott ordered Posada's deportation to "any country but Cuba or Venezuela," a decision based on fabricated reports alleging that Latin America's most dangerous terrorist would be tortured in Venezuela. The only evidence supplied was the testimony of Posada's Cuban-American attorney and co-conspirator, Joaquin Chaffardet. Based on this bogus legal ploy, Posada Carriles may soon be sipping piña coladas with fellow criminal Bosch in Miami, since immigration law requires that an "undocumented alien be granted conditional liberty if he cannot be removed from the country within a reasonable period."[3] The US appears to be doing everything in its power to prevent Posada Carriles's release to the Chavez administration. Perhaps partly because Posada Carriles is a former CIA agent, undoubtedly with intimate knowledge of the agency's inner workings, in this case the Bush administration is not interested in pursuing a terrorist. Indeed, the administration is more concerned about defying Chavez than in complying with international law or seeking justice in this case.

Such blatant irregularities and contradictions serve as eye-openers to the international community, and people are becoming more astute as time goes by and more of the US regime's hypocrisy is exposed. In other nations around the world where regime change glitters in the eyes of the US government, strategies and methodologies both old and new are being and will continue to be applied. But advance knowledge allows for preparation, and the interventions may be foiled, as the Venezuelans have successfully done thus far.

Declassifying Venezuela

Utilizing the Freedom of Information Act (FOIA) in the US, independent journalist Jeremy Bigwood and I submitted numerous requests to various agencies and entities in the US government regarding different issues pertaining to Venezuela. FOIA is a body of US law passed after the Watergate scandal that enables journalists and others to access and declassify secret US government documents. Information requested through the FOIA is first analyzed by the government agency possessing the relevant documentation and then released or withheld in entirety, or a combination thereof.

The US government is made up of many different entities. In order to find out how deeply involved the US has been in Venezuela it was necessary to file hundreds of requests with a range of agencies: Department of State, Department of Defense, Department of the Army, Central Intelligence Agency, US SOUTHCOM, Department of Agriculture, National Endowment for Democracy, US Agency for International Development, and others.

The investigation was initiated in 2003 and is ongoing. Most likely it will extend for decades to come. Generally, the government takes a long time to respond to FOIA requests and typically engages in delay tactics and censoring intended to prevent information from reaching the public at large. Often, documents or information withheld or unlawfully delayed can be appealed, but the appeals process itself can continue for an indeterminable period, therefore hampering critical information from reaching public scrutiny.

FOIA investigations generally occur years or decades

after the intervention has occurred, such as in the case of Chile, when it is too late to act in a preventative or precautionary manner. This investigation, however, is occurring in "real time" and therefore has the privileged opportunity of effectuating change in US policy on Venezuela. To date, the results of the investigation have already impacted US–Venezuela relations and have opened the eyes of millions of Venezuelans who were unaware of the extent of US meddling in their nation. The details of what the investigation has uncovered so far follow.

I must issue a disclaimer, however, because the investigation is not yet near completion. Due to the timeliness and importance of the information, I believe it is critical to conduct immediate analyses and make the documents available to the public domain as they are obtained. But it must be clear that as more documents are acquired, more facts about the US role in the events of the past few years in Venezuela are revealed and could alter the present understanding of this investigation. Also, many documents have been heavily censored and appeals have been submitted when appropriate. The appeals process will delay the release of information for a longer, unpredictable period. Therefore, I withhold conclusions regarding the full extent of US intervention in Venezuela at this time.

CHILE AND NICARAGUA: THE COUP COOKBOOK

Present US intervention in Venezuela has been implemented in three stages, each adapting to the circumstances presented by the failure of the previous attempt to garner any success. The strategy in Venezuela has followed a textbook outline of intervention in Latin America. The tactics used in Venezuela appear to be a metamorphosed version of those previously applied in Chile (1970s), Nicaragua (1980s), and Haiti (1990s), which all resulted in the ouster of democratically elected presidents, either through coup d'etats (Chile and Haiti) or through heavily influenced electoral processes (Nicaragua).

The past few years in Venezuela have shared common histories with Chile during the late 1960s and early 1970s. Distant cousins of the coup and strikes that plagued Chile have also beleaguered Venezuela, yet the latter was able to resist and overcome the attempts of the right-wing opposition movement financed and politically backed by the US government. The former, unfortunately, was forced to succumb to a violent takeover that resulted in the assassination of a democratically elected and popularly supported president, Salvador Allende, and the installation of one of the most brutal dictatorships in Latin American history. The bloodied hands of the US government were stamped all over the 1973 coup d'etat in Chile, and later, declassified documents attained by the National Security Archives (NSA) revealed the intricate plots Henry Kissinger and his cohorts had enacted to crush the growth of socialism in the region.

In Chile, the US employed tactics that have subsequently proven successful time and time again. Before the coup, the US had succeeded in funneling hundreds of thousands of dollars to labor unions, business associations, and social organizations willing to band together to oppose Allende. The US attempted to prevent Allende's election in 1970 by strengthening and supporting opposition parties and candidates, but the overwhelming popularity of the socialist leader left the US government with little choice but to go the violent route. Still, after Allende's election, the US instigated acts of economic sabotage through massive strikes led by its financed counterparts and it attempted to isolate the Allende government from the international community. The US also applied a strategy, later known as "Chileanization," which involved organizing internal right-wing forces to destabilize the elected government. This concept ensured that as opposition forces incited violent confrontations with the government, international scandals and reactions would form over "Allende crackdowns," the nation would spiral into civil disorder and instability, and the government would be labeled a "human rights violator" or international pariah. It wasn't until all these efforts had failed three years later that the coup plan proceeded.

The tactics used in Chile were preserved for future use. The embarrassment of some members of Congress over the US role in Allende's overthrow and its unconditional support for a brutal dictator who went on to commit human rights atrocities for more than a decade merely affected the tone of future interventions, not the substance. In Venezuela, the US applied many of the same tactics it had used in Chile—the formation of a movement bringing together labor unions, business associations, political parties, and social organizations; the economic sabotage; the strikes. And of course, the bloody coup. But the failure of this strategy to take root in Venezuela led the US government to alter its tactics, to merge together strategies it had successfully applied in other Latin American nations, and to modernize its methodology.

The Nicaragua Model

During the 1980s, the US government was heavily involved in Nicaragua. More than $1 billion was invested in removing the Sandinistas from power, first through armed struggle and later through electoral intervention.[1] The NED, the USAID, and the CIA shared terrain in that small Central American nation and these entities used a number of techniques that had been successful in prior interventions in Chile, the Philippines, and Panama, to name a few.

The US started a dirty war in the late 1970s in Nicaragua against the Sandinista government, making the tiny nation the "test case" of its new strategic operations. Ronald Reagan's administration created the "Contras," a 15,000-strong armed counterrevolutionary force that brutalized and terrorized Nicaraguan citizens at the behest of the US government. Alleging fears that "communism" would "spread throughout the region," the Reagan administration justified the widespread human rights abuses and atrocities committed at the hands of its CIA-trained counterrevolutionaries. After several years of armed combat that resulted in strengthening, rather than weakening, the Sandinista government, the US government had to resort to even more desperate measures: It sold arms to Iran illegally in order to support its billion-dollar conflict in Nicaragua. Seeing its own failure in Nicaragua, officials in the Reagan Administration proposed a change in US policy—a move toward a "democratic" solution rather than an armed conflict.

Coming out of the 1970s, the US Congress was hesitant to finance covert operations in Latin America after the harsh revelations of the US role in the overthrow of Allende were made public through Congressional investigation.[2] The Congress had imposed substantial restrictions on CIA funding and support of private groups and organizations in other nations, therefore hampering the capacity of the US government to covertly build networks that supported US interests abroad. The Iran–Contra scandal made financing of such groups even more difficult and it became obvious that a new approach was necessary.

The National Endowment for Democracy

In the late 1970s, a coalition of labor, business, political, and academic leaders formed the American Political Foundation (APF), with the objective of seeking new methods of achieving US foreign policy goals abroad despite the Congressional restrictions in place. The APF, funded by Congress and composed of ultra-conservative think tanks such as the Center for Strategic and International Studies and the American Enterprise Institute, together with representatives from the National Security Council (NSC) and the USIA, the propaganda office of the US government, proposed the creation of an institution funded by Congress to provide financial and political support to groups and organizations working in US interests abroad. The institution would focus on "promoting democracy" abroad through financial support intended to foster the "infrastructure of democracy" that would enable a free press, unions, political parties, universities, and social organizations to function in the interests of US foreign policy.

In 1983, resulting from APF recommendations, the National Endowment for Democracy (NED) was established by Congress with the "National Endowment for Democracy Act" (P.L. 98–164), and funding was authorized to ensure its success. At the time of the NED's creation, the APF had also recommended the formation of "core grantees" to act as funnels for funds to reach political parties and partisan groups in other nations. The core grantees, which included the Center for International Private Enterprise (CIPE), the National Democratic Institute (NDI), the International Republican Institute (IRI), and the Free Trade Union Institute (FTUI), overseen by the AFL-CIO and later denominated the American Center for International Labor Solidarity (ACILS), were all connected through an interlocking board of directors that shared influences within the NED and the US Congress.[3]

The NED was created to serve as the perfect conduit for funds from the US government to provide international political aid that would support its interests abroad and influence foreign and domestic policy in nations of strategic importance. Established during the Cold War, the NED's objectives reflected a neoconservative agenda that prioritized its global struggle against communism over democratic notions of sovereignty and self-determination. Hence, the NED's premiere in Nicaragua provided a major dose of US intervention on a political and electoral level and its technique was perfected over the course of nearly a decade.

The NED's leadership clearly reflects its goals. Carl Gershman has been the president of the NED since its founding. A former member of the Socialist Party USA, Gershman split off to lead a right-wing faction, Social Democrats USA. He is known as a neocon and linked to the old-school hawks' network; he worked in the early 1970s with several key neoconservatives figures, including Richard Perle, Elliot Abrams, and Paul Wolfowitz, deputy secretary of defense under Donald Rumsfeld.

In Nicaragua, the CIA had originally been the principal conduit for financing the anti-Sandinista movement (the Contras), but after their failure to unseat the Sandinistas during the 1984 elections, the NED was employed to ensure success in the 1989–1990 ballot. In fact, during the 1984 elections, the US was so sure of their defeat that they advocated widespread voter abstention on the opposition side in order to discredit the elections, which, despite US power and influence, still failed. The second time around, the US decided to take a thoroughly proactive role in the electoral process. Through the formation and crafting of an opposition movement comprised of social organizations, political parties, and NED affiliates, the US government was able to shape the outcome of the Nicaraguan elections.

The US pushed for the unification of the various political parties and social organizations that opposed the Sandinistas, many of which were far right and shared conservative agendas with the Reagan–Bush administration.

The US made financing through the NED to these organizations contingent upon their formation of a unified group, the Coordinadora Democrática Nicaragüense (CDN), that would be capable of winning the 1989–1990 elections. The CDN was comprised of four conservative political parties, two trade union groups affiliated with the AFL-CIO, and a private business organization, COSEP, which had close links to influential US corporations and figures in the business community.

Closer to the elections, the NED blackmailed the fourteen opposition parties in Nicaragua into forming one party, UNO, that would endorse the US-chosen candidate, Violeta Chamorro, for the presidency. By threatening to deny all funding sources to these parties, the NED was able to achieve its goal. Chamorro became the leading candidate, with full opposition support, to confront Sandinista President Daniel Ortega.

The Nicaragua–Venezuela Connection

Control of media was a major tool in the propaganda war intended not only to win over supporters for Chamorro and UNO in Nicaragua but also to filter news and information to the international press with a guaranteed anti-Sandinista and pro-US spin. The CIA had been financing Nicaragua's main newspaper, *La Prensa*, during the Sandinista–Contra war and passed on the baton in large part to the NED and its international affiliates during the late 1980s. The Venezuelan government, then headed by Carlos Andrés Pérez (in his second term), played a major role in the funneling of funds and support from the US government to the CDN, UNO, and *La Prensa*.

Pérez had developed close ties to the Chamorro family while in exile in Costa Rica during the Pérez Jiménez dictatorship in Venezuela. He also had ties to other influential Nicaraguans developed during his first presidential term from 1974 to 1978, and he was eager to offer Venezuela's support for US efforts to oust the Sandinista government through the strengthening of an anti-Sandinista civil opposition.

Beginning in 1989, the CIA rerouted a minimum of $200,000 monthly through Venezuelan private foundations in order to fund *La Prensa* and campaign materials for the UNO. Pérez maintained close contact with President Bush during the electoral process in Nicaragua and even appointed his secretary of the presidency, Beatríz Rángel, as his personal representative in his contacts with Bush. According to one source, Rángel was observed carrying a suitcase "stuffed with secret funds from Washington and Miami to Caracas" destined for the Nicaraguan opposition's campaign.[4]

Venezuela's largest union, the Confederación de Trabajadores Venezolanos (CTV), worked in connection with the NED and the AFL-CIO to establish ties with workers and unions in Nicaragua, with the goal of incorporating them into the opposition movement.[5] Pérez also recommended the use of the US polling firm, Penn and Schoen Associates, to conduct a polling program in Nicaragua as part of the electoral intervention agenda. Penn and Schoen had, with the Venezuelan firm DOXA, done polling for Pérez's presidential campaign and had also been a successful part of US electoral intervention in Panama.

Penn and Schoen later became the polling firm of choice for these types of interventions and has subsequently been used in the former Yugoslavia during the elections that ousted Milosevic from power and, most recently, in Venezuela during the August 15, 2004 recall referendum against President Chávez. In fact, in Venezuela, Penn and Schoen came under international scrutiny for allegedly producing fraudulent exit poll results with Venezuelan NED-grantee, Súmate, that were intended to discredit the official results of the referendum. (See Chapter 9.)

The Venezuela connection to the NED and CIA intervention in Nicaragua in the late 1980s evidences the strong bond formed between those entities and the politicians of that period. Such relationships have clearly been integral to the recent interventions the US government has pursued in Venezuela during the Chávez era. Pérez, particularly, has played an interesting role in the three different US interventions in Venezuela, serving as a liaison between old-school officials and other influential individuals in the US, as well as a facilitator of funds to those who led the coup against Chávez and an international propagandist spreading harsh critiques of the Chávez administration.

In Nicaragua, the US utilized a variety of tools and methodologies to remove the Sandinistas from power. Once armed conflict proved unsuccessful, the US unfolded a skillfully crafted electoral intervention plan that involved the formation of a capable opposition movement, the selection and molding of an opposition candidate, the unification of diverse opposition parties, the buying of media to win the propaganda war,[6] the financing of the opposition's electoral campaign, and the use of international networks to covertly funnel additional funds to the opposition and media in Nicaragua and ensure regional support for the candidate chosen by the US. The intervention scheme also involved the use of polling firms selected by the US to influence opinions about the electoral process and the creation of a "neutral" Nicaraguan non-profit entity dedicated to "electoral education" during the campaign.

Vía Cívica, as it was called, was created at the behest of the NED to function as a conduit for funds to finance the electoral process directly. Since Nicaraguan law prohibited the direct financing of political parties and campaigns (as does US law), the NED had to seek alternative routes to channel its funds. NED's "core grantees" were used to finance the opposition parties, as were the pathways provided by the Pérez administration in Venezuela, but the creation of Vía Cívica offered an overt and direct channel. As the elections neared in late 1989, the US government managed to trap the Nicaraguan government into permitting the financing of the opposition's campaign to the tune of $9 million, despite the prohibitions in place by law.[7] Vía Cívica, an alleged "non-partisan civil society" organization, was additionally utilized to influence the electoral process in favor of the opposition by preparing and distributing electoral material and conducting "electoral education" workshops and conferences that clearly showed bias toward the opposition.

The major US investment and intervention in Nicaragua was successful. In 1990, Violeta Chamorro was declared the winner of the elections and the Sandinistas were officially removed from power. As a result of the layers and networks the US had built to cover its influential role in the electoral process, the elections were widely viewed as "transparent and democratic" and were accepted internationally. The US, satisfied with the outcome of its efforts, proceeded to expand and implement its new "democratic intervention" model in other nations.

US Agency for International Development (USAID)

Another entity that existed prior to the Nicaragua intervention was also utilized to enable the financing of US interests abroad. USAID, an international funding entity officially established by the US Congress in 1961, was originally intended to aid humanitarian development around the world. Similar to the NED, USAID had large portions of its funds diverted to support foreign political movements aligned with US interests. Though USAID was created to separate military aid from humanitarian and development aid, it merely became an additional fund for the CIA to dip into for covert interventions. USAID is overseen and directed by the Department of State, which exercises make-or-break authority over its actions.

One of the first documented misuses of USAID funds was during the early 1960s in Brazil. The CIA was heavily involved in attempts to thwart João Goulart from succeeding in the Brazilian presidency because he was viewed as a leftist who supported "social and economic reforms" that in the eyes of the CIA had "communism" written all over them. The CIA and USAID spent approximately $20 million to support hundreds of anti-Goulart candidates for gubernatorial elections in 1962. USAID was used as a cover to invest heavily in the Brazilian labor movement. The funds were filtered through the international branch of the AFL-

CIO, then American Institute for Free Labor Development (AIFLD), now known as the American Center for International Labor Solidarity (ACILS), and were controlled on the ground by the CIA. In 1964, President Goulart was overthrown by a CIA-backed coup that resulted in a brutal US-sponsored dictatorship that lasted nearly twenty years.[8]

In the 1980s, as part of the move toward "democratic intervention" models, the State Department established the USAID Office of Democratic Initiatives, with the goal of supporting and "strengthening democratic institutions." From 1984 to 1987, USAID utilized that office to filter more than $25 million into electoral processes in Latin America. Although the NED later assumed similar operations, USAID has continued to use the office, now known as the Office of Transition Initiatives (OTI), to intervene in nations involved in crises that "threaten democracy." USAID and the NED also overlap in funding initiatives for the IRI and the NDI, both core NED grantees. A large portion of USAID and NED funds are channeled into electoral intervention efforts and civil society penetration. In the case of Venezuela, more than $20 million has been invested by USAID and NED since 2001 to foment conflict and instability in the name of "promoting democracy."

CHÁVEZ'S RISE TO POWER SPURS VISA DENIAL

With much of Latin America, Venezuela shares a history of corrupt governments, dictatorships, US intervention, and stark economic divisions.[1] Venezuela's democratic political system was born in 1958, after a popular uprising overthrew the dictatorship of General Pérez Jiménez.[2] The country's first democratic constitution was ratified in 1961 and granted vast rights that had been denied under decades of dictatorship. Throughout the 1960s and 1970s, Venezuela's oil wealth greatly enriched the nation, and despite ample corruption in the elected governments, the populace was relatively unengaged in political discourse since the administrations throughout those decades provided for substantial basic infrastructure needs and social services.

The 1980s saw the first decline in Venezuela's booming economy and poverty levels began to rise. The political parties, Acción Democrática (AD) and the Social Christian party (COPEI), that had held a tight reign on the country's politics since the overthrow of Pérez Jiménez in 1958, were beginning to be seen as corrupt and blamed for the changes in the distribution of the oil wealth, which was caused primarily by the institution of a neo-liberal economic agenda. Venezuelans' distrust in their government slowly began to rise.[3]

In 1988, AD candidate Carlos Andrés Pérez was elected on a platform of returning the country to its 1970s wealth and economic distribution, a promise Venezuelans believed because of his successful presidential reign in the late 1970s. During that term, he had nationalized the oil industry and Petroleros de Venezuela, S.A. (PDVSA), the state-owned oil company, was born. But soon after assuming office in 1989, Pérez backtracked on his campaign promises and instituted a neo-liberal economic program based on International Monetary Fund (IMF) and World Bank doctrines that was set to increase domestic petroleum prices by 100 percent in the first quarter of 1989, as well as significantly affect other social and economic issues throughout the nation.[4] In reaction, transportation prices immediately rose, and an enraged citizenry reacted violently and angrily. The result was the *Caracazo*, the worst incident of violence in contemporary Venezuelan history, which left thousands dead. Human rights abuses were rampant and became the norm, and constitutional guarantees and rights were suspended indefinitely.

Nevertheless, as a result of the neo-liberal free-market reforms Pérez instituted, from 1990 to 1992 Venezuela had the highest rate of economic growth in the Americas—as well as its sharpest ever increase in economic inequality and record levels of poverty and malnutrition.

On February 4, 1992, Lieutenant Colonel Hugo Rafael Chávez Frías led an attempted military rebellion against the Carlos Andrés Pérez government. Although the rebellion failed, it was widely supported, and Chávez's Bolivarian Revolutionary Movement-200 grew and gained national media attention and sympathy. (The "200" is in honor of the 200th anniversary of the birth of Simón Bolívar, which was in 1983, the year Chavez formed the party.) Chávez was detained and imprisoned as a result of the coup effort, but he left an impression on many Venezuelans. A political figure had taken responsibility for his actions. In the two minutes of national television he had on the day of his arrest, Chávez famously admitted failure only *"por ahora"* (for now). He left Venezuelans with the hope that he and his revolutionary movement would return someday, stronger than ever.

Later that same year, on November 27, another attempt against the Pérez administration was led by members of the Bolivarian Revolution Movement-200 (MBR-200) while Chávez was imprisoned; it also failed. As fate would have it, several months later, in May 1993, Carlos Andrés Pérez was indicted and impeached on charges of corruption by his own political party. He fled the country and took up residences in New York and Santo Domingo.

After a brief interim government following Pérez's impeachment, new elections in 1994 brought one of the founders of COPEI, also a former president from the 1970s, Rafael Caldera, to the presidential palace. During these elections, more than 40 percent of the voting population abstained. Though Caldera won only 30 percent of the votes, he had won a higher percentage of votes than any of the other three candidates. The level of interest and trust among Venezuelans in government had drastically declined. Though he arrived in office by campaigning against them, once installed in the presidency, the same neo-liberal policies Pérez instituted, aligned with the International Monetary Fund and World Bank policies and commitments, won the day. During Caldera's presidency, the economic divisions throughout the country skyrocketed, and Venezuelan currency, the bolivar, was rapidly devalued. Poverty levels grew to an all-time high and the country's national debt reached over $23 billion dollars.

During his first year as president, Caldera pardoned Hugo Chávez and his compatriots for their roles in the 1992 coup attempts against Carlos Andrés Pérez, and they were released from prison. During his two-year prison term in San Francisco de Yare, Chávez had solidified his political party and found supporters. Upon his release from prison, Chávez began strengthening his party, changing its name to the Fifth Republic Movement (MVR), and aligning with Movimiento al Socialismo (MAS) and a new leftist party called Patria Para Todos (PPT) to create the Polo Patriótico (PP), a populist multiparty alliance. By the 1998 presidential elections, Chávez, backed by the PP, was the leading candidate. The traditional parties that had long dominated

Venezuelan politics, AD and COPEI, lost significant support throughout the country because of charges of corruption and failed policies. As a result, despite last-minute dirty political maneuvers and corrupt campaigning by the other candidates, Chávez won the 1998 presidential elections by a substantial majority: 56 percent, with the rest of the votes split among three other candidates.[5]

Chávez had pledged to make substantial and significant economic and social changes within Venezuela. The movement was well received by a majority of Venezuelans during a time in which they had been experiencing declining living standards and drastic drops in the price of oil, the country's principal export commodity.

Chávez, a former military lieutenant colonel, based his movement in large part on the philosophies and ideology of Simón Bolívar, the great liberator of South America, who had attempted to unite the continent to become a major power against imperialist forces. Chávez's movement sought to implement similar ideas by encouraging the political unification of Latin America through the creation of a sovereign and powerful economic block. These concepts were applauded by a citizenry suffering the effects of a neo-liberal agenda that had crippled the economy and drastically increased poverty.

Visa Denial

In the early days of the presidential campaign in 1998, a Peruvian journalist invited Chávez to be interviewed on a Miami television program. Just like any other citizen, Chávez applied to the US embassy in Caracas for a visa to enter the US. His request was denied on the grounds of "prior terrorist activity," due to the 1992 coup attempt against Peréz. Chávez had been placed on the US government's "terrorist watch list." In addition to denying his visa request, the US embassy issued a public statement regarding the reasons for the rejection, making clear their distaste for his candidacy. Chávez was not surprised. Soon after, during a local Venezuelan news interview, a reporter made a condescending remark about the visa denial. Candidate Chávez responded humorously, "What do you mean? I have a Visa," as he pulled a Visa credit card from his wallet.

The day after he won the presidential elections in December 1998, President Chávez was dining with his family when he received a phone call from the US embassy in Caracas. The ambassador, John Maisto, had authorized an immediate issuance of his US visa. It was hand delivered.

Before his inauguration on February 2, 1999, President-elect Chávez had planned an international tour to Spain, Cuba, the US, and the Dominican Republic. In Washington, DC, he was to meet with President Bill Clinton on January 27, 1999, at the White House. During his meeting in Spain, he received an unexpected phone call from a State Department official. To Chávez's surprise, the official had called to urge him to cancel his visit to Cuba before arriving in the US. The official claimed that it would not be in Chávez's interests to visit President Fidel Castro in Cuba before coming to the White House. He even threatened to cancel the Washington visit if Chávez did not comply. Chávez decided to preserve the sovereignty and right of self-determination of the nation he had been chosen to lead, and he firmly told the US representative that he had no intention of canceling his Cuba visit, despite the cost in Washington's eyes.

From Spain he traveled to Havana and met with Castro. From Havana he traveled to Washington and met with Clinton. But not officially. Clinton had decided not to receive Chávez in an official capacity, but rather through the "back door." According to President Chávez, Clinton met with him in an informal room in the White House with no press or photographers allowed. Dressed in jeans and a tee-shirt, Clinton received the Venezuelan President with a soda in hand and an intentionally casual attitude. The meeting lasted about fifteen minutes and it went unannounced to the world. There was no protocol involved. Chávez had been treated as though he were an unimportant visitor and not the president of one of the most important nations in the Americas.

Clinton later sent his secretary of energy, Bill Richardson, to lead the US delegation to Chávez's inauguration ceremony, instead of attending himself. Clearly, this was a sign of how the US's view of Venezuela was clouded with thick petroleum.

The grounds had been set for his relationship with the US government. Chávez, a meticulous student of Simón Bolívar, believed the liberator's conviction that the "United States is destined to plague the Americas with misery in the name of liberty."[6]

FROM TRAGEDY IN VARGAS TO PREMONITIONS OF A COUP

Relations between the US and Venezuela were relatively uneventful in the first year of Chávez's administration. After the initial visa quandary, things had settled down, and Washington had taken more of a wait-and-see approach to the new government. But in December 1999, things got a little tense. December 14, 1999 started out as a normal day in Caracas and its coastal regions. But by the afternoon, torrential rains had begun to fall that seemed as if they would never cease. The state of Vargas, on the coast northwest of Caracas and home to the main airport in Venezuela, Maiquetia's Simón Bolívar International Airport, saw the worst of the rains. Massive flooding and mudslides brought tragedy.

Tens of thousands of Vargas residents lost their homes and all of their belongings. As often happens, it was the poor, whose homes were built of earth and tin, who suffered the most. Hundreds were killed by the rains and flooding, trapped on mountainsides, crushed by mudslides, and drowned by the forceful floods. The airport was flooded and shut down for more than a week. The National Guard and army were called in to rescue whomever and whatever could be rescued. It was Chávez's first tragedy as president, and it was of major importance.

The rains were so powerful and intense that they washed away part of Venezuela's geography. After the Vargas floods, new maps had to be drawn up, reflecting the changes in

Venezuela's territory. A majority of those who survived but lost their homes and belongings lived in a state of homelessness and desperation for months while Chávez's "Plan Bolívar" built the Vargas residents new homes in other parts of the country.

International assistance came from many nations around the world, the US among them. Venezuela was open to receiving financial assistance to rebuild the area devastated by the tragedy and to construct new homes and lives for the survivors. But the Venezuelan government was startled when the US announced it had sent in naval ships and helicopters to aid in the rescue—despite the fact that no request had been made by the Chávez administration for military assistance. Chávez told US Ambassador John Maisto "no thanks," declaring that while Venezuela would accept financial assistance, it was not about to open its coasts and borders to US military teams for an unspecified period. President Chávez, fully aware of US interventions throughout Latin America, believed that Washington was eager to get its military on Venezuelan terrain and saw the Vargas tragedy as a perfect opportunity.

The rejection of US aid was exploited by a growing private media industry in Venezuela opposed to President Chávez's policies. National papers and television stations declared it an "outrage" that Chávez had denied foreign aid in a time of need. An article in *El Universal* carried a political cartoon portraying two workers carrying a statue of a hand giving the finger with the caption, "Where do we put this new international aid?" But despite the media's siding with the US government on the issue, the State Department was concerned about repercussions. After all, it had rushed in military ships with no authorization, under the guise of "humanitarian aid." Chávez had caught them before they could make ground, literally.

A cable from the US embassy in Caracas on January 20, 2000, revealed a level of concern regarding the situation. In order to distract attention from the naval ships scandal, the embassy engaged in a media ploy to bring favorable coverage to US intentions in Venezuela. According to the cable,

A highly-successful January 19 media trip arranged by the embassy and the joint task force has significantly shifted coverage to a different topic: US efforts to bring water to affected areas. The Ambassador accompanied a group of eight international and national journalists... on visits via land and Black Hawk helicopter to four separate water purification sites... coverage was immediate and highly favorable.[1]

And lo and behold, the naval ships incident became a distant memory. In any case, Venezuela had its hands full with the worst natural tragedy in history ever to hit the nation.

In July 2000, Ambassador Maisto was removed and Donna Hrinak became the new US ambassador to Venezuela. Hrinak had joined the Foreign Service in 1974 and served at posts in Caracas, São Paulo, Bogotá, Poland, and Mexico City until 1991, when she was named deputy assistant secretary for Inter-American Affairs, responsible for overseeing relations between the US, Mexico, and the Caribbean. Prior to her appointment at the US embassy in Venezuela, she held posts as the ambassador in Bolivia and the Dominican Republic. Hrinak was to remain in Caracas until the weeks before the 2002 coup.

Just one month after Ambassador Hrinak's arrival, relations between the two nations became shakier when President Chávez, as the new head of the Organization of Petroleum Exporting Countries (OPEC), made clear his dissatisfaction with the status quo.

Venezuela was one of five founding members of OPEC in 1960, along with Iran, Iraq, Kuwait, and Saudi Arabia. Today OPEC has eleven member countries, all of which are heavily reliant on oil revenues as a main source of income. (Indonesia, Libya, Nigeria, Qatar, the United Arab Emirates, and Algeria have joined the founding five.) After a significant decline in OPEC's power and influence throughout the 1990s, by the time President Chávez came to office in 1999, oil was selling for about eight dollars per barrel. Venezuela was elected to head OPEC in June 2000 and through its representative, Ali Rodriguez Araque, began a series of measures intended to boost oil prices and control production output. This resulted in bringing the price of oil up to approximately thirty dollars per barrel.

As the new head of OPEC, President Chávez decided to embark on an international tour to visit fellow OPEC nations. The trip included visits to all other ten member countries, including Iraq. Chávez was to become the first democratically elected head of state to visit Iraq and its leader, Saddam Hussein, since the 1991 Gulf war. The US was up in arms. The State Department threatened the Chávez administration in the days proceeding the Iraq visit, suggesting that the trip "contravened United Nations political sanctions, as the Venezuelan leader had not sought advice from the UN sanctions committee before his visit... It's Venezuela's obligation, as a UN member state, to observe all the Security Council resolutions regarding Iraq and the sanctions regime," said State Department spokesman Richard Boucher in early August 2000.

Right after Chávez's trip to Iraq, Secretary of State Madeline Albright omitted Venezuela from a tour of South American nations. The US denied any connection between the two matters.

Nothing much happened during the remainder of the Clinton administration in terms of US–Venezuela relations. But though they weren't yet too noticeable, alliances were being forged between a growing opposition movement in Venezuela and sectors of the US government. It wasn't really until George W. Bush took office in 2001 that relations between the two countries started going downhill rapidly.

Chávez Opposes the Free Trade Act and Ejects the US Miliary

In April 2001, at the Summit of the Americas meeting in Quebec, Canada, President Chávez manifested his opposition to the Free Trade of the Americas Act (FTAA), a hemispheric trade bloc proposed by the United States. He began advocating for a South American regional trade organization capable of negotiating with the powerful United States economy. The FTAA would create the world's largest "free trade zone" and would encompass 34 nations in the Western Hemisphere, including 800 million people. Corporate rights would become a hemispheric priority, leaving sovereign nations and governments with little or no say in decisions affecting internal politics and issues.

Chávez became the most outspoken head of state opposing the FTAA throughout the region and was championed by anti-globalization activists and movements for his posture. His position clearly endangered the possibility that the US proposed agreement would take root immediately and even threatened its future implementation. The drift widened between the countries.

In September 2001, just before the attacks on the World Trade Center in New York City, the Venezuelan government announced that it would not renew a 50-year old bilateral military cooperation agreement with the US. Ambassador Donna Hrinak made no comments to the press on the decision. The Venezuelan defense minister at that time, José Vicente Rángel, also requested that the US military mission in Venezuela vacate the space they had been occupying on the Fort Tiuna Defense Ministry headquarters.

The news was a blow to US foreign military policy in Venezuela, which had enjoyed a position that enabled infiltration of and influence over Venezuela's armed forces and defense department. But despite the Venezuelan government's actions, the US still had other roads of access into the Venezuelan armed forces.

A cable from the military section in the US embassy in Caracas dated June 2000 revealed the true intentions behind the International Military Education and Training (IMET) program the US had been running in Venezuela: "Expand United States government access and influence at all levels of the Venezuelan Armed Forces... Increase the number of Venezuelan Armed Forces Officers at all levels receiving instruction in US military schools..." (see Appendix 2).

Furthermore, the cable revealed the training program was contingent on the US requirements that the Venezuelan government place IMET graduates in "key positions as general staff officers or as commanders of key tactical units." This placement would guarantee the US access to the Venezuelan Armed Forces at the highest levels. The program had been going on for years and Venezuela boasted a military force with the highest percentage of officials trained in the School of the Americas and other US military institutions.

The State Department cable cited as an example of "one of the biggest supporters of adopting US proposals..." the US-trained retired Major General Raúl Salazar Rodríguez. Salazar Rodríguez was Chávez's first Minister of Defense and also commanded the Armed Forces. At the time of the April 2002 coup, he was the Venezuelan ambassador in Spain. The retired major general was one of the key figures in the coup plotting from that Iberian nation, which would also be fingered in the coup.

Regardless of Venezuela's demands, the US took its time. Only after three years did it finally withdraw its military commando from Fort Tiuna. But the US IMET training program survived, although President Chávez did suspend the training of Venezuelan military at the Georgia-based School of the Americas.

A Fateful Flare-Up

On October 29, 2001, President Chávez went on national television to deplore the US bombings in Afghanistan that had been initiated as part of the Bush-declared "war on terror." At a time when most nations were expressing allegiance to the United States, Venezuela was the first democratic nation to demonstrate disagreement with the Bush administration's tactics. Showing photographs of Afghani children killed in US bombing attacks, Chávez defiantly stated, "Terror cannot be fought with more terror... This has no justification, just as the attacks in New York didn't either."

The US did not hesitate in its response. Ambassador Donna Hrinak was called immediately to Washington for "consultations," which, in government lingo, means a problem is brewing. On November 2, 2001, State

Department spokesperson Richard Boucher affirmed the US government's growing concern about Chávez:

> I think a lot of things are going on down there. We have seen comments by President Chávez that we, frankly, found surprising and very disappointing. And I think we want to look at the relationship, because we do believe this relationship is an important and longstanding one between the United States and Venezuela. (Daily Press Briefing, 2 November 2001).

After Hrinak returned to Caracas, she requested a meeting with President Chávez. In that closed-door meeting, the nervous ambassador read from a document addressed to the Venezuelan leader. The text was a request sent from Washington demanding that Chávez officially and publicly retract his statement about the bombings in Afghanistan. Before Hrinak could get even a quarter of the way through the document, President Chávez interrupted her. "You are speaking to the head of state of this nation. You are an ambassador in my country. You are out of line. Please leave my office now."

Hrinak was shocked. She did not expect such a firm and defiant reaction from the Venezuelan president, in light of the fact that she was making a request on behalf of the most powerful nation in the world. Embarrassed and uneasy, Hrinak apologized and requested humbly that the president at least allow her to read through the entire text, then she would go. Chávez agreed, and dismissed her when she was done.

It was becoming clearer that the relationship the US government had enjoyed with earlier Venezuelan governments was over. The new Venezuelan government had no plans to be subservient to US interests and this did not sit well in Washington.

It was around that time that the NED quadrupled its funding in Venezuela and opposition to Chávez began to grow aggressively.

US TAXPAYER DOLLARS CREATE PRIMERO JUSTICIA

In 2001, the National Endowment for Democracy (NED) gave the International Republican Institute (IRI) a $340,000 grant for its work in Venezuela training "national and/or local branches of existing and/or newly created political parties on such topics as party structure, management and organization, internal and external party communications and coalition building" (Appendix 2). (During the previous year, IRI's grant from the NED for its work in Venezuela was a mere $50,000, so the amount from 2000 to 2001 was almost sextupled.)

The NED, which had maintained a minimal presence in Venezuela during the previous years, all of a sudden began investing heavily in political party strengthening and civil society "political" education and orientation. IRI, known officially as the international branch of the Republican Party, became a major player in Venezuela. During 2000–2001, its Venezuela funds appeared to come exclusively from the NED, although it also received substantial funding from USAID.

Run by a board of directors that reads like a right-wing parade, the IRI is headed by former national security advisors, corporate executives, State Department officials, former ambassadors, and directors of conservative think tanks, such as the American Enterprise Institute. At the time of the increase in financing for its Venezuela programs, Georges Fauriol, a former colleague of Otto Reich and a staunch anti-Chávez Bush advisor, was in charge of IRI's Latin America program.

IRI's work in Venezuela during 2000 had been focused on an organization by the name of Fundación Participación Juvenil (Youth Participation Foundation), but IRI canceled the program because it determined that the "goals for the youth program in Venezuela can be better achieved if IRI administers the program directly."[1] IRI had clearly decided that it needed a more hands-on approach in Venezuela.

IRI went through a series of trial periods with opposition parties in Venezuela to determine which was worth the most investment. Although a new party, Primero Justicia would eventually win, early on in its grant program in Venezuela, IRI engaged in an interesting collaboration with another new political party, Unión por el Progreso (Union for Progress), led by Francisco Arías Cárdenas.

Arías Cárdenas was involved in Hugo Chávez's attempted coup in 1992 against the government of Carlos Andrés Pérez. An old friend of Chávez, he shared many of the same objectives and ideas as the Bolivarian leader, but he also had deep political aspirations. In 1995, he was elected governor of Zulia, the most important state in Venezuela. Zulia lies at the heart of Venezuela's oil industry, built around huge Lake Maracaibo in the center of the state. When Chávez was elected president in 1998, Arías Cárdenas stood by his side. This loyalty did not last long, however. Just one year later, after the new Constitution had been ratified by popular vote and new elections had to be held, he decided Chávez was incapable of governing the nation and ran against him. Thus began the train of betrayal Chávez was to face from those close to him, even inside his government.

Arías Cárdenas's abrupt and public departure from the Chávez ranks made headlines. And they must have been international, because IRI heard them loud and clear. Immediately, IRI began working with Arías Cárdenas and his newly formed party, Unión por el Progreso, shaping and molding it in preparation for the upcoming presidential elections. It was an interesting choice for IRI, because Arías Cárdenas claimed to be a progressive. Clearly, IRI was ready to back any party capable of beating Chávez.

IRI could boast relative success. Arías Cárdenas, while losing the elections, garnered nearly 38 percent of the vote, despite his fairly last-minute decision to challenge the popular president. IRI had tapped into a part of the populace that had looked to Chávez for change, but feared following his more radical agenda.

But Unión por el Progreso and Arías Cárdenas lost ground and credibility after those elections and momentum within the opposition again dropped. It was around this time that IRI received the $340,000 grant for "Strengthening Political Parties." It was clear that COPEI, AD, MAS, Proyecto Venezuela, Unión por el Progreso, and Primero Justicia needed a big boost. And though the other parties still had lingering potential, Arías Cárdenas's party had suffered a big defeat, as had Proyecto Venezuela, which posted its leader, Henrique Salas Römer, as a candidate against President Chávez in the 1998 elections. AD and COPEI were getting support in the single digits.

Primero Justicia (Justice First), which had garnered important seats in the 2000 regional elections, appeared to be IRI's—and the US government's—Venezuelan hope. A new political party, Primero Justicia was first inscribed in 2000 in Venezuela's Consejo Nacional Electoral (CNE), the National Electoral Council. It had at first been an NGO focused on judicial reform. The IRI must have been attracted to its mostly young membership and its conservative politics. The switch from IRI's work with the Fundación Participación Juvenil to its focus on Primero Justicia was effortless, as the two entities actually shared many of the same members and goals. Based on IRI's disagreement with the Chávez administration policies and its desire to find a counterpart in Venezuela, it was logical that the right-wing organization would find solace and potential in an emerging conservative youth party willing to be shaped and directed by its financiers. Taking advantage of the lack of leadership and popularity of the traditional parties in Venezuela, Primero Justicia successfully landed itself key political positions in the 2000 regional elections, including 5 National Assembly seats in the state of Miranda, 23 municipal council member seats in Miranda, and 2 key municipal mayoral offices in the wealthier sectors of Caracas.

In early 2001, IRI began intensive training programs for all opposition parties in Venezuela. The sessions were not limited to Primero Justicia leaders and members, but included other opposition parties, such as the traditional AD and COPEI, and MAS, Proyecto Venezuela, and lesser-known parties. One of the first training sessions in March brought the executive director of the Mississippi Republican Party, George Fondren, to Venezuela to teach these failing opposition parties about "political communication." Fondren preached to anti-Chávez leaders such as Francisco Arías Cárdenas, Henrique Salas Römer, Governor Henrique Fernando Salas Feo, William Ojeda, Julio Borges, Governor Eduardo Lapi, Liliana Hernandez, Antonio Ledezma, William Davilia, and Sergio Omar Calderón about the fundamentals of campaign communications, "how to connect with people to convince them to vote for you, and how to relate with them on an emotional level."[2] The IRI helped to set up training programs and party strategies that could be implemented throughout the country by the party leaders themselves—"Strengthening Political Parties," as the NED grant was aptly titled.

The IRI's initial focus was on rebuilding these traditional parties that had dropped the ball during the 1998 presidential elections and had truly lost power. IRI's objective was to provide a base from which these parties could spring back into the political sphere, with the ultimate goal of reassuming the national government. After all, Venezuela's largest oil exporting company was owned by the state. Whoever was in power controlled a multi billion-dollar oil industry with limitless reserves. Having that kind of influence was well worth the sextupling of IRI's funding in Venezuela.

In early December 2001, IRI brought Mike Collins, the former press secretary for the Republican Party, to teach communication strategies to Primero Justicia and other opposition parties, including the two traditional parties, AD and COPEI, the anti-Chávez Caracas Mayor Alfredo Peña's growing movement, and Unión para el Progreso. Collins gave sessions focusing on "crafting a message for the party, finding a target audience and developing an image that will attract that target."[3] In short, the Republicans came in to help the opposition develop its image and message, essential aspects of successful political parties.

The IRI training sessions were not just limited to political parties. On December 5, 2001, just five days before the first opposition "general strike," Collins directed a session with the Centro de Divulgación del Conocimiento Económico (CEDICE), the Center for the Dissemination of Economic Information, a "free-market think tank similar to the CATO Institute in Washington, DC." The IRI training was directed toward local journalists and focused on reporting on politicians and political movements.[4] By that period in Venezuela, the private media (non-state channels) had banded together in open opposition to the Chávez administration. IRI's training sessions enhanced this position, and media coverage subsequently became more biased and inaccurate.

In 2001, IRI underwent substantive changes in its Venezuela team in the Washington headquarters. Stanley Lucas, who had been the senior program officer for Venezuela, moved to the IRI strategic planning team. Former NED officer Elizabeth Winger Echeverri took over the senior program officer position for Venezuela and Ecuador.

Lucas was also simultaneously running IRI's Haiti program, which had been financing activities to seek removal of Haitian President Jean Bertrand Aristide. USAID funded IRI to the tune of more than $3 million from 1998–2003 to destabilize Haiti under the guise of "promoting democracy," the usual term put forth by such programs. Lucas, wealthy and Haitian-born, was hired by IRI in 1992 to run their Haiti program. As in Venezuela, Lucas and IRI hosted training sessions for Aristide's most virulent opponents. IRI's millions and Lucas's genius applied the US intervention model formerly used in Nicaragua: unification of opposition parties.

In Haiti, IRI crafted and built the "Democratic Convergence," a group of disparate opposition parties, social organizations, and groups in the country. The Democratic Convergence was elemental in provoking the ongoing tension and violence in the nation, eventually leading to the illegal and violent overthrow of President Aristide. IRI's role was beyond pivotal.

In Venezuela, Lucas was encouraging the same tactics and strategies to be implemented through IRI's programs. IRI sessions promoted dialogue and compromise between the opposition parties, bringing together disparate viewpoints and crafting a solid opposition to the government. But the Venezuela circumstances were different from those in Haiti. Venezuela's traditional parties were weak, but they were still breathing, and IRI saw the potential for resuscitation. IRI had decided initially to work on strengthening them all.

Primero Justicia has been the most successful of IRI's endeavors in Venezuela. As a party comprised primarily of young professionals with little or no political experience, IRI has been able to form and mold party leaders and determine and shape the party goals, strategies, and platform, essentially building the party from scratch. With the hundreds of thousands of dollars IRI has pumped into Primero Justicia from NED and USAID funds, the new conservative party has left the traditional political parties in Venezuela in the dust. Primero Justicia has become the number one opposition party and by far the most outspoken. Its leaders and members have played key roles in the major destabilization attempts against the Venezuelan government, and one of its most powerful figures, the municipal mayor of Baruta, Henrique Capriles Radonsky, was even formally charged by Venezuela's attorney general for aiding and abetting in the assault against the Cuban embassy in Caracas that occurred on April 12, 2002 during the coup.

Primero Justicia Assaults the Cuban Embassy

In a vicious act of aggression, Venezuelan anti-Chávez extremists and Cuban exiles in Venezuela stormed the Cuban embassy in the Baruta section of Caracas, destroying property and automobiles and cutting off the embassy's electricity, gas, and water. Live on television, the aggressors threatened to kill embassy diplomats by "starving them" and forcing them to "eat carpet," depriving them of water and food. Mayor Capriles Radonsky, in charge of the municipal police, made no effort to stop the assault and in fact encouraged it by arriving at the scene and interacting with the aggressors.

Capriles Radonsky violated diplomatic law by forcing entry into the embassy, where he attempted to persuade Cuban Ambassador German Sanchez Otero to turn in Vice President Diosdado Cabello and other Chávez government officials whom the opposition believed were taking refuge in the embassy. Though Ambassador Sanchez Otero permitted Capriles Radonsky on the premises to engage in dialogue, he made it clear that the actions were violating diplomatic law. The Primero Justicia mayor attempted to force a search of the inside of the embassy by threatening the ambassador that the situation would only worsen if a full search were not allowed.

When the ambassador stood firm, Capriles Radonsky left the embassy. If it hadn't been for the growing pro-Chávez demonstrations appearing all over Caracas and the rapid fall of the coup government, the Cuban embassy might have suffered substantially more damage and injury. Capriles Radonsky denied that his actions were unwarranted and illegal and claimed Ambassador Sanchez Otero "invited" him inside the embassy. He was later charged by the attorney general's office for the assault and detained for four months. The case was subsequently dismissed by a sympathetic judge.

During the actions leading to the coup d'etat on April 11, 2002, the municipal mayor of Chacao, Leopoldo Lopez, a leading Primero Justicia party member, played a key role. As revealed on the Venevisión morning program *24 Horas* with Napoleon Bravo on April 12, 2002, Leopoldo Lopez, hand in hand with coup leader Rear Admiral Carlos Molina Tamayo, led the opposition march on an illegal route to the Miraflores Presidential Palace, where violence broke out. On that morning program, Lopez spoke in detail of his important role in those events.

Lopez, Capriles Radonsky, and other leading Primero Justicia members, such as coordinator Gerardo Blyde and national coordinator and assembly member Julio Borges, made frequent trips to Washington during the pre-coup period to visit IRI headquarters and meet with officials in the Bush administration. NED was a frequent host to these ultra-conservative Venezuelans, as was the Colombian ambassador in Washington.

Primero Justicia national assembly members Julio Borges and Liliana Hernandez have generally been the most outspoken critics of all legislation proposed by government party lawmakers. IRI's training has been relatively successful, though it has still failed to consolidate national support for the party. Primero Justicia is viewed as more of a Caracas party than one with national reach.

IRI's Coup-Time Blooper

Although it pledged to be non-partisan, IRI's objective in Venezuela was clearly to support and build the opposition movement with the goal of removing President Chávez from office. This was clear on April 12, 2002, during the coup d'etat against President Chávez, when IRI President George Folsom issued a press release entitled "IRI President Folsom Praises Venezuelan Civil Society's Defense of Democracy":

> Last night, led by every sector of civil society, the Venezuelan people rose up to defend democracy in their country. Venezuelans were provoked into action as a result of systematic repression by the Government of Hugo Chávez. Several hundred thousand people filled the streets of Caracas to demand the resignation of Lt. Col. Hugo Chávez. Chávez responded with sharpshooters and his paramilitary Bolivarian circles, killing more than 12 civilians and wounding more than 100 others. In contrast, IRI commends the patriotism of the Venezuelan military for their refusal to fire on their countrymen.
>
> IRI also applauds the bravery of civil society leaders— members of the media, the Church, the nation's educators and school administrators, political party leaders, labor unions and the business sector—who have put their very lives on the line in their struggle to restore genuine democracy to their country. IRI will remain engaged for

the long term with political parties and our civil society partners to help rebuild Venezuela's fractured political system and restore elected democracy to the country.

IRI has promoted the strengthening of democracy in Venezuela since 1994 and recognizes that Venezuela's future is not a return to its pre-Chávez past, but instead the development of accountable, non-corrupt, and responsive government.

Today, the National Assembly is expected to meet to lay the groundwork for the transitional government to hold elections later this year. *The Institute has served as a bridge between the nation's political parties and all civil society groups to help Venezuelans forge a new democratic future, based on accountability, rule of law and sound democratic institutions. We stand ready to continue our partnership with the courageous Venezuelan people.*

IRI is a nonprofit organization dedicated to advancing democracy worldwide. IRI's programs span the globe and include training on civic responsibility and the legislative process, and strategies for building political parties and election campaigns. IRI is a nonpartisan organization, federally funded through the National Endowment for Democracy (NED) and the US Agency for International Development (USAID), as well as privately funded by donations from individuals, corporations and foundations.[5] (Emphasis added.)

After April 14, 2002, once it was clear that President Chávez had been returned to power and a coup had occurred, Carl Gershman, president of the NED, wrote a scathing memo to George Folsom, stating, "By welcoming [the coup]—indeed, without any apparent reservations—you unnecessarily interjected IRI into the sensitive internal politics of Venezuela."[6] Gershman's statement to Folsom was rather ironic, considering the NED had been funding IRI to train and build the opposition movement during the prior year, clearly itself an interjection into "sensitive internal politics." What Gershman meant, of course, was that Folsom had made that interjection unnecessarily public. In any case, Gershman's remarks to Folsom were mere puffery. Instead of cutting back financing to IRI, NED increased it right after the coup.

DECODING VENEZUELA

In September 2001, the US embassy in Caracas began sending signs to Washington that a change in government would soon be possible and the man to fill the president's shoes was Pedro Carmona, president of Fedecámaras, Venezuela's chamber of commerce. In a September 2001 cable from the embassy in Caracas to the Departments of State, Commerce, and Energy, Ambassador Donna Hrinak announced an upcoming Washington visit by selected members of the Council of Venezuelan–US Businessmen, Consejo de Empresarios Venezuela–Estados Unidos (CEVEU). Pedro Carmona, one of the selected members, was labeled as "a highly regarded and influential business leader who has consistently played a critical role in advancing US commercial interests in Venezuela."

The embassy cable strongly recommended that the Department of State arrange meetings between the CEVEU representatives and the undersecretary of commerce for international trade, the assistant secretary for policy and international affairs, the Department of Energy, and the assistant secretary of state for economic and business affairs. Ambassador Hrinak also requested appointments be arranged between Carmona and his fellow travelers and Representative Cass Ballenger, Representative Gregory Meeks, Representative Mark Souder, and Senator Bob Graham. With an endorsement from the embassy and State Department, Carmona was sure to be received in Washington with open arms.

After Ambassador Hrinak returned from consultations in Washington in early November 2001 and relations were still brittle between the two countries, she sent a cable up to Washington informing the secretary of state that the Carmona-led Fedecámaras had announced the suspension of dialogue with the Venezuelan government. Hrinak mentioned the possibility of a nationwide work stoppage to be announced on November 28, 2001. In the cable, the ambassador sided with Carmona's version of events, justifying the harsh reaction from the business community:

> Carmona, only recently elected as president of Fedecámaras, had been attempting to establish a dialogue with the Chávez government. The cut-off of communication and the threat of a national work stoppage are a strong reaction to what is widely perceived to be a disregard for the views of the private business sector by President Chávez and his cabinet. While discontent with Chávez has been widespread in the private sector since his election, Chávez's October 29 speech coupled with the GOV's[1] failure to respond to private sector concerns over the new laws appears to have brought the discontent to a head.[2]

Hrinak's frame made it sound as though the growing conflict was all Chávez's fault.

"The Right Man for the Right Time in Venezuela"

In a highly censored and classified cable from the US embassy in Caracas at the end of November 2001, Ambassador Hrinak reported on the decision made by Fedecámaras to declare a national strike as of December 10, 2001. But in the few areas left uncensored, the cable made clear that the US government shared the opposition's views entirely on the driving issue behind the strike: the 49 laws President Chávez had enacted under the "Enabling Act" earlier that month. "President Chávez acted beyond his enabling act authority in decreeing certain laws," wrote Ambassador Hrinak. "The Land Law is an attack on the right of private property."

A few days later, an embassy official by the name of

Cook sent another cable, this time addressed to the State Department, the CIA, Defense Intelligence Agency, National Security Council, and other US embassies in Bogotá, Quito, La Paz, Lima, Mexico, Buenos Aires, Brasilia, and the US Interests Section in Cuba, referring to Pedro Carmona as "statesman-like" and "the right man for the right time in Venezuela" (see Appendix).

Clearly, the stage was being set for a US-backed change of leadership in Venezuela.

In the months that followed, Carmona and fellow union leader Carlos Ortega took several trips to Washington, accompanied by other prominent opposition leaders, including Leopoldo Lopez and Gerardo Blyde of Primero Justicia and other NED grantees.[3] But it was during that first "strike" on December 10, 2001, that a solid bond was formed between two traditional opponents, Fedecámaras and the Confederación de Trabajadores Venezolanos (CTV), historically the leading workers union in the nation.

In 2001, the NED grant to the American Center for International Labor Solidarity (ACILS), the international branch of the AFL-CIO, was tripled. Though ACILS had had an relationship with the CTV since the early 1990s, its average grant for work with the Venezuelan union was about $60,000. But in 2001, this amount was increased to $154,375 with the goal of defining "a new mission and role for the union movement in the development of the nation" (see Appendix).

This new role and mission, it seemed, was a joint venture with the bosses' organization, Fedecámaras, to build a movement capable of ousting the Chávez government. In order to achieve this goal, the NED was the number one financier.

As 2001 came to a close, the NED had pumped up its spending in Venezuela to a whopping $877,435. In addition to ACILS's tripled budget with the CTV and IRI's sextupled grant for its work with Primero Justicia and other parties, the National Democratic Institute (NDI) had jumped on board. While NDI had been absent from the 2000 NED–Venezuela budget, it received a $210,500 grant to work with the social organization Momento de la Gente (The People's Moment) to "engage citizens in the policy-making process" and to focus on "government accountability and transparency." Momento de la Gente was one of the leading civil society groups in the growing opposition movement to President Chávez. The generous $210,500 grant was sure to boost their national projection and mission.

Momento de la Gente was also a direct NED-grantee in 2000. Headed by the well-connected, wealthy Mercedes de Freitas, Momento de la Gente had received a mere $16,747 from the NED in 2000. But by 2001, as their political efforts to oppose Chávez were gaining ground, NED increased their direct grant to $40,000, over twice what they were previously receiving just months before. The grant specifically noted that the NED funding would be "used to cover core institutional costs." Basically, NED was funding the functioning of the organization as it was taking on a leadership role in the opposition coalition forming between labor, business, and civil society. Together with the NDI–NED grant, more than $250,000 was made available to Momento de la Gente in 2001—almost fifteen times what they had been granted the year before.

Momento de la Gente's Mercedes de Freitas made a plea to NED program director Christopher Sabatini during the days of the coup against Chávez to accept the Carmona government and dismiss any notions that a coup had occurred. Her organization had just received an additional $64,000 in the run-up to the coup.

By the end of February 2002, Fedecámaras and the CTV, along with opposition-aligned political parties and social organizations, were calling for massive marches in the streets of Caracas.

The Growing Coalition of Unlikely Friends

Months before the April 11, 2002, coup, the US government had put into action a skillfully devised plan to aid the anti-Chávez movement. The unlikely allies—Venezuela's largest labor union, CTV; the chamber of commerce, Fedecámaras;

leaders of the traditional political parties, Acción Democrática, COPEI, Movimiento al Socialismo, and others; the new parties, Primero Justicia and Proyecto Venezuela— shared a common complaint against the Chávez administration's policies about their own loss of political and economic power. This opposition, including the CTV, was primarily comprised of individuals and organization from Venezuela's elite, or, as it is commonly called in Venezuela, the oligarchy. Even though the CTV was Venezuela's major union, it primarily represented upper level and white-collar workers antagonist to Chávez's policies, which favored the vast poor majority.

Although tension and animosity were stirring among Venezuelan elites soon after President Chávez won his second term under the newly ratified Constitution in 1999, it wasn't until 2001 that the opposition coalition began solidifying and making its voice heard. History shows that this wasn't the first time this alliance between the CTV, Fedecámaras, and the traditional political parties had been formed. In the late 1980s, during Carlos Andrés Pérez's generous collaboration with the US government, these same entities came together to form the National Democratic Foundation, which had been used to funnel NED monies from the US to Nicaragua. Once again, labor, business, and political parties were unified to promote US interests in Latin America.

The NED had been present in Venezuela, though minimally, since the late 1980s when they began financing the CTV. But from 2000 to 2001, the NED's budget in Venezuela quadrupled, and funding (more than $877,000) began flowing to large and small organizations with one characteristic in common: a public aversion to President Chávez. Several Venezuelan organizations were awarded direct grants from the NED with no intermediaries. Numerous other organizations were given funding through the four NED core grantees, IRI, NDI, CIPE, and ACILS. Some of the entities directly funded by NED in 2001–2002 included the Asamblea de Educación (Education Assembly), Asociación Civil Comprensión de Venezuela (Venezuelan

Civil Association for Understanding), and the Asociación Civil Consorcio Justicia (Justice Consortium). All of these organizations were aligned with the opposition movement; all of the money was given to "promote democracy."

The Asamblea de Educación worked on opposing all Chávez-promoted legislation involving education reform. Its leader, Leonardo Carvajal, was a staunch Chávez opponent who disagreed with Chávez's educational goals and vowed to do his best to prevent the proposed changes from being enacted. By 2001, the Chávez government had already built more than 1,000 new "Bolivarian" schools in neighborhoods and areas with traditionally little or no access to quality education. The government was also promoting the implementation of a new "Bolivarian curriculum," which would alter the previous school curriculum to include more accurate historical information about Venezuelan and Latin American history, as well as change the Eurocentric approach to education to a more South American one.

So, in addition to providing $55,000 of funding for Carvajal's and his organization's opposition activities and attendance at marches, the NED grant also funded efforts to oppose legitimate legislation that had been lawfully debated and enacted by Venezuela's National Assembly. In fact, Carvajal admitted later that the NED funding was the primary source of income for his organization. He even received a salary from the NED grant to finance his lifestyle (see Appendix 2).

The grant to Asociación Civil Comprensión de Venezuela (ACCV) in the amount of $57,820 from the NED came at a peculiar moment. The focus was on "initiating a national debate on the newly changing role of the military in the country." President Chávez is a former military colonel. A large percentage of his cabinet members and top-level government officials are retired or active military officers. While the NED grant to ACCV may have seemed timely, it was also rather unusual. As NED was financing efforts to raise awareness on the negative aspects of military involvement in government, Venezuela had just elected, twice, a government with a strong military presence. It doesn't seem odd then that around the time of the ACCV NED project, dissident military officers began aligning themselves with the opposition movement.

In the years 2000, 1999, and earlier, the primary recipients of NED funds in Venezuela were the ACILS for its work with the CTV, CIPE for its work with counterpart Centro de Divulgación del Conocimiento Económico (CEDICE: Center for the Dissemination of Economic Information), and the IRI for its ongoing training and shaping of political parties in the nation. Direct NED grantees in Venezuela during those years included groups such as Centro al Servicio de la Acción Popular (CESAP: Center for the Service of Public Action), Programa para el Desarrollo Legislativo (PRODEL: Program for Legislative Development), Fundación Momento de la Gente, and Sinergia, an organization dedicated to strengthening other social organizations aligned with the opposition. All of these entities had leanings toward the opposition, some more than others. Even so, the NED role in Venezuela was relatively minor prior to 2001. Then the Bush administration authorized an increase in spending on organizations capable of forming a solid opposition movement to Chávez.

These contributions are couched in high-minded language: "strengthening political parties," "the National Endowment for Democracy," and so on, appearing to be nothing more than well-intentioned efforts to help democracy take root. But imagine being subjected to an equivalent amount of "aid" from a foreign country, shoveling billions of dollars into the US to build parties and educate candidates who are sympathetic to that government's interest. Such an effort would be immediately exposed as an attempt to subvert the democratic process, not build it.

The First Signs

On December 10, 2001, the first "general strike" was called by the loose coalition of the CTV, Fedecámaras, private media, NED-funded social organizations, and opposition political parties with the objective of opposing the Chávez government's proposal of a set of 49 laws that would implement many of the new rights represented in the 1999 Constitution. Prior to the strike, high-level officials of the US government, including Colin Powell, George Tenet, and Roger Noriega, had made statements indicating a possible break in relations with the Chávez administration, basing such attitudes on Chávez's overt opposition to the bombing of Afghanistan in October 2001. Ambassador Hrinak's call to Washington in early November 2001 for consultations was an indicator of a change in relations.

The December 10th opposition-led strike paralyzed the nation for one day and set the stage for the months to come. The opposition organized multiple protests and acts of civil disobedience and a faction of senior military officers began to "defect" and publicly declare a state of rebellion. The private media upped its tone of aggression toward the government and overtly gave complete coverage to the opposition, rarely presenting balanced news accounts. The private media channels ran continuous advertisements promoting the strike and calling on citizens to participate in marches and demonstrations against the government.

"US Policy Toward Venezuela: November 2001–April 2002," a report from the office of the inspector general at the State Department, completed after the April coup at the request of Senator Christopher Dodd (D-CT), concluded that

> during the six month period [November 2001–April 2002], NED, the [State] Department, and DOD provided training, institution building and other support programs totaling about $3.3 million to Venezuelan organizations and individuals, some of whom are understood to have been involved in the events of April 12–14. Further, the federal assistance programs involved numerous contacts between NED, the Department, and DOD and these organizations and individuals during the six months period.[4]

In fact, the report affirmed that NED funding for programs

in Venezuela during that same six-month period totaled over $2 million. The report also showed something that NED's own internal documents released under the Freedom of Information Act (FOIA) had attempted to cover up: an additional $622,000 the NED had funneled into ACILS for its work with the CTV from February 2001 to January 2002—more than $150,000 every three months. On top of the $622,000, NED had given another grant to ACILS in the amount of $154,400 to support the CTV.

The $2 million figure was astonishing. The year before, NED's total grant program in Venezuela was just a little more than $200,000. Twelve months later, it was ten times that amount. And those receiving the financing—all of it—were building a movement opposed to the democratically elected and popularly supported Venezuelan government. Democratic? Popular? Who cares? The US government wanted Chávez out and through financial and political support for the growing coalition of business, labor, political parties, and social organizations, they thought his demise would be plausible.

Groups receiving direct NED financing in Venezuela during the 2002 pre-coup period included the Consorcio Justicia, which received two grants, one for the amount of $84,000 and another for $11,000; Acción Campesina, $35,000; Asamblea de Educación $57,000; Centro al Servicio de la Acción Popular (CESAP), $63,000; Momento de la Gente, $64,000; CIPE-CEDICE, $90,000, $66,266 and $116,525; Instituto Prensa y Sociedad, $25,000; Asociación Civil Justicia Alternativa, $10,000; Fundación Justicia de Paz del Estado Monagas, $11,000; and NDI, $50,000.

All of the groups receiving NED monies were involved in the opposition movement in early 2002. Most were spending a majority of their time marching in the streets calling for Chávez's resignation and focusing their energies on seeking out ways to force regime change. Such activities are a far cry from where US taxpayer dollars should be spent.

US Public Funds for "Promoting Democracy" in Venezuela

Year	NED in US $	US AID in US$
2000	232,831	—
2001	877,435	—
2002	1,698,799	2,197,066
2003	1,046,321	8,903,669
2004	874,384	6,345,000
2005	930,274	5,000,000
2006*	2,000,000	7,000,000
Total Public Funds:		$34,175,505

* approximate

A COUP BY ANY OTHER NAME

On February 25, 2002, Charles Shapiro was officially sent to Caracas as the new US ambassador. But Washington's decision to replace Hrinak with Shapiro had been made back in December 2001, as the opposition consolidated and showed potential, yet clearly needed some experienced support and guidance. Shapiro's history with the State Department gave a sense of the tone the US government now chose to set with Venezuela. A 24-year veteran of the Foreign Service in Latin America, Shapiro had worked in the US embassy in El Salvador for five years during the tumultuous 1980s when US intervention was at an all-time high. From 1999 to 2001, he was coordinator of the Bureau of Cuban Affairs office in Washington, responsible for monitoring and overseeing US policy toward Cuba and upholding US-imposed restrictions on travel and commerce between the two nations. The Chávez administration was known as an open ally of Fidel Castro and Chávez made no attempt to conceal or alter his relationship with Cuba despite Washington's insistent requests and demands that he do so. Sending Shapiro to Caracas was a clear sign that the US was losing patience with Chávez and his Castro-friendly policies.

Ambassador Shapiro wasted no time at all acclimating to the Venezuelan political scene and getting Venezuela in tune with the US agenda. By the time he was officially installed in the embassy in Caracas, three top-ranking Venezuelan military officers had publicly denounced President Chávez and threatened a military rebellion. On February 7, 2002,

Venezuelan Air Force Colonel Pedro Sota demanded Chávez's resignation. Colonel Sota's call was followed the next day by National Guard Capitan Pedro Flores, who claimed the majority of Venezuela's armed forces was ready to rebel against the government. Then, on February 18, Vice-Admiral Carlos Molina Tamayo accused President Chávez of "seeking to impose a totalitarian regime in Venezuela and placing the nation in danger by soliciting closer ties to Cuba and distancing itself from the United States." He demanded Chávez's resignation and spoke of a "rising military rebellion in the armed forces."

Earlier that month, the opposition had staged several large protests, gathering hundreds in the streets to demand President Chávez's resignation. On January 31, 2002, the Catholic church declared its opposition to Chávez, refusing to engage in dialogue with the government and instead expressing support for the growing opposition movement. The public military rebellion, and in particular the position of Vice-Admiral Molina Tamayo, was a clear indicator that the situation was becoming more unstable each day. Rumors of a possible coup began circulating across the country.

Otto Reich Comes onto the Scene

Toward the end of February 2002, Carlos Ortega, then president of the CTV, which had clearly emerged as one of the leaders of the opposition movement, led a small delegation of AFL-CIO and CTV members to Washington to meet with top government officials. Of particular note was a meeting between Ortega and Otto Reich, who at the time had just been named the assistant secretary of state for Western Hemisphere affairs.[5] What is important to understand is that Reich had been a key player in the decade-long intervention in Nicaragua, and during his later tenure as ambassador to Venezuela, he had been implicated in securing the release and entry into the US of one of the most notorious terrorists in Latin America, Orlando Bosch. In short, Reich had a long history of aiding overthrows of democratic governments or those governments not working in US interests. A vehement anti-Castro Cuban American who had long worked to support the ousting of Fidel Castro, Reich considered Chávez's government to be on the path to "Castro-communism." As far as he was concerned, Chávez needed to be stopped at all costs.

During the Reagan administration, Reich had headed the Office of Public Diplomacy for Latin America, a Reagan creation that was declared illegal after a 1987 investigation by the US comptroller general. Reich's office was charged with disseminating "White Propaganda," covert mis-information designed to influence public opinion against Nicaragua's Sandinista government. The office attempted to influence US reporters and mainstream media to portray the Sandinistas in a negative light and to run deceptive op-ed articles drafted by Reich and his office, but signed by university professors and anti-Sandinista Nicaraguans.

The Senate Foreign Relations Committee blocked Reich's appointment in January 2002 as assistant secretary of state for Western Hemisphere affairs. But President George W. Bush exercised executive privilege and appointed Reich on an interim basis for a one-year period. Subsequently, failing Senate confirmation, Bush named Reich his special advisor on Latin American affairs. Reich resigned on June 16, 2004 to return to the private sector, leaving a career of intervention and "regime change" behind him. But back in early 2002, he was frequently meeting with opposition leaders and putting forth the US's desire for a change in Venezuela's government. Among others, Reich met frequently with Fedecámaras head Carmona, who was already well on the radar screen of the US government. Reich's role would only expand as the coup rumors gained credibility.

Bogus Intelligence Reports

On March 20, 2002, a Secret Intelligence Assessment was prepared by the US Southern Command Joint Intelligence Center, entitled "Venezuela: Growing Evidence of an Insurgent Partnership." Though heavily censored in old-style black marker, it is still plain to see that the report analyzed the alleged connections between the Chávez government and Colombian terrorist organizations (the FARC and the ELN). The assessment made reference to an agreement between Chávez and the FARC to provide free access to Venezuelan territory in exchange for a FARC promise not to kidnap or extort Venezuelan citizens. The source for this hardcore intelligence was the Bogotá daily, *El Tiempo*. No other credible source was provided.

The intelligence assessment further cited a letter published in Venezuela's daily, *El Universal*, from the dissident military officers calling for Chávez's resignation, charging that the Venezuelan government had allowed the FARC to establish two large camps on Venezuelan territory in the Perija Ridge, and that additional FARC camps were under construction in San Joaquin de Navay. The only source provided was the letter in *El Universal*.

The report further cited multiple accounts of Chávez's collaborations with the FARC and the ELN, including an alleged channeling of $1 million dollars into a FARC-ELN front company, Cootraguas. The source? *El Universal*, Globovisión television station, *El Nacional* newspaper. What do all these media outlets have in common? An open and explicit dislike of the Chávez government and a notorious manipulation and distortion of information. Maybe Otto Reich's Office of Public Diplomacy had been re-hatched.

The "intelligence" report even claimed that according to *El Universal*, $2 million were used to purchase weapons "through Nicaragua's Sandinista Front in order to arm the members of the Bolivarian Circles and to create a special military force to defend the regime."[6] The Bolivarian Circles are community and neighborhood-based grassroots organizations formed to coordinate local issues and to foster community relations. No concrete evidence has ever been provided to prove claims that the Venezuelan government has armed such organizations.

Despite the lack of credible sources, this intelligence assessment was sent to Washington and circulated among members of Congress to influence opinion. It was no wonder that soon after, US Congress members were declaring they had evidence of Chávez's collaborations with the FARC and the ELN. Not one single member of Congress has ever presented any evidence to prove such claims.

In any case, the bogus intelligence report was offered as justification for increasing US government efforts to support an illegal ouster of President Chávez. Surely if a link was made between Chávez and a terrorist group, his removal from office, however conducted, would be accepted.

The CIA Knows All

On March 5, 2002, CIA operatives in Venezuela prepared and sent a Senior Executive Intelligence Brief (SEIB) to approximately 200 top-level representatives at the Defense Intelligence Agency (DIA), the National Imagery and Mapping Agency (NIMA), the CIA, the State Department, and the National Security Agency (NSA). The SEIB was labeled "Top Secret" and "Not for Foreign Dissemination." The top-secret brief detailed how "Opposition to President Chávez is mounting... Calls for his resignation by public officials and private-sector leaders are becoming daily occurrences... The military is also divided in its support for Chávez... A successful coup would be difficult to mount."[7]

The SEIB brief also mentioned, "Opposition leaders are not unified and lack a singular strategy for replacing Chávez." Clearly, the CIA was well aware of the opposition's downfalls, hence the need for more than $1 million in NED funding to "strengthen political parties" and anti-Chávez NGOs. And it was just around that time that NED gave IRI that extra $300,000 to "strengthen political parties." ACILS also received that additional $116,001 to back the CTV. Leaders of those very same political parties and labor unions were precisely the ones the CIA was referring to as "not unified" and "lack[ing] a singular strategy for replacing Chávez." So the US believed that a substantial influx of US taxpayer dollars into these groups could aid them in unification and strategizing.

"Another Piece Falls into Place"

On March 5, 2002, something happened that pleased the US government. A cable sent by the US embassy in Caracas to Washington—to the CIA, DIA, NSC, and others—carried the subject line "Labor, Business, and Church Announce Transition Pact." The summary of the cable read,

> With much fanfare, the Venezuelan Great and Good assembled on March 5 to hear representatives of the Confederation of Venezuelan Workers, the Federation of Business Chambers and the Catholic Church present their "Bases for a Democratic Accord," ten principles on which to guide a transitional government... This accord represents an important step for the opposition, which has been quick to condemn Chávez but had so far offered no vision of its own.[8]

The language of the embassy cable is extraordinary—"the Venezuelan Great and Good" apparently means everyone in Venezuela but the Chavistas; all those assembled to hear the opposition leaders present their "Transitional Government" pact were firmly in the anti-Chávez camp. At the same time, the CIA had been sending briefs to top intelligence and government officials about the difficulties of mounting a coup and the divisive opposition, so the leaders of the CTV, Fedecámaras, and the Catholic Church were doing their best to come together and agree what to do after they got Chávez out of office. According to the cable, Carlos Ortega, CTV president, stated, "This accord is a pact for us... to guide us through the transition and to establish a Government of Democratic Unity."

If it had any doubts before, as of March 5, 2002, the US embassy must have been absolutely clear that the opposition was planning to get rid of Chávez. While the US government may have liked this idea on its premise, they also knew full well that Chávez's constitutional term was not up until December 2006, four years away. Therefore, unless they truly believed Chávez was just going to step down, despite the fact that he gave no signs whatsoever to make anyone believe he would voluntarily resign, they must have thought there would be a coup d'etat. Considering that high ranking military officers such as Molina Tamayo were threatening military rebellion, it was not far-fetched for the US government to think a coup was in the works.

The US government appeared to have been thoroughly pleased by the March 5th accord reached by the opposition— after all, it had pumped in a couple of million dollars to help strengthen and unify the opposition parties. A comment in the embassy cable revealed such satisfaction with the investment: "Another piece falls into place," wrote Embassy Official Cook. "This accord... may well form the frame of reference and code of conduct for a transitional government..."

The "another piece falls into place" comment should raise some eyebrows. Many eyebrows. If the opposition agreement of a post-Chávez transitional government is another "piece" in the plan, then the plan must really have been the ouster of Chávez.

If on March 5th, the US government could possibly have believed that Chávez's removal would come through resignation, by Monday, March 11, 2002, they could no longer sell that story. Another SEIB was sent by the CIA folks in Venezuela to the five intelligence agencies in Washington, this time in the form of a warning. The warning was prepared by the DCI Strategic Warning Committee, a highly secretive and top-level group chaired by the National Intelligence Officer for Warning and comprised of representatives from the directors of the NSA, the DIA, and NIMA, as well as the assistant secretary of state for intelligence and research and the deputy director for intelligence at the CIA. The top-secret warning was more specific: "There are increased signs that Venezuelan business leaders and military officers are becoming dissatisfied with President Chávez... the military may move to overthrow him."[9]

More Pieces in Place

The military was preparing a coup and the opposition leaders had agreed on a post-Chávez transitional government agenda. The highest levels of the US government knew this in early March 2002. Despite the fact that coups against democratic governments are illegal, the US did nothing to dissuade the plotters from acting. In fact, their actions were encouraged. No threats were made to cut NED financing to its grantees, despite their open ties with coup plotters. Instead, the monies were increased during the period when the conspiring was at a head.

Furthermore, the US military had substantial control and influence over the Venezuelan armed forces, particularly those officers who had declared rebellion, all of whom had received training in the US at academies such as the School of the Americas. Yet, no attempts were made to dissuade the officers from coup plotting.

By April 1, 2002, the US government knew the coup was fast approaching. A SEIB brief of that date, again from the DCI Strategic Warning Committee, stated, "President Chávez is facing continued strong opposition from the private sector, the media, the Catholic Church and opposition political parties... Reporting suggests that disgruntled officers within the military are still planning a coup, possibly early this month."[10]

Ten days before the coup, the US government was aware of who was planning it—the private sector, the opposition parties, the Church, and now the media were involved too, and that the dissident military officers would be the ones most likely to carry it out.

Within five days, the US government knew how the coup was going to play out, in detail. A top secret SEIB from April 6, 2002, headlined "Conditions Ripening for Coup Attempt" informed:

> Dissident military factions, including some disgruntled senior officers and a group of radical junior officers, are stepping up efforts to organize a coup against President Chávez, possibly as early as this month... the level of detail in the reported plans targets Chávez and 10 other senior officials for arrest...

The phrase "level of detail in the reported plans" implies that the CIA had the "reported plans" in their possession on that day, five days before the coup actually took place. Is there any other conclusion to draw than that they were in close contact with the plotters?

The April 6th SEIB further revealed that "To provoke military action, the plotters may try to exploit unrest stemming from opposition demonstrations slated for later this month or ongoing strikes at the state-owned oil company PDVSA."[11]

To summarize, as of April 6, 2002, the US government had clear, explicit information about the approaching coup:

What: A coup d'etat against President Chávez
When: Early April 2002
Who: The private sector, the media, the Catholic Church, the political opposition, and dissident military officers
Where: Venezuela
How: Exploit violence in the opposition march, provoke military action, and arrest Chávez and other top-level officials

Let's look at what happened after April 6th.

On April 7, 2002, President Chávez announced the firing of seven PDVSA managers, the forced retirement of twelve managers, and the removal of an additional five from their positions. The workers were dismissed largely due to mismanagement of the industry, embezzlement of finances, and a difference in policy from the Chávez government. Since PDVSA was a state-owned company, President Chávez legally had full decision-making authority over its operations and employees. But the decision sparked immediate protest from the opposition. The CTV called for an April 9 general strike, which was also supported by Fedecámaras. The fired PDVSA workers called for an "indefinite strike."

By April 10, the PDVSA workers had shut down several operations within the state-owned oil industry, placing the lifeblood of the nation in danger. The shutdowns were directed mostly at operations affecting the internal Venezuelan markets for fuel and gas, intended to induce panic and unrest among Venezuelans and encourage protest. All activities related to fuel production at the Puerto La Cruz refinery were halted. Operación Morrocoy (Operation Turtle, or slow down) was implemented in the José Complex near Puerto la Cruz and affected liquefied petroleum gas production. Work at several refineries near Puerto Cabello stopped, including the largest fuel distribution plant in Venezuela, Yagua, and the El Palito refinery, which provided fuel to most of the Venezuelan market. PDVSA Caracas was closed down.

To say the least, the country was in a state of turmoil; the "pieces were falling into place" as planned.

On April 10, Pedro Carmona and Carlos Ortega announced in a televised press conference that the "general strike" would be "indefinite." The US-financed opposition leaders also declared the "immediate establishment" of a "coordinating committee for democracy and liberty" intended to "rescue Venezuela's freedom and liberty and coordinate all opposition activities." The political parties comprising the committee included AD, COPEI, MAS, Proyecto Venezuela, Primero Justicia, and Alianza Bravo Pueblo, all parties funded by the NED and IRI. They announced an opposition march scheduled for the morning of April 11, from Parque del Este in the eastern side of Caracas to the PDVSA headquarters in Chuao.

A lot happened—or was supposed to happen—on April 10 and on the days to come. That day, a NED-sponsored conference to "promote democracy" in Venezuela had been planned by grantee Consorcio Justicia. One of the headline speakers programmed for the conference was Fedecámaras's Carmona, outspoken opposition leader, coup plotter, and favorite of the US government. But the conference, which was financed by Consorcio Justicia's $84,000 NED grant, never took place due to the strikes and protests occurring throughout Caracas that day.[12]

Highlighting the increasingly tense situation, the private media channels aired a speech by General Nestor González González declaring rebellion and publicly calling for President Chávez to "step down." This was the very same González that US military attaché Rodgers had been looking for days before the coup, with his mysterious message. Two days later, on live television, it was revealed that General González González had pre-recorded that media moment in order to keep Chávez from attending an Organization of American States (OAS) meeting in Costa Rica, so that the coup plan could be activated. The general succeeded in his efforts.

The Coup

On April 11, 2002, CTV, Fedecámaras, and the NED-supported opposition parties held one of the largest rallies and marches Venezuela had ever seen.

The night before, Ambassador Shapiro had cabled to Washington:

> Five to seven thousand opposition supporters held a loud and jubilant rally at PDVSA headquarters until late in the evening... Virtually all prominent opposition figures including Pedro Carmona, Alfredo Peña and Carlos Ortega gave impromptu speeches... Carmona seemed particularly energized by the size and mood of the crowd... It was a celebratory atmosphere, not unlike after Venezuela defeated Paraguay in World Cup qualifying.[13]

Shapiro's likening of the opposition rally in preparation for a coup d'etat to a soccer game demonstrates the patronizing and belittling attitude the US had assumed in the grave matter of the overthrow of a democratic government in South America.

About midday on April 11, speakers at the opposition rally, including Carmona and Ortega, began calling for supporters to march on the presidential palace, Miraflores, to demand Chávez's resignation. No official permit or authorization had been requested or given for this change in route. Caracas Mayor Freddy Bernal appeared on the state television channel, Channel 8, pleading with Carmona and Ortega not to direct marches toward the palace, fearing violence would ensue.

A pro-Chávez rally was happening at the same time in front of Miraflores; thousands of Chávez supporters had been alerted to the opposition's movements and objectives. The Presidential Guard was called out to ensure that the two sides, now riled up, would not clash. Before the opposition marchers even reached the side of Miraflores where the pro-Chávez supporters were gathered, two anti-Chávez marchers were shot. The bullet wounds showed the shots came from within the opposition march itself. But no warnings were given to other marchers that violence had erupted from within their own crowd.

Instead, the march continued aggressively toward the palace. Led by Rear Admiral Carlos Molina Tamayo, who had publicly denounced the president just weeks before and threatened a military rebellion, the crowd managed to pass through several metropolitan police barriers that had been set up to prevent the march from reaching Miraflores. The metropolitan police were under the control of Greater Caracas Mayor Alfredo Peña, who just minutes before had been addressing the anti-Chávez rally, calling for marchers to head to the palace. Joined by the ex-President of PDVSA, retired General Guaicaipuro Lameda, Molina Tamayo was able to break another police barrier that had been set up in the El Calavario section of Caracas, close to the palace and the pro-Chávez rally. The National Guard came out to prevent a confrontation between the two groups, and eventually Molina Tamayo and Lameda ceased calling for a raid on the pro-Chávez rally. Unfortunately, the plan had already been set into motion and the resulting violence could not be stopped.

At 2:15PM, the high military command was broadcast on national television, attempting to diffuse rumors of violence that were circulating throughout the country. Earlier that day, in the eastern part of town, ten high-level military officers had summoned CNN correspondent Otto Neustald to a residential location to record a prepared statement for subsequent broadcast. Read by Vice Admiral Héctor Ramirez Pérez, who was subsequently named Minister of Defense by the Carmona coup government, the testimony deplored the massacre of innocent civilians, announcing that a macabre conspiracy had been implemented by Chávez, resulting in the death of six Venezuelans, killed at the hands of government forces. Ramirez Pérez called for a military insurrection, citing the violence as justification. Neustald had to do two takes of the vice admiral's testimony. It was recorded before any violence had erupted in the opposition or pro-Chávez demonstrations.

A few months later, Neustald, participating in a forum entitled "Journalism in Times of Crisis" at the Bicentennial University of Aragua in Venezuela, revealed that

> On the 10th at night they called me on the telephone and said, Otto, tomorrow the 11th there will be a video of Chávez, the march will go toward the presidential palace, there will be deaths and then 20 military officials of high rank will appear and pronounce themselves against the government of Chávez, and will request his resignation. They told me this on the 10th at night.[14]

He affirmed that at the time of the recording, which specifically cites deaths caused by Chávez forces, no violence had yet happened. The US media had in effect been in the service of the coup.

Venevisión, the most popular station in the country, had installed a correspondent on the rooftop of a building nearby the palace, with a view of Puente Llaguno, the area where the pro-Chávez rally was concentrated. Nevertheless, throughout the greater part of the day, the private media had been exclusively broadcasting images from the opposition demonstration and march. The lack of balanced coverage appeared to be part of the plan. (According to a CIA SEIB, the media had also joined in the coup plotting.)

By about 3PM, violence had erupted in various places on the outskirts of the palace. At about that time, Molina Tamayo, Guaicaipuro Lameda, Pedro Carmona, and Carlos Ortega were called to a meeting at the Venevisión headquarters. In fact, most of the opposition leaders disappeared from the march, one by one, leaving the masses to confront the planned massacre on their own. Shortly after, shots began ringing out from atop buildings surrounding the palace and from the metropolitan police, stationed on Avenue Baralt, right beneath Puente Llaguno. The first to fall were in the pro-Chávez crowd—twelve people were killed. After 3:10PM, more than 20 deaths and injuries occurred in the space of just a half hour. But no television stations were reporting these events.

Soon, innocent victims from both sides were hit, and before it was clear what was happening on the ground, the private stations began to broadcast the pre-recorded Ramirez Pérez statement, blaming the deaths on Chávez and calling for a military insurrection.

Just as the call for military rebellion began, at 3:44PM, President Chávez initiated a broadcast on national television, what is called a *"cadena"*—the government broadcasts on all channels, per decree. But as he was speaking, the private television channels illegally captured alternative transmitters and were able to split the television screens to show the president on just half a screen and the opposition on the other side, or in some cases, block the president's *cadena* altogether and broadcast the military call for insurrection.

The images taken by the Venevisión cameraman and correspondent stationed on a rooftop nearby Puente Llaguno had been manipulated back at the studio. The full scene of the metropolitan police below and snipers on rooftops above the bridge was cut and the only footage left was that of the pro-Chávez demonstrators firing at targets below the bridge. The Venevisión reporter recorded a voiceover claiming Chávez supporters stationed on Puente Llaguno were firing on peaceful, unarmed opposition marchers at the orders of President Chávez. The video failed to pan to the full image to show that no opposition marchers were even in that area. The manipulated footage was picked up and broadcast over and over again by all the private channels, and even sent around the world to justify the ouster of President Chávez.

The author of the video, Luis Alfonso Fernández of Venevisión, won the top journalism prize in Spain (Premio Rey 2003) for that same news video. He later admitted to the newspaper *Panorama* (31 August 2003) that "in reality, that day I did not see the Chávez supporters firing at the opposition march." Journalist Ricardo Márquez of *Últimas Noticias* wrote that Luis Alfonso Fernández stated he could not see who the Chávez supporters were firing at and that the voiceover on the video was added after the events. Another journalist from a private channel, Del Valle Canelón of Globovisión, initially affirmed that in the video, the group of civilians were seen firing, but against the Metropolitan Police.[15]

The truth of the manipulation would emerge in time; on the day of coup, the video served its purpose. Utilizing the television reports as justification, the military officers who had already declared rebellion, together with opposition leaders, stormed Miraflores and attempted to force President Chávez's resignation.

The discussion about the Avenue Baralt and Puente Llaguno violence in a cable on April 11 sent by Ambassador Shapiro to Washington is completely censored. But the cable did remark that

> On the morning of April 11th, the opposition's "Coordinating Committee for Democracy and Liberty" decided to go for broke—to seek the immediate departure of President Chávez by popular acclamation... The following opposition rally held in front of PDVSA headquarters in Chacao was an overwhelming success...[16]

Clearly, Shapiro considered it an "overwhelming success" that the coup was occurring as planned and the opposition was actually accomplishing its objective.

Meanwhile, President Chávez, refusing to resign, was detained and imprisoned in Fort Tiuna. The palace was taken over by opposition leaders and the state-owned television Channel 8, which had broadcast a substantially different account of events than the private media, was shut down by force. Pedro Carmona, the Fedecámaras chief, was named by an unknown party as "interim president" later that day and to the understanding of most, a transition team was to be named to govern through the following weeks.

Wasting no time at all, the PDVSA board and managers were reinstated to their positions.

"No Oil Will be Sent to Cuba"

One of Ambassador Shapiro's first cables up to Washington after the intense events of the day began thus:

> Televised scenes of joy have marked the return of Petroleos de Venezuela (PDVSA) employees to their La Campiña headquarters building... PDVSA executives underline that the company should return to normal operations by early next week. Shipments are expected to resume today. PDVSA spokesperson stated publicly that no oil will be sent to Cuba...[17]

Evidently, the least of the US government's concerns was the harsh disruption of constitutional order instigated by a coup d'etat led by its benefactors. The primary preoccupation of the US government appeared to be Venezuela's oil flow. As the fourth largest exporter of oil in the world, Venezuela is also the nearest major oil supplier to the United States. Venezuela also owns eight oil refineries in the US and the CITGO gas chain, which has franchises across the country.

The US was also rather concerned about the flow of oil to Cuba. Under the Chávez administration, Cuba and Venezuela shared an amicable trade relationship. Venezuela provided oil to Cuba at specific tariffs and Cuba provided medical doctors, sports trainers, and other expert services at special rates. The US embassy cable referencing the cutoff of oil supply to Cuba is heavily censored under the heading "Cuba Connection to end?" The only piece left uncensored was a quote from reinstated PDVSA worker Edgar Paredes: "'We are not going to send even one barrel of oil to Cuba,' which drew thunderous applause."

Venevisión's Contributions

Several accounts indicated that multinational media mogul and close Bush family friend Gustavo Cisneros, a Cuban-Venezuelan, hosted Carmona, CTV head Carlos Ortega, and other opposition leaders and media owners at his Venevisión television headquarters for briefings and meetings throughout the day on April 11. Also, several phone calls and visits were made between Otto Reich, Elliot Abrams, Ambassador Shapiro, and Pedro Carmona. All of these contacts were verified later, but excused as merely "normal communications" during a time of heightened risk.

On April 12, Venezuelans awoke to television personality Napoleon Bravo, host of Venevisión's *24 Horas* morning show, declaring "Good morning Venezuela—we have a new president." During this extraordinary television moment, the guests thanked the private media channels for their integral role in making the coup happen and explained in detail the plans leading up to the coup.[18] They specifically underlined the key role of the private media in broadcasting the images that justified the coup. On that same program, in an interview with Rear Admiral Carlos Molina Tamayo and Victor Manuel Garcia, director of the private polling company Ceca, Bravo confessed to having facilitated in his own house the recording of the call to military rebellion by General González González on April 10th.

Later on that same program, Bravo hosted Rear Admiral Carlos Molina Tamayo, Leopoldo Lopez, Victor Manuel Garcia, and other coup participants, who gave an in-depth account of the coup plotting and plans. Garcia revealed that he had headed a civilian commando at Fort Tiuna that was in constant contact with the two military commandos also at the Fort, led by General Efrain Vasquez Velasco and General Nestor González González. Garcia spoke of his constant contacts with Rear Admiral Molina Tamayo and their close coordination during the opposition march. Garcia's live commentary, though reckless, made clear that the events the day before had been meticulously planned.

But the US government already knew that. The CIA's April 6 briefing had come to fruition, exactly as planned.

The US Supports the Coup

The US role was not to just sit back and remain dormant in this conspiracy. On the morning of April 12, President Bush's spokesman Ari Fleischer publicly announced the US government's support for the "Carmona administration" and its condemnation of "ex-President" Chávez for inciting the violence that forced him to "resign." In fact, the White House, the State Department, and the US embassy in Caracas all issued similar statements blaming Chávez for the massacre and recognizing Carmona as a legitimate leader:

> Let me share with you the administration's thoughts about what's taking place in Venezuela. It remains a somewhat fluid situation. But yesterday's events in Venezuela resulted in a change in the government and the assumption of a transitional authority until new elections can be held.
>
> The details still are unclear. We know that the action encouraged by the Chávez government provoked this crisis. According to the best information available, the Chávez government suppressed peaceful demonstrations. Government supporters, on orders from the Chávez government, fired on unarmed, peaceful protestors, resulting in 10 killed and 100 wounded. The Venezuelan military and the police refused to fire on the peaceful demonstrators and refused to support the government's role in such human rights violations. The government also tried to prevent independent news media from reporting on these events.
>
> The results of these events are now that President Chávez has resigned the presidency. Before resigning, he dismissed the vice president and the cabinet, and a transitional civilian government has been installed. This government has promised early elections.
>
> The United States will continue to monitor events. That is what took place, and the Venezuelan people expressed their right to peaceful protest. It was a very large protest that turned out. And the protest was met with violence.[19]

The US role seemed to be convincing the world that Chávez was the instigator of the violence, thereby justifying his overthrow. In fact, according to the White House and the State Department, there was no ouster—Chávez had resigned, and he had even dismissed his entire cabinet beforehand. Considering the CIA had reported to the State Department, the National Security Agency, and other top level officials in Washington of the detailed coup plan, the US reaction on April 12 itself rings of conspiracy. The White House knew the opposition and dissident military officers were planning to overthrow Chávez by exploiting violence in an opposition march and arresting the president. The fact that the coup events played out almost identically to the plan made it simple for the US to be ready with a response that would help legitimize the coup government.

The US was also in charge of pressuring other nations in the region to recognize the Carmona government as legitimate. The US, backed by Colombia and El Salvador, attempted to convince other nations gathered at a Rio Summit to issue a statement recognizing Carmona as Venezuela's new president. Not only did other nations in the region refuse to succumb to US pressure, but they decided to issue a statement condemning the illegal ouster of President Chávez, "Venezuela's constitutional and legitimate President," and rejecting the Carmona government as "a disruption in Constitutional order." The OAS followed suit.[20]

The US was one of the only countries in the world to rush to judgment on the muddled events of April 11 and to openly laud and recognize Carmona as legitimate president. The fact that officials of the US government had been prepping Carmona for this moment for months explained the immediate level of confidence they had in him.

Carmona the Brief

Soon after, the Fedecámaras chief was sworn in as "interim president." To the surprise of many, during a sweeping first act on April 12 in the Salon Ayuacucho in Miraflores Palace, Carmona issued a decree dissolving all of Venezuela's democratic institutions, including the National Assembly, the Supreme Court, the Public Defender's Office, the Attorney General, the Constitution, and the 49 laws Chávez had decreed in December. Carmona also changed the name of the country from the Bolivarian Republic of Venezuela back to the "Republic of Venezuela."

The reading of the "Carmona Decree," which instituted those undemocratic changes, as the text was later referred to, was broadcast by the private media and endorsed by more than 395 Venezuelans present in the palace. In the meantime, pro-Chávez legislators such as Tarek William Saab and other supporters were brutally attacked and detained by the Caracas police force, which was still under the control of opposition leader Mayor Peña. An April 13 cable (see Appendix) from Shapiro to Washington confirmed

> To date, several members of Chávez's MVR party have been detained by Police Forces. These include MVR Deputy William Tarek Saab and former Interior Minister Rodriguez Chacin. We have also heard reports that Tachira Governor Ronald Blanco La Cruz and Mérida Governor Florencio Porras, both of MVR, were being held. We do not know what charges, if any, have been filed against them.

Yet despite the US government's clear knowledge that former Chávez government officials, governors, and congress members were being politically persecuted, no statement was issued to condemn such human rights violations or call for the immediate release of those detained. Instead, the State Department and White House publicly lauded Carmona.

New York Police Department (NYPD) Connection?

More than 60 Venezuelans were killed in the violence that ensued after the coup, primarily at the hands of the metropolitan police. The IRI had worked closely with Peña during 2001 to "shape his image" and the NED-funded Liderazgo y Visión organization had received a $42,207 grant to work with the Caracas police force, several members of which were later charged with the homicides of pro-Chávez supporters killed during the events of April 11, 2002.[21]

In 2000, Peña entered into a contract with ex-NYPD Chief William Bratton, who was brought to Venezuela by the NED-funded opposition group CEDICE to train and improve the capacity and quality of the metropolitan police force. Bratton, known for cleaning up New York City during the years Rudolph Giuliani was mayor, was the creator of the "quality of life crime." Bratton's success in New York was due in large part to his harsh treatment of the Big Apple's immense homeless population and street culture. Under Bratton's direction, the NYPD became notorious for human rights violations and multiple brutal killings of innocent victims. Bratton's contract was renewed by Peña at the end of 2000 despite objections from the Venezuelan government.

A Change of Events

The events of the following 48 hours drastically altered the old-school coup plan that had at first appeared successful. Millions of Chávez supporters filled the streets on April 13 demanding his return to office. At the same time, President Chávez was being held captive in another military base close to Maracay, La Orchila, where allegedly a plane was set to take him outside of the nation. The presidential guard, along with other factions of the military that had remained loyal to Chávez, swiftly forced Carmona and his advisors into detention and returned the palace grounds to the Chávez cabinet members, who then initiated Chávez's rescue.

There are many different versions of the events of April 11–14. According to a CIA Spot Commentary issued at 2:00AM on April 14, 2002,

> Escalating public protests and signs that his military support was flagging prompted interim President Pedro Carmona to resign late Saturday night... Carmona's support unraveled quickly yesterday as political parties, labor unions and the military sensed he was moving too quickly and without their consultation. Disbanding Congress and scrapping the constitution left Carmona operating without a legal framework and ruling by decree—a move condemned by many regional leaders and the international community.

That is, except the United States, which had hastily expressed its approval of the Carmona regime, despite its blatant illegality.

Shapiro's cables to Washington also confirmed the disagreement within the opposition as to how the coup government should function. The embassy political office (POLOFF) has received several phone calls from party members who are concerned about the new government's course of action, especially the dissolution of Congress. They resent not being included in the new government, and fear that the Carmona government is proceeding undemocratically. Although many party representatives were involved in the decision to name Carmona interim president, the party representatives who are now expressing concern say that the party leaders themselves were not consulted.[22]

The concern within the opposition parties and the US government was not about the disruption in constitutional order that had just occurred—the ouster of a democratically elected president by force. The opposition political parties were resentful that they were not playing a bigger role in the coup government. The concern over the dissolution of Congress was not because it represented a highly undemocratic act, but rather because many of their own congressional representatives had been deposed by the measure. So Carmona's actions in many ways provoked his own failure—not because of their undemocratic nature, but rather because of his selfishness.

The US Was "Absolutely Not" Involved in the Coup

Ambassador Shapiro visited Carmona several times during the course of the coup. He claimed that his visits to Carmona on April 12 were intended to persuade him to reactivate the Congress and other institutions he had dissolved. But Shapiro's responses to questions about his relations with opposition leaders and coup participants were highly crafted and thought out.

Not by him, of course.

Shapiro received a cable from the State Department on April 16, 2002, containing "Western Hemisphere Affairs Press Guidance," drafted by L.S. Hamilton and approved by Richard Boucher, State Department spokesman.

When asked, "Did US officials meet with Venezuelan opposition officials prior to the April 11 removal of President Chávez from power?" the answer to memorize was

US officials have met with a broad spectrum of Venezuelans over the past several months both in Caracas and in Washington. US officials met with business community representatives, labor union officials, Catholic Church leaders, opposition political leaders and a wide array of Venezuelan Government officials.

Anticipating questions about meetings with Carmona, the press guide prefaced its suggestions with "If Asked," — in other words, don't offer any information unless pressed. The extended response:

> In the course of normal diplomatic contacts, US officials met with Pedro Carmona... Our message to all Venezuelan contacts has been consistent. The political situation in Venezuela is one for Venezuelans to resolve peacefully, democratically and constitutionally. We explicitly told all of our Venezuelan interlocutors on numerous occasions and at many levels that under no circumstances would the United States support any unconstitutional, undemocratic effort, such as a coup, to remove President Chávez from power.

It is hard to imagine how strongly or "explicitly" this "no coup" message was being relayed, as the US government funneled a couple million dollars into the pockets of the coup plotters and met with them on a regular basis to discuss their plans.

But it was no surprise that the response to the question "Was the United States involved in the effort to remove Venezuelan President Chávez from power?" was "ABSOLUTELY NOT."

Media Blackout

Chávez's return to power in the early morning hours of April 14 came too late to stop the headlines and editorials in the *New York Times*, *Chicago Tribune*, and other international press, which all praised the Venezuelan president's undemocratic ouster in the same tone as the Bush administration.[23] The Venezuelan papers had become remarkably silent, though some carried outdated coup-praising headlines, such as *El Universal*'s "A Step in the Right Direction!"

After multiple outbursts of joy and elation for Carmona's takeover and Chávez's forceful removal, the media was silent on April 13 and 14, imposing a blackout on information and news about developing events.

Andrés Izarra, former managing producer of *El Observador* (a news program on the private station RCTV), testified to the Venezuelan National Assembly that he received clear instructions from Marcel Granier, the owner of RCTV, on the day of the coup and the following days to air "[n]o information on Chávez, his followers, his ministers, and all others that could in any way be related to him." Furthermore, Izarra confirmed that on the day of the coup, RCTV had a report from CNN that Chávez had not resigned but had been kidnapped and jailed, yet the station owner refused to report the story.[24] In fact, all the private channels disseminated the news that President Chávez had resigned, despite their knowledge to the contrary.

The very same private stations that had just provided 24-hour coverage of the Chávez opposition broadcast Tom and Jerry cartoons, with occasional movies such as *Pretty Woman* in between, as Chávez supporters piled into the streets to demand his return. The media did not cover the popular uprisings all around the country in support of Chávez. The blackout was intentional. The media was in mourning; the coup on which they had pinned their hopes had failed.

More Money in the Pot

As calm and normalcy were established in Venezuela in the following days, the US government was forced to issue a statement minimally recognizing the legitimacy of the Chávez government. But, the US has never backtracked on its statement about the version of events that took place on April 11, 2002. It stood by the claim that Chávez ordered the violence against "peaceful opposition marchers," despite ample evidence proving otherwise, including declassified US government documents.

Even on April 17, 2002, when it was clear that a majority of Venezuelans supported President Chávez and that an illegal coup had occurred, the US government still stuck to its "story." In remarks to the North-South Roundtable at the Carnegie Endowment for International Peace, then principal deputy assistant secretary for Western Hemisphere affairs, Lino Gutierrez, stated

> We know that supporters of President Chávez fired on anti-government protestors resulting in more than 100 people wounded or killed... We know that the government prevented five independent television stations from reporting on events... President Chávez allegedly resigned the presidency... The roots of the present crisis lie, we think, with the polarization that occurred under President Chávez and his confrontational policies. President Chávez has attacked freedom of the press, interfered in labor union elections, criticized the Church, stacked the judiciary and attempted to cow any opposition... Let me say now, categorically: the United States did not participate in, inspire, encourage, foment, wink at, nod at, close its eyes to, or in any way leave the impression that it would support a coup of any kind in Venezuela. The record is crystal clear...

The CIA SEIB reports show not only that the US knew about the detailed plans of the coup, but it also augmented the financing of the opposition—and those specifically involved in coup plotting—in the months and weeks prior. Clearly, such support qualifies as "participating in, encouraging, fomenting, and closing its eyes." Furthermore, its subsequent endorsement of the Carmona government and its attempts to induce other governments to recognize Carmona as a legitimate leader constitute clear support for the coup.

Gutierrez's statement that "supporters of President Chávez fired on anti-government protestors resulting in more than 100 people wounded or killed" was intentionally inaccurate. It was quite clear during and after the coup that the majority of those killed and injured were in the Chávez camp. Footage shot by independent journalists in the area at the time clearly got the procession of victims on tape. Most that fell during the violence on April 11 were in the pro-Chávez demonstration. In the days subsequent to the coup, more than

60 Chávez supporters were killed by metropolitan police officers during rebellions in the *barrios* that protested Chávez's arrest. Police records, morgue reports, and witness testimony affirm this fact. But no evidence was ever provided to support claims that "supporters of President Chávez fired on anti-government protestors" except a manipulated video image, later discovered to be a complete farce.

The tape, filmed and produced by Venevisión, which is owned by ardent anti-Chavista and billionaire Gustavo Cisneros, intentionally cut footage and featured a voice-over recorded in the studio well after the events had occurred. The narrator claimed the Chávez supporters were firing on "peaceful" opposition protestors when in reality, those Chavistas who fired guns that day were shooting back at metropolitan police and snipers firing at them. Mayor Peña's metropolitan police were major players in the coup. It was later discovered through forensic investigations that snipers had fired from the roofs of buildings surrounding Puente Llaguno and the presidential palace.

The US government was forced at this point to admit that Chávez was the "legitimate leader" of Venezuela, but it vowed to keep "close watch on him." The efforts to oust Chávez through other means continued.

In April 2002, shortly after the failed coup, the State Department issued a grant of $1 million in "Special Venezuela Funds" to the NED. If the NED really was set up to foster democracy, it seems odd that they would receive these extra funds. At this juncture in time, Venezuelans had just shown themselves to be masters of democracy—they had reversed a coup. That is an Olympian feat in the annals of democracy. But instead of recognizing Venezuela's tremendous advances in democracy and ceasing the US-imposed "promotion of democracy," the US government augmented its presence in Venezuela.

The fact that the NED gets sizable new funding at this juncture clearly reveals that its real objectives don't match the spin. Moreover, NED's choice of recipients for the funds showed the US position: The extra funds were distributed to the very same groups that had just played key roles in the coup against President Chávez. Asamblea de Educación, whose president, Leonardo Carvajal, had been named education minister by Carmona, was given a new grant of $57,000. Fundación Momento de la Gente, whose director, Mercedes de Freitas, had tried her best to explain to the NED that a coup never took place by claiming that Carmona was a "legitimate leader placed by civil society," was awarded $64,000. Asociación Civil Liderazgo y Visión, a group dedicated to promoting alternative models to the Chávez government and providing leadership training, received $42,207. At the time, it was directed by Oscar Garcia Mendoza, who not only published two congratulatory declarations to the Carmona government in national newspapers on April 12, but also signed a civil society decree recognizing Carmona's legitimacy as president.

CEDICE, through NED core grantee CIPE, was awarded $116,525, despite the fact that its director, Rocio Guijarro, was one of the first signers and endorsers of the ill-fated Carmona Decree. And the IRI, which had issued a laudatory statement in favor of the coup and Carmona's takeover on April 12, was given $116,000 to continue its work with Primero Justicia, despite the fact that several of the parties' leaders had signed the Carmona Decree and one, Leopoldo Martinez, had even been named minister of finance under Carmona. The ACILS was given an additional $116,525 to finance the CTV, despite the union's visible participation in the coup.

The NED's bias against Chávez was quite clear. A June 2002 memorandum from Christopher Sabatini, program director for NED in Latin America, stated

> Chávez has done little to demonstrate his good faith or desire for a mediated solution and has continued to inflame popular passions and class tensions... There are rumors... that the government has distributed Uzis to the Bolivarian circles... most people I spoke to recognize that the government is anti democratic and is driving the country to ruin through a misguided revolutionary plan and sheer incompetence...

Sabatini admitted that the groups financed by NED were in the opposition camp: "My general impression is that the NED's program is working with some of the most serious civic groups in the country... many of them have very clear (oppositionist) positions toward Chávez...."

The failure of the coup resonated uncomfortably with the US government. The $1 million special grant from the State Department for NED projects in Venezuela clearly was not going to cover future efforts at regime change in Venezuela. A new strategy was necessary that could adapt to the peculiar circumstances in that South American nation. Therefore, just a few months after the coup, the State Department ordered the placement of a USAID Office of Transition Initiatives (OTI) in Venezuela.

AN OFFICE FOR A TRANSITIONAL GOVERNMENT

"We don't need an Office for Transition Initiatives because this is not a government in transition."
—Tarek William Saab, then National Assembly member from the MVR party, on the news that OTI was being established in the US embassy in Caracas in July 2002, three months after the reversed coup

In 1994, USAID developed the concept of the Office for Transition Initiatives (OTI) "to respond to countries experiencing a significant and sometimes rapid political transition, which may or may not be accompanied by a social and/or economic crisis." The OTI "assesses, designs and implements programs that have characteristics of being fast, flexible, innovative, tangible, targeted, catalytic and overtly political, focusing on the root causes of the crisis."[1] According to USAID annual reports, OTIs have been used previously in Kosovo, Haiti, Indonesia, Peru, Guatemala, the Philippines, and Colombia, among other nations.[2] In Bolivia, the OTI was set up to "support Bolivia's fragile democracy" and to "promote a peaceful and informed dialogue between the government and the people." In Haiti, the OTI was set up in February 2004 "in response to the political turmoil resulting in, and from, the resignation of President Jean-Bertrand Aristide." While these efforts may appear noble at first sight, in the case of Haiti, it was widely known and accepted that Aristide did not "resign," but rather was forced out in a coup d'etat that was supported and facilitated by the US government. The fact that the OTI would come to the rescue right afterward based on claims that Aristide's "resignation" had sparked a political crisis clearly evidences bias. If the OTI were truly dedicated to promoting democracy, it would have aided Aristide's return to his constitutional position instead of facilitating the "transition" to an unelected coup government.[3] Similarly, it was notable when the OTI was established in Venezuela—in a period of stability, three months after a coup had been roundly defeated. Its appearance signaled either a new kind of support for another coup, or the knowledge that other coups were in the making.

USAID generally engages its OTI to establish on-the-ground relationships with political organizations, media, and NGOs and to provide necessary funding and training to obtain desired results. As a rapid response operation, the OTI falls under the special authority of International Disaster Assistance account funding. "Time is always of the essence" in an OTI operation and its general timeframe is two years. Venezuela was no different. Ronald Ulrich, head of the OTI in Venezuela at its commencement, affirmed publicly in March 2003: "This program will be finished in two years, as has happened with similar initiatives in other countries, the office will close in the time period stated."[4]

According to the OTI's calculations, its closing date was August 2004, two years after its official inauguration. Despite President Chávez's transparent electoral victories on August 15, 2004 in a recall referendum on his mandate and again on October 31, 2004 when his party, MVR, won 21 out of 23 governorships in regional elections and a majority of mayoral offices throughout the nation, the OTI in Venezuela extended its stay indefinitely.

The OTI's continued presence in Venezuela was not made public. It should be noted that USAID operations in general are highly secretive. No DAI or USAID representatives or workers would respond to any questions about work in Venezuela. The USAID website has no link to a program description of the OTI's operations in Venezuela, though all 28 other OTI offices worldwide have links and program information on the website.[5] When the US government sees a need to spend millions in taxpayer dollars to fund a "transition office" in a country that has overseen nine electoral processes in the past five years that have all ratified the authority of its current government, it is hard not to read that as an ominous signal that more US-backed efforts to topple the government are in the works.

Ambassador Shapiro wrote a press bulletin explaining the OTI's purpose back in 2002. He brushed off the meaning of the name "Office for Transition Initiatives" and wrote,

> I know, I know—the name of this office has created a controversy... I could explain that we never had the intention of using this name formally in Venezuela, knowing full well that the word "transition" could result in misunderstandings... Some will believe me, others won't.... So I make just one request: forget about the bureaucratic name used in Washington, and in its place, concentrate on what our efforts represent.[6]

Here was Ambassador Shapiro appealing to Venezuelans to ignore the fact that the US had just set up a transition operation in their nation, the kind usually reserved for nations in crisis, such as the former Yugoslavia, the Congo, and East Timor, and instead, to accept the "intentions" of the office with open arms.

Well, what were those intentions? A document establishing the OTI's operations in Venezuela clearly outlines the feelings of those pushing its creation:

> In recent months, his popularity has waned and political tensions have risen dramatically as President Chávez has implemented several controversial reforms. The tensions came to a head in April when protesters were shot outside the presidential palace... The current situation augers strongly for rapid US government engagement.[7]

Note that the word "coup" is not mentioned. And according to this statement, which is consistent with all others made by the US government, the coup and resulting violence were all Chávez's fault. Even more revealing is the blatant remark that Venezuela is in need of "rapid US government engagement." There is no other term for that than "intervention."

"These programs exist where there are conflicts, like in Burundi and the Congo," affirmed Ronald Ulrich and Jack McCarthy, representatives of the OTI program in Venezuela. Apparently the program directors didn't have any problem with exposing the true intentions or origins of the office.

Since a real crisis didn't exist in Venezuela—not like the horrors occurring in the Congo where thousands were being massacred—the US government had to help create one. By now, entire opposition organizations and leaders were living off the millions the US was pouring in to "promote democracy" and the only assurance that these funds would keep rolling in was to agitate the conflict and ensure an ongoing crisis. US interests believed this ongoing conflict and "crisis situation" would chip away at the Chávez government's credibility and support and eventually result in the president's ouster.

The OTI was a way to penetrate civil society even further than the NED was capable of, with a budget five times as large. Its arrival in June 2002, post-coup, was no coincidence. The OTI had been originally been programmed for Venezuela in March 2002, but the coup prospects put its establishment on hold. If the coup had succeeded, the OTI would have been unnecessary, as its ultimate goal had always been to facilitate the removal of President Chávez from office.

But Shapiro's plea seemed to find resonance in the majority of Venezuelans, and the government, including President Chávez, accepted the OTI and its proposal at face value.

Development Alternatives, Inc.
The OTI set up shop in the US embassy in Caracas in June 2002. The program was closely coordinated with the US

embassy, and in fact, the OTI program director fell under the authority and supervision of the US ambassador. With $7 million dollars allotted for the two-year project, during its first six months the OTI's budget was $2,197,066—more than double that of the NED's for just half a year. Soon after its founding in Venezuela, the USAID awarded Development Alternatives, Inc. (DAI), a private US consulting company, a $10,061,062 contract to establish and monitor a $7 million grant fund and program in "direct response to increasing political polarization in Venezuela."

USAID, through its OTIs, often uses contractors to provide additional support and administer funds. As a protective measure, the contractor sets up a parallel office, hires staff, establishes communications systems, and selects and monitors grantees. According to USAID, contractors are "critical to the success of OTI programs because they are expected to overcome the significant challenges posed by 'war-torn' or otherwise unstable countries in which OTI operates."[8]

Was Venezuela a "war-torn" nation or "otherwise unstable"?

Despite the contractor's separate status from the OTI, all of its operations and employees fell under the authority of the OTI field officer and the US ambassador. According to the contract, "The field representative will maintain close collaboration with other embassy offices in identifying opportunities, selecting partners and ensuring the program remains consistent with US foreign policy." In other words, the US embassy was intimately involved in the decision-making process and operations of the OTI and its private contractor.

DAI moved quickly to establish its office in the swanky El Rosal sector of Caracas, right down the road from the IRI's headquarters. DAI also promptly complied with its contractual obligations and announced the creation of the Venezuela Construction of Confidence Initiative, or Venezuela: Iniciativa para la Construcción de Confianza (VICC). DAI claimed its purpose, along with the OTI, was to step in "to assist Venezuelans in fostering political conditions that would preclude violent conflict and systemic breakdown."[9]

But the operations of OTI, USAID, and DAI were highly secretive. Though word of the OTI had resonated in the political sphere in Venezuela when it was first established, no one had ever heard of DAI before. For that matter, the Venezuelan government was also completely unaware that NED and USAID were financing political activities in the country. This is an astonishing fact considering that USAID has invested more than $15 million in Venezuela since mid-2002, and NED had given out more than $4 million, exclusively to opposition groups, since 2001.

The relationship between USAID and DAI was peculiar. At the time the contract was made between the two organizations, USAID had already designated all the top-level program directors and officers DAI was to employ in Venezuela. DAI was subject to the determinations made by USAID and therefore the choice of employees was non-negotiable. Other lower-level employees that were to be hired by DAI before project commencement had to first be approved by the OTI field officer at the US embassy in Venezuela. It seems that USAID had an inordinate amount of control over its contractor.

The designated employees were listed by first initial and last name only:

J. McCarthy:	Chief of Party
H. Mendez:	Program Development Officer
L. Blank:	Program Development Officer
G. Diaz:	Program Development Officer
G. Fung:	Financial Management Specialist
J. Jutkowitz:	Local Program Manager

The assignment and selection of these individuals by a government agency for employment with a private contractor was highly unusual. Obviously, they had to be highly trained and knowledgeable of Venezuela's political situation and the US foreign policy objectives in the region. Most likely, the individuals chosen were former or current USAID or US government employees specializing in this type of operation.

From the requirements listed in the 40-page contract with DAI, it was clear that USAID had an intrinsic interest in protecting its OTI employees and its private contractor, as well as its assets in the country. The contract obligated DAI to lease offices and residences for employees that met OTI standards: "the required setback from public thoroughfares; rebar grates on first floor windows, and a fenced perimeter or compound and secure parking with flood lighting for vehicles." Before leasing offices or residences and purchasing security equipment, DAI was obligated to consult with the OTI officer and seek inspection and documented prior approval. Furthermore, DAI was required to supply its employees with global positioning systems (GPS) technology and other high-tech security equipment as instructed by the OTI. Such requirements seem a bit extensive and unusual for a private contractor charged with dispensing grants to local groups working to "promote democracy and support dialogue."

But if the OTI's requirements revealed a heightened security interest in its operations with DAI, the actual grant-making procedures seem oddly easygoing and unrestricted. "For those who request our help, it is only necessary to bring a proposal that meets one of the two objectives of the program... the requirements are not high... Two pages are sufficient to specify the details and identification of the organization soliciting the funding, along with its mission, objectives and methodology of the proposal... " confirmed Ronald Ulrich, OTI program manager, in statements made to the Venezuelan press.

A two-page proposal that included the organization's information was sufficient to receive up to $100,000 of US taxpayer money? Such low standards are unheard of among expert grant writers in the United States. Moreover, the USAID-DAI contract required "immediate availability of liquid funds" since local grants would need to be issued "on an urgent basis."

It is hard to understand how a forum entitled "Electoral Solutions to the Political Crisis in Venezuela" at the ritzy J.W. Marriot Hotel in Caracas, attended by Venezuela's wealthiest and most influential members of the business community, and not a Chávez supporter in sight, was an "urgent" matter in need of funding from the United States. Particularly considering that at that time, Venezuela's next constitutionally permitted elections were not for another four years.

On the OTI website, the Venezuela program "exit" date has been changed from August 2004 to "TBD" (to be determined). Other OTI programs with a "TBD" end date include Sudan, Afghanistan, Iraq, Haiti, and Bolivia—all nations with a heavy US presence, to put it mildly. And the extension of the OTI in Venezuela was revealed on the OTI's budget for 2005, which had $5 million authorized for Venezuela.

MEDIA CONTROL AND
OIL INDUSTRY SABOTAGE

After the launch of its Venezuela: Initiative to Build Confidence (VICC) program, DAI chose to fund many of those very same groups that had openly participated in and even led the coup against President Chávez just a few months prior. One of the first few grants DAI distributed in Venezuela, under its VICC program, was for the purpose of "promoting social dialogue and citizen formation" using mass media. The project involved the creation of television and radio commercials to promote "democratic and modern values, rupturing with the patterns of paternalism and populism."[1] The project assured the collaboration of the new Fedecámaras president, Carlos Fernandez.

After the failed April coup, Carmona had escaped from his home arrest and fled the country, seeking and obtaining political asylum in neighboring Colombia. The Colombian government had been quick to endorse Carmona as "interim president" during the coup. According to a heavily censored cable of April 12, 2002, from the US ambassador to Colombia, Ann Patterson

> [Clemencia Forero, then Colombian foreign minister] Spoke warmly about Venezuelan interim president Pedro Carmona. Ferero said she has known Carmona for many years, that Carmona is well known to the Colombian business community, is committed to regional integration, and is a great friend of Colombia.

A few days later, after the coup crumbled, Foreign Minister Forero denied she had ever expressed public support for Carmona. But when Carmona came running for asylum a month later, Colombia received him with open arms. From Colombia, he was able to make frequent trips to Washington and Miami until the US could no longer defend itself against the protests from the Venezuelan government, and his visa was revoked in August of that year. From Bogotá, Carmona was still closely working with Fedecámaras and the opposition.

Ah, the irony: the US had once prevented Chávez from entering the country when he was a presidential candidate because of his involvement in a coup years earlier, in 1992. If any doubt remained, the US's immediate open door policy to Carmona made clear that its stand against Chávez was not a principled one against coups; in the US's eyes, Chávez had simply attempted the *wrong kind* of coup. Carmona's attempt was just fine.

Back in Venezuela, Fernandez was left holding the reins of the nation's most powerful business association, and he continued Carmona's efforts to seek premature removal of President Chávez from office.

Media War against the People

The DAI project focusing on radio and television commercials was timed to help Fedecámaras, the CTV, and the opposition parties, now known as the Coordinadora Democrática (CD), or Democratic Coordinator, organize a December 2, 2002, national "general strike" intended to destabilize Venezuela's economy and force President Chávez to resign. In support of the opposition's objectives, the private media symbolically joined the strike by suspending all regular programming and commercials and donating all air space to strike coverage and promotion. Though the strike was not supported by a majority of Venezuelans, many were forced to stay home because business owners and "bosses" closed shops and companies, inhibiting workers from fulfilling their duties. For 64 days, many Venezuelans suffered from the effects of the forced "bosses" strike, particularly because high-level oil industry managers and employees reduced oil production to dangerously low levels, forcing an oil and gas drought that made transportation to anywhere nearly impossible.

The CD, with the help of Venezuela's top public relations firms and USAID, produced some of the most highly crafted anti-Chávez commercials Venezuelans had ever seen. These commercials, often broadcast ten at a time in between coverage of opposition marches, speeches, and interviews, contained varying messages on Chávez's failures, alleged human rights abuses, and the overall political crisis and poor state of the nation. Some of the commercials exploited images of children singing and stamping red colored handprints, symbolizing blood, on walls, with messages about the "future of the nation," the "safety of children," and the "need for a new Venezuela."

The following is a transcription of one such television advertisement that played on a Venezuelan private media channel during the December 2002 strike. During the 64-day stoppage, approximately 700 similar, yet varied, ads were broadcast daily.[2]

> A big "NO" appears in red letters. Smaller letters state "Don't be deceived," as a man narrates the same. The same voice continues, as the written words appear: "In this country, our country, there is only one person responsible for so much abuse, impunity, anarchy, and lack of governance." [Fast-paced music builds in the background.] A women narrates now, as written words appear over an image of thousands of opposition marchers in the streets, "Venezuela, don't be deceived." Return to man: "The only one responsible for the violation of the Constitution..." [Words pasted over scenes of national guard repression and violence.] Woman: "... of financing the circles of terror created in the shadow of his government..." [Scenes of violence among people in the streets, tear gas in the air, people running, members of Bolivarian Circles speaking and gesturing.] Man: "... to give away our petroleum..." [Image of PDVSA, the state-owned oil company.] Woman:

"... of the taking of our merchant marines by mercenaries..." [Scenes of armed individuals mounting oil tankers.] Man: "... of the torture of PDVSA..." [Image of violence in the streets, tear gas, people screaming, running.] Woman: "... for politicizing our armed forces..." [Image of armed forces in the streets, violence.] Man: "... disrespecting our institutions..." [Image of armed forces firing tear gas on civilians, chaos in the streets.] Woman: "... for the stoppage in the nation... " [Scene of marches in the streets, armed with sticks and rocks, yelling, fighting one another.] Man: "... for the division of Venezuela... " [Violent street protestors yelling, fighting.] Woman: "... for the hate among brothers." [Continue fighting in the streets, violence, chaos.] Man: "Venezuela, don't be deceived." [Image of a giant Venezuelan flag held by opposition marchers.] Woman: "In this country, our country, there is only one person responsible for so much horror... " [Image of opposition marchers in the background yelling and signaling "get out."] Man: "... for so much sadness..." [Image of Venezuelans carrying a coffin through a crowd.] Woman: "... for so much terror..." [Image of individual captured for firing at opposition protestors, bloodied and half naked, carried by police.] Man: "... for so much violence..." [Image in background of man with a stick, swinging it violently in the street.] Woman: "... for so much intransigence..." [Scene of armed guards and police in the streets, harassing civilians.] Man: "... for so much insensibility." [Same scene of armed forces in the streets.] Woman: "You, who have been judged in five elections in two years, what is the fear of being judged again?" [Background image of polling machines, voters voting, election volunteers with ballots.] Cut to image of animated map of Venezuela with a big "HERE" written on it. Man: "Here, there is only one responsible..." Cut to yellow screen, with words appearing as they are yelled by a chorus of angry people: "Not one step back! OUT, GET OUT NOW!" Ends with the Coordinadora Democrática logo.

The DAI radio and television commercial project in collaboration with Carlos Fernandez began on December 9, 2002, just a week after the strike and the propaganda war commenced.

One Venezuelan described it like this:

Disinformation, flashing negative imagery, fear and stress induction techniques, quasi-hypnotic suggestion, excessive repetition and falsification and forgery are just but a few of the mindshock techniques deliberately being used, not just in overtly political spots but also in regular programming... Numbing repetition, relentless slandering, and demonizing of Chávez supporters. Exaggeration, negative spinning and saturation coverage of any minor fact or event that can remotely make the Chávez government look bad. Loud, rapid-fire, invariably negative interviews. Excessive use of panic-inducing words ("Castro-Communism" is a favorite of Venevisión, along with "mobs," routinely used to describe Chávez supporters). Deliberate use of loaded terms like "crimes against humanity" or "genocide" in the wrong contexts, to describe current events in Venezuela. Exploitation of children in interviews to stir up anti-Chávez sentiment... Venezuelans are being subject to a massive Chávez-aversion therapy program, 24 hours a day, seven days a week, month after month, ad nauseam. People wake up and go to sleep with it...[3]

In Nicaragua and Chile, the US had to buy the press. *El Mercurio* in Chile and *La Prensa* in Nicaragua were heavily funded and controlled by the CIA. But in Venezuela, the US lucked out. With little investment and encouragement from the US government, Venezuelan media owners voluntarily jumped aboard the anti-Chávez bandwagon.

The mere existence of these commercials is telling. A truly popular uprising, such as that which toppled Ferdinand Marcos in the Philippines, doesn't generally have the resources to buy air time on TV and radio. Such massive commercial campaigns cost money and resources, suggesting that their agenda serves those who financed them. In Venezuela's case, the donation of air time by those controlling media meant that the media's owners were, along with the creators of the commercials, essentially financing— and intending to benefit from—these efforts.

In Venezuela, five major private television networks

control at least 90 percent of the market and smaller private stations control another 5 percent. This 95 percent of the broadcast market began to outwardly express its opposition to President Chávez's administration as early as 1999, soon after Chávez began his first term in office. After President Chávez came to power in 1998, the five main privately owned television channels—Venevisión, Radio Caracas Televisión (RCTV), Globovisión, Televen, and CMT—and nine out of the ten major national newspapers, including *El Universal, El Nacional, Tal Cual, El Impulso, El Nuevo País*, and *El Mundo*, took over the role of the losing traditional political parties, Acción Demcrática (AD) and COPEI. The investigations, interviews, reports, and commentaries of these mass media all pursued the same objective: to undermine the legitimacy of the government and to severely damage the president's popular support.[4]

A small group of businessmen own fifteen television stations in Venezuela. Only six of these stations are national; the rest are local channels. Three of the local stations, Televisora Andina de Mérida, Canal de los Niños Cantores del Zulia, and Vale TV, belong to the Catholic Church. There is only one public television station with a national broadcasting frequency, Venezolana de Televisión (or Channel 8); another with UHF frequency, VIVE TV; and growing community media stations, such as Catia TVe and Boconó, have an extremely limited range.[5] For several decades, commercial television in Venezuela has belonged to just two families: the Cisneros, who own Venevisión (the largest station in the country), and the Bottome & Granier Group, which owns Radio Caracas Televisión (RCTV) and Radio Caracas Radio. Against the determined opposition of these two families, Televen, Globovisión, CMT, and La Tele were able to enter the private media market, although the latter two only have VHF frequency, with limited reach.

This same small group of media owners are not just the proprietors of broadcast circuits but also own advertising and public relations agencies that operate for the benefit of the stations, as well as record labels and other cultural industries that produce material to be promoted, released, and broadcast on the stations. Cisneros also owns, in addition to Venevisión, over 70 media outlets in 39 countries, including DirecTV Latin America, AOL Latin America, Caracol Television (Colombia), the Univisión Network in the US, Galavisión, and Playboy Latin America, as well as beverage and food product distribution (Coca Cola bottling, Regional Beer, Pizza Hut in Venezuela, dairy distributors, and other local food products) and cultural entities such as Los Leones Baseball team of Caracas and the Miss Venezuela Pageant. These are precisely the types of monopolies that some developed nations seek to prohibit. These media monopolies broadcast to more than four million television screens in Venezuela, reaching millions upon millions of Venezuelans.

Print media are similarly concentrated in the hands of just a few wealthy families. For example, the six largest dailies are owned by specific family groups. There are 200 magazines and 50 daily papers circulating in Venezuela. Owners of tabloids are also proprietors of magazines, dailies, and public relations agencies. One of the original opposition leaders against President Chávez, Teodoro Petkoff, later founded the daily *Tal Cúal*, another print mechanism of opposition propaganda that has played a key role in the media war against Chávez.[6]

With the private media so willingly and adamantly on the side of the opposition, it was no wonder that the strike lasted 64 days.

Media mogul Cisneros contributed more to the strike than mere television coverage. He ordered the closure of his beverage and food product distribution companies so that no commodities were available in markets. With food shortages abounding, Venezuelans might become desperate and be forced to join the call for Chávez's ouster. At Cisneros's milk farm in the state of Mérida, witnesses saw workers pouring milk into the rivers instead of bottling it for sale. Cisneros had decided that depriving Venezuelan children of milk was fair game in the war to get rid of Chávez.

Despite the fact that the strike was a lockout, originating and imposed by bosses, owners, and managers—not workers—the private channels portrayed it as a massive general workers' strike. This news was picked up around the world and perceived, although mistakenly, as an oil industry workers' strike, supported by laborers and business owners throughout the nation. In reality, high level managers and executives in the oil industry sabotaged equipment, changed access codes, and locked workers out of computer information systems, halting production. Workers were forced off jobs, businesses closed. The sabotage in the oil industry led to the most severe gas shortage in Venezuelan history, crippling the economy and destabilizing the nation for more than three months.

As millions of Venezuelans were unable to work and had no gas to travel, they were forced to remain at home and engage in the one free activity still available to them: watching television. The private media snatched up the opportunity to launch the most massive information war ever experienced in modern times. The four primary stations suspended all regular programming throughout the duration of the 64-day strike: no product commercials, no soap operas, no movies, no cartoons, no sitcoms. According to media expert Luis Britto Garcia,

> No less than four television channels [not to mention radio and print media] joined together 24 hours a day in December 2002 and January 2003, and broadcast 17,600 propaganda announcements against the government, dedicating all of their programming, without a second of rest, to denigrate the government through yellow journalism, to cause all classes of alarm and rumors to invoke terror, precisely.[7]

The situation was so severe during those 64 days that Venezuelan citizens did not know which information source to rely on: the private channels or the government. On the state-run Channel 8, the minister of education would state in a press conference that all public universities and schools were open and functioning normally, while the private media would broadcast announcements claiming all public universities and schools were on strike and closed down. In the end, Venezuelans were left with a government denied access to media and a private media functioning as a de facto government.[8]

Perhaps most damaging was the broadcast of violent images and opposition propaganda by all the private stations during children's viewing hours, in explicit violation of Venezuelan law.[9] One Venezuelan testified how dramatically the media war had affected his child:

> Last night I made the mistake of not checking if my six-year old was watching TV. He woke up in the middle of the night in a cold sweat, hyperventilating, unable to breathe. He pleaded to be allowed to sleep with his mother and me. He was afraid the "Chavistas" would come in the middle of the night and kill him.[10]

Another successful, principled use of US taxpayer dollars.

The "Democratic" Coordinator

After the failure of the coup in April and the installation of the OTI in June, the Coordinadora Democrática (CD) emerged. Interesting timing, familiar name. Born in the image of the Coordinadora Democrática Nicaragüense—that NED-funded anti-Sandinista coalition—the Venezuelan CD was composed of Fedecámaras, the CTV, numerous civil society organizations, and about ten different political parties, many of which were ongoing NED recipients. Instead of reflecting on the incidents of April 11–14 that had paralyzed the nation and altered Venezuela's future, the CD immediately began working on the next phase of getting rid of Chávez. Although the OAS had sent a delegation to help "negotiate" a solution, led by Secretary General Cesar Gaviria, the opposition was set on just one way out of the crisis: Chávez's removal from the presidency.

In October 2002, dissident military officers, many of whom had played key roles in the coup, declared a state of rebellion and claimed a plaza in the wealthy eastern section of Caracas, declaring it a "liberated zone." The CD and the private media, which publicly supported the military rebellion, utilized the growing chaos as a platform to call for a "national strike" in early December.

On the second day of the strike, Secretary of State Colin Powell met in Bogotá, Colombia with former interim coup president Carmona, who, according to Colombian papers, had met frequently with the US ambassador in that nation, Ann Patterson.[11] Considering that Carmona was still in contact with his successor at Fedecámaras, which was the principal instigator and promoter of the strike, the meeting between the US secretary of state and an exiled coup leader playing an ongoing role in destabilizing a democratic nation seemed out of place.

The CD-led strike lasted into February 2003. The economic damage exceeded US$10 billion. The strike, which in many areas was more of a lockout, with business owners shutting down companies so that employees could not work, had focused on the oil industry, Venezuela's lifeline and principal source of income. A faction of workers in PDVSA, primarily high-level management employees led by Juan Fernandez, formed an entity called "Gente de Petroleo" (oil people) that became a part of the CD. Gente de Petroleo received indirect funding from both NED and USAID.

Intesa: A Shoddy Deal

The high-level managers and other workers in PDVSA who joined the strike not only violated their own contracts, but also made it impossible for supplemental workers to access codes and authorized areas in order to run the refineries and other industry operations. INTESA, a little known but strategically important venture between a US company with CIA ties, Science Applications International Corporation (SAIC), and PDVSA, played a key role in crippling Venezuela's oil industry.

INTESA, the information and technology enterprise that was formed to run all electronic operations at PDVSA and to update many of the older, analog systems, not only promptly joined the strike, but also intentionally sabotaged essential equipment and networks necessary to run the industry. From remote locations, INTESA employees altered access codes and programming, making it impossible for remaining PDVSA workers to run computers, machines, and refinery equipment. As a result, Venezuela's oil production was brought to a halt, and the losses were devastating. Not only were common Venezuelans denied gas and oil, but also Venezuela's contracts with international partners were severely threatened.

It's easy to see why the oil industry would benefit in the long term from shutting down. The strike made it look to outsiders as though Chávez had lost control and that a new leader was needed to restore order. The fact is the shutdown was quite ordered—the opposite of the chaos it was meant to imply. For the short term costs of losing revenue, the industry would get a new head of state more sympathetic to its agenda.

Venezuela had to purchase petroleum from other nations in order to minimally cover its contractual obligations. Lines for gasoline in some parts of Venezuela were more than five miles long. As the strike continued through the end of December, many taxi drivers and car owners spent Christmas eve staked out in their cars, waiting in line for a ration of gasoline. Millions of citizens with no electric appliances were forced to cook with wood fires, even in the middle of Caracas, throughout the 64-day strike.

INTESA's majority shareholder, SAIC, which owned 60 percent of the company to PDVSA's 40 percent, is a major contractor for the US government. With former chiefs of staff, ex-CIA agents, and high-level government employees comprising its board of directors, SAIC is closely linked to the US government, and not just through contracts. Cables sent from the US embassy during the negotiations between PDVSA and SAIC regarding the formation of INTESA stated that the joint venture was of "critical importance" to the United States.

Right before President Chávez took office in 1998, SAIC was negotiating a similar venture with Venezuela's ministry of defense. Such a contract would have given a company led by former CIA officers and high-level US officials complete control over Venezuela's defense systems and national security. President Chávez nixed the deal before it could be solidified. But the PDVSA-SAIC venture INTESA was already in place, and the government could only wait for the contract to expire in late 2002.

PDVSA's president, Ali Rodriguez, tried to amicably resolve the situation with INTESA during the strike by informing the company of its contractual obligations, requiring it to continue its provision of services despite exterior occurrences. Once INTESA's management refused to comply with PDVSA, Rodriguez requested they turn over access codes to equipment so that PDVSA employees could operate the machinery and get the industry off the ground. This exchange went on for several weeks. INTESA continued to refuse cooperation with PDVSA, and eventually PDVSA employees had to enter INTESA headquarters and seize operating equipment in order to return Venezuela's oil industry to a functional state.

SAIC later sued PDVSA for "expropriation" of its equipment and won. The case was heard at the Overseas Protection for International Companies (OPIC), a US government agency that provides insurance to US companies investing overseas. It was hardly surprising that a US government agency would rule in favor of another US government-connected company. PDVSA was ordered to pay approximately $6 million in damages to SAIC.

"Early Elections"—What about the Constitution?

As the strike was at its peak, the White House called for "early elections" in Venezuela in order to end the political crisis. The US government, which had supported the coup just nine months prior, now again supported an unconstitutional solution in Venezuela. The Venezuelan Constitution has no provision for calling "early elections" when political crises arise, just as the US constitution has no provision for early presidential elections. Nevertheless, on December 13, 2002, the White House issued a statement declaring, "The United States is convinced that the only peaceful and politically viable path to moving out of the crisis is through the holding of early elections."[12]

On that same day, State Department spokesperson Richard Boucher made a revealing comment in a daily press briefing: "… an early election, we think, is the kind of solution that's needed. And I guess you could say that's our objective…"[13] Clearly, the US had an objective in mind: undermine the Venezuelan Constitution by calling for unconstitutional elections in order to push Chávez out of office under the guise of a democratic electoral process.

The public relations spin was neatly organized: since elections are inherently essential to democracy, calling for early ones is obviously an attempt to safeguard democracy. In fact the call for early elections was an attempt to subvert Venezuelan democracy. Only by ignoring both the unconstitutional nature of early elections and the US role in attempting to force Chávez out could anyone believe the call for elections to be simply a move to strengthen democracy.

During that same period, the Department of Defense was sending bogus intelligence reports to Washington in an attempt to make a pariah of President Chávez, once again justifying any actions taken against him. One December 2002 cable falsely claimed that Chávez had "ordered the destruction of television stations Globovisión, Televen, Canal Dos, and possibly other media outlets. These attacks are scheduled to take place on the evening of 12 December." Such allegations were entirely false. President Chávez had never ordered such attacks, nor were these stations ever destroyed. In fact, those very same television outlets were broadcasting 24-hour a day, uncensored anti-Chávez messages that in many cases were violent and aggressive, and the state had taken no action to inhibit freedom of expression.

But those receiving the information in Washington did not know that the report was false. The same report discussed "Cuban troops and Revolutionary Armed Forces of Colombia guerrillas in Venezuela to support Chávez," clearly intending to link the Venezuelan leader to Colombian terrorists, opening the door to international intervention.[14]

ELECTORAL INTERVENTION: THE US'S LAST HOPE

In a strange coincidence of time, place, and fact, a new entity was born in Venezuela. As SAIC was pushed out of PDVSA, losing its grip on the most important oil industry in the Western hemisphere, the NED-financed Súmate, a technologically advanced, elections-focused non-profit led by opposition-aligned wealthy Venezuelans, was established.[1] In August 2004, when a reporter visited the Development Alternatives, Inc. (DAI) office in Caracas, the DAI representative told the reporter, "I can't give you any information on [grant funding]. Because of our work with Súmate, we have to be careful." This chapter will show why the DAI had good reason to be careful.

Súmate began at the tail end of the strike, which had failed in its objective of ousting Chávez, but had succeeded in making Venezuelans' lives miserable through economic devastation. The opposition was heeding the "early elections" calls of the US, but the government rightfully refused to permit such an unconstitutional gesture. Súmate offered an alternative to a desperate opposition movement and an eager US government: a referendum.

Venezuela's 1999 Constitution includes a provision in Article 72 to request a recall referendum on any public official's mandate after the halfway point of the term has been met. The referendum must be solicited by 20 percent of the electorate, and then a greater number of voters than elected the official in the first place must vote to recall, and those recall votes must be more than those voting to keep the official in office. It is a complex process. Unfortunately, Súmate, riding high on its clever proposal, perhaps forgot to read the content of Article 72 and in early February 2003, began a signature drive to petition for a referendum.

In early 2003, more than 3,000 laptop computers had been shipped to Súmate headquarters in Caracas from an unknown source in the United States. On the day of the petition drive, Venezuelan authorities discovered several hundred laptops with PDVSA tags in the possession of Súmate workers—they had been stolen from the oil industry offices during the strike.

Claiming they had collected 27 million signatures in just one day—out of Venezuela's 24.5 million citizens—in support of a recall referendum on President Chávez's mandate, Súmate demanded the government immediately convene an election. Súmate's demands fell on deaf ears at the Venezuelan government—the halfway point of President Chávez's term had not even yet been reached.

Another government heard their cries loud and clear. The US government handsomely rewarded Súmate for their brave and bold actions. Both the NED and USAID granted Súmate funds to continue their fight for the referendum.[2]

Súmate, much like Vía Cívica in Nicaragua, was held by the US government to be a neutral entity devoted to electoral education, but Súmate's own website clearly stated the organization's objective was to "promote a recall referendum against President Chávez."[3] Furthermore, Súmate's vice-president and treasurer, Maria Corina Machado, had signed the infamous Carmona Decree during the coup, evidencing a clear anti-Chávez bias and undemocratic tendencies. And Súmate's president, Alejandro Plaz, was the director of the Andean office of McKinsey & Company, a consulting firm notoriously linked to the CIA.

The Referendum

For fiscal year 2003, USAID's OTI requested $5,074,000 for

its Venezuela operations. NED gave out more than $1 million to its Venezuela grantees and counterparts, many of which were the very same organizations that had just spearheaded the illegal 64-day strike that devastated Venezuela's economy. DAI also continued to dish out grants to projects falling within its VICC program.

After the strike failed when people became fed up with the business closures and economic losses, it became clear that the opposition needed to consolidate and focus on an electoral solution that would appear legitimate in the eyes of the world. The Constitution opened the possibility of recall referendum, and in May 2003, after more than nine months of brokering by the OAS, the opposition agreed to seek a "peaceful and constitutional" solution to the crisis. Since early elections were unconstitutional, the referendum would be the only possible way of prematurely removing President Chávez from office.

Súmate immediately began a campaign to force the government to accept the signatures it had gathered back in February 2003. The private media and international press, encouraged by the US government, supported this demand. Claims that the Chávez government was preventing a constitutional referendum from occurring were continuously repeated by US government spokesmen, despite the fact that the Article 72 requirements had not been met. Venezuela's National Electoral Council (CNE), an autonomous governmental body, pronounced that it would not accept signatures gathered in clear violation of referendum requirements. The CNE then released a clear set of rules and guidelines that would regulate the referendum process. A date was set in late November for a petition drive to be held in support of a recall referendum. If the required 20 percent of registered voters' signatures, approximately 2.4 million, were obtained, then a recall referendum on President Chávez's mandate would be held.

Súmate promptly launched a massive media and propaganda campaign in support of the petition drive, referred to as the *Reafirmazo*. Utilizing NED and USAID funding, Súmate mass-produced anti-Chávez and pro-referendum materials, which were distributed nationwide. The organization also produced little blue cards that affirmed a voter had signed the petition for a recall referendum. The cards were distributed at petition drive tables and voters were told to turn them in to employers or else face termination. It was blackmail paid for by the United States government.

In fall 2003, the OTI requested and was authorized an additional $6,345,000 for use in Venezuela during 2004.

USAID also gave $1.75 million to the Carter Center, run by former US President Jimmy Carter, to observe and mediate the referendum. (In fact, the Carter Center did later verify the referendum results—in favor of Chávez.)

That same fall, USAID awarded the IRI and the NDI more than $2 million for "ensuring credible electoral processes" and "strengthening political parties" in Venezuela during 2003–2004.

In one grant to NDI totaling $769,000, USAID required $300,000 to be distributed to local sub-grantees. Súmate was the primary local group referred to in the grant. The grant project called for local organizations to engage in electoral observation, voter registration monitoring, and training of polling site officials—activities that when conducted at the behest and supervision of a foreign government are sure signs of intervention. Moreover, it is hard to believe a grant program aimed at "conducting pre-election, election day, and post-election monitoring, including a quick count" for a recall referendum on President Chávez's mandate, premised on the notion that Chávez is "populist," "authoritarian," and "controversial," would be fair and balanced.

With USAID money, NDI helped Súmate build its organization and volunteer-based structure. The $769,000 grant permitted NDI to "design observer manuals for the Venezuelan context," "work with groups to establish an effective 'train-the-trainers' pyramid training structure," and "help groups build alliances with other institutions and sectors to strengthen their volunteer base." NDI helped

Súmate develop training materials, "observer forms, software, public education information, and other tools in Spanish." Basically everything Súmate needed to run the recall referendum campaign was paid for by the US.

While NDI was focusing on Súmate and the recall referendum campaign, IRI was making use of a $450,000 USAID grant to train opposition political parties for the anticipated upcoming elections that would take place once Chávez lost the recall referendum. Working with parties such as Primero Justicia, Proyecto Venezuela, AD, COPEI, MAS, Alianza Bravo Pueblo, and others, IRI provided training in campaign organization and structure, message development, grassroots campaigning, membership and recruitment fundraising, and other aspects of professional campaigning.

From the looks of its heavily financed preparation and training for a post-Chávez government, the US government certainly was banking on Chávez's removal. As Roger Noriega, assistant secretary of state for Western Hemisphere affairs, affirmed shortly before the referendum, "We have invested a lot of money in this process..."

The Venezuela Terrorist Connection

Right around the time of the "Reafirmazo," in fall 2003, the US launched another attack against the Chávez government, this time claiming Venezuela was harboring terrorist training camps and was collaborating with the Colombian FARC and ELN, two groups on the US list of international terrorist organizations. An October 6 article in *US News and World Report* by Linda Robinson, entitled "Terror Close to Home," claimed that al-Qaeda, FARC, and ELN terrorists had training camps scattered throughout Venezuela. The article included a big map of Venezuela with markings identifying the training camps.

> The oil-rich but politically unstable nation of Venezuela is emerging as a potential hub of terrorism in the Western Hemisphere, providing assistance to Islamic radicals from the Middle East and other terrorists, say senior US military and intelligence officials... Middle Eastern terrorist groups

are operating support cells in Venezuela and other locations in the Andean region...Venezuela is supporting armed opposition groups from neighboring Colombia; these groups are on the official US list of terrorist organizations and are also tied to drug trafficking...

The allegations were based on comments by an "anonymous US official" and an "exhaustive" investigation conducted by the magazine, which was never substantiated.

In fact, Brigadier General Benjamin R. Mixon, director of operations at the Pentagon's Miami-based US Southern Command, later confirmed to the *Miami Herald*, "the Southern Command has no information about Venezuela supporting terrorists."[4]

A United Press International article also claimed there was a connection between the Venezuelan government and Islamic terrorist networks. The UPI article went so far as to claim that Chávez was harboring al-Qaeda suicide bombers that were involved in the September 11, 2001, attacks in the United States:

> Investigators name two Venezuelan-based al-Qaeda suspects: Hakim Mamad Al Diab Fatah who was deported from the US on suspicion of involvement with the Sept. 11, 2001 attacks and Rahaman Hazil Mohammed Alan who is jailed in the UK for smuggling an explosive device onto a British Airways flight. American and British officials complain that their investigations are stymied because the government of President Hugo Chávez has dismantled US-trained intelligence units which tracked terrorist connections among the half-million strong Venezuelan Arab community... Chávez has instead brought in Cuban and Libyan advisors to run his security services according to American, British, and other European diplomatic officials in Caracas.[5]

The UPI article mentions no official sources by name nor provides any substantive evidence for its claims. Moreover, subsequent to this round of articles making outrageous claims about Venezuela's alleged connections to al-Qaeda and other terrorist groups, no further mention was made of the issue. Were the allegations true, the world would have learned of such sinister terrorist networks freely functioning in South America. But in the end, the claims were merely scare tactics and part of a strategy to isolate the Chávez government in the international community and provide a justification for intervention.

Yet again, the strategy failed.

The Guarimba

Despite these international pressures, the signature collection process to institute the referendum went smoothly. The CNE later determined that only 1.9 million signatures were valid, while another nearly 1 million were set aside and questioned for fraud. More than 800,000 signature lines had been filled out with duplicate handwriting in violation of CNE regulations. The opposition reacted to the news with violence.

In February 2004, newly formed extremist factions in the CD launched the "Guarimba," a plan allegedly created by Cuban-Venezuelan Robert Alonso. The Guarimba called for right-wing groups to engage in widespread civil disobedience and violence in the streets of Caracas and other metropolitan areas, provoking repressive reactions from state forces that would then justify cries of human rights violations and lack of constitutional order.

The Guarimba lasted from February 27 to March 1, 2004, and during that period, numerous Venezuelan citizens were injured and arrested for violations of law. Provocateurs burned garbage in the streets, blocked roadways, and threw Molotov cocktails and other homemade bombs at security forces. The opposition-controlled media in Venezuela quickly broadcast to the world a prepared version of events that cited the government as the "repressor" and portrayed claims of those arrested during that period as "victims of torture and unlawful arrest." The Guarimba starkly resembled the "Chileanization" strategy applied in Chile and Nicaragua, using similar tactics and provoking identical results.

As a result of the violence and instability again caused by the opposition, the Venezuelan government agreed to allow those signatures that had appeared fraudulent to be "reaffirmed" by the signers over a four-day period regulated by the CNE. The opposition was provided with a second opportunity to legitimately obtain the necessary 2.4 million signatures needed to hold the recall referendum. The signature repair period, "reparo," as it was known, was held at the end of May 2004. The Carter Center and the OAS provided international observation, paid for by USAID.

Finally, the opposition obtained the necessary 2.4 million signatures and the referendum date was set for August 15, 2004.

"Plan Consenso" (Plan Consensus)—Made in the USA

About five days after the announcement confirming the referendum, the opposition released an alternative plan for a transitional post-Chávez government. Entitled "Plan Country Consensus," the project appeared as the first attempt by the opposition to offer Venezuelans anything beyond a strict "get Chávez out of office" position. The opposition had been highly criticized internationally for having no concrete plans, no viable candidates to oppose Chávez, and no platform on which to campaign. The "Plan Consensus" was a magic solution. But of course Plan Consensus's polished offerings were not born independently. They were the result of a NED grant to CIPE–CEDICE in 2003, combined with USAID funding that had gone through DAI to several opposition groups, including Liderazgo y Visión and Queremos Elegir.

Additionally, both IRI and NDI had played roles and had financed the crafting of this "alternative agenda." It was the goal of the US to win the referendum and install a transitional government that would work best in its interests. As such, the referendum campaign, via Súmate and the CD, and the alternative agenda, via NED and USAID grantees, were financed and overseen by US government agents.[6] The NED chose as the principal drafter of an agenda for a "transitional government" CEDICE, an organization whose president, Rocio Guijarro, was one of the initial signers of the Carmona Decree. In fact, Carmona had chosen him to represent NGOs at his swearing-in ceremony. CEDICE was one of the most fervently outspoken anti-Chávez groups in Venezuela—its leaders actually attempted several times to convince NED program director Christopher Sabatini that a coup d'etat did not take place on April 11, 2002, but rather, a popular uprising against a "dictator."[7]

But the Plan Consensus project represented nothing to Venezuelans that they hadn't heard before: shallow promises and a return to a neo-liberal agenda. The NED-funded project brought together representatives from almost every organization and political party connected to the opposition umbrella group, the CD, and even included members of the Catholic Church and former PDVSA executives. Many of these same individuals and their organizations had just participated in two illegal and destructive activities against democracy: the coup and the strike.

The CEDICE Plan Consensus project was based on the premise that a "national agenda that induces the adoption of free market reforms is particularly important at the present time." It included this assertion: "The one thing separating the country from full revolutionary control are [sic] the fact that the Chávez government was the result of free elections, as was the Nazi regime in its inception…"

The US government was funding an organization that nonchalantly compared the Chávez administration to the Nazi regime and was working to implement the type of free market reforms the Venezuelan government had been elected to avoid. Furthermore, a list of the Plan's committee members reads like a who's who of coup participants and organizations feverish to get rid of Chávez by any means.

Maxim Ross of Asamblea de Ciudadanos, Domingo Alberto Rangel of Resistencia Civil, Cipriano Heredia of Visión Emergente, Tomás Páez of Red Universitario, and Rocio Guijarro, who supervised the project, were Carmona Decree signors. Elias Santana, head of Alianza Civica, signed the public civil society document recognizing the legitimacy of Carmona's coup government. Hugo Fonesca Viso, Jorge

Botti, and Albis Muñoz were representatives of Fedecámaras, which spearheaded both the coup and the strike. Jesus Urbieta and Nelson Landáez represented the CTV, the labor union responsible for teaming up with Fedecámaras during the coup and the strike. Nelson Benitez represented Gente de Petroleo, the PDVSA worker organization responsible for initiating the illegal oil industry strike. Representatives from the opposition parties COPEI, AD, Un Solo Pueblo, Alianza Bravo Pueblo, and Primero Justicia were also participants in the project. (See Appendix 2 for full document and list of individuals and organizations involved.)

Once it was revealed that Plan Consenso had been financed by the US government, Chávez went wild. "Plan Consenso Pa' Bush" (Plan Consensus for Bush) he called it—"Made en USA" (Made in the USA). Diego Urbaneja, representative of CD and spokesman for the Plan Consensus project, conceded defeat almost immediately. Though initially launched with great enthusiasm by the opposition as "the alternative to Chávez," within a week there was no mention at all of the infamous Plan Consensus. The opposition's own misjudgment, and the US government's, had once again led to their failure.

The Petare Experiment

Meanwhile, DAI had distributed 67 grants totaling $2.3 million over the previous few months, more than half of which were focused on the referendum and a post-Chávez Venezuela. When USAID responded to the FOIA request for information on its Venezuela projects, it purposely decided to withhold the names of all organizations and recipients of US taxpayer dollars in Venezuela. In a few cases, administrative errors were made and beneficiaries such as Súmate, Carlos Fernandez, and Mirador Democrático were revealed. But for the majority of the 67 grants, only project names and program descriptions were left uncensored. Some projects were easy to decipher, such as the "Un Sueño Para Venezuela" (A Dream for Venezuela), a proposal of the NED-funded organization Liderazgo y Visión for yet another alternative to Chávez, but most were identifiable by project name only.

Of the 67 grants for 2003–2004, one thing in particular stood out: 6 grants focused on the community of Petare, one of Venezuela's most populated neighborhoods and a major pro-Chávez support base.

Petare is the most populated area of greater Caracas. Located in the municipality of Sucre in the state of Miranda, Petare is primarily a poor working-class barrio with a few middle-and upper-class zones. Although known as a Chávez stronghold, to the surprise of many, something different happened in Petare during the recall referendum against President Chávez on August 15, 2004: The opposition "yes" vote received higher numbers than expected in contrast to the "no" vote to keep Chávez.

The six USAID–DAI grants in Petare were primarily focused on "citizen development and political formation" and improving community relations. One grant worth $22,081, titled "Teniendo Puentes Comunitarios para Fortalecer la Vida Democrática en Nuestra Comunidades" (Building community bridges to strengthen democratic life in our communities), was allegedly to help mend relations between the upper- and middle-class communities in the Petare sector and the majority lower class. Another grant to the tune of $53,000, "Mi Barrio: Un Espacio Democrático para el Consenso y el Desarrollo" (My Neighborhood: A democratic space for consensus and development), was focused on helping poor community members develop democratic values.

"Diálogo y Resolución de Conflictos" (Dialogue and conflict resolution) was another Petare-based USAID–DAI effort allegedly to teach the working poor how to communicate in a democracy. And the flowery "Acciones Vecinales Para la Armonia y El Entendimiento" (Neighborhood actions for harmony and understanding) was a $34,215 project to help community members get along better. The more obscure "Experiencia local de negociación y legitimación de consensus en torno. Los derechos de la ninfancia en Sucre." (Local experience in negotiation and consensus legitimatizing. The rights of infants in Sucre) brought in another $6,000, and the more general "Prevención de la Violencia Cotidiana" (Prevention of everyday violence) brought a whopping $49,830 into the neighborhood.

There are two striking aspects to these Petare-based grants. For one, the USAID–DAI grants in Petare were not only condescending and patronizing to community members, treating them all as poor, uneducated, and valueless citizens, but they were also attempts to teach democratic values and development methodologies not native to Venezuela. The grants brought in US-imposed values and notions to attempt to sway public opinion. The idea behind these grants was to influence the ideology and political formation of Venezuela's base: its vast poor majority, which also just happens to be Chávez's largest support base. In Petare, a true "battle of ideas" was taking place, and by the looks of the referendum results, the US was winning.

The other thing worth noting about the grants was that a majority of Petare community members had never heard of a single one of them. More than $200,000 was invested in their community for democratic and political formation and conflict resolution and most Petare residents never partook in the projects. Even more intriguing were the many eyewitness accounts of Primero Justicia's deputy in Miranda, Carlos Oscariz, going door-to-door with his aides in Petare's poorest neighborhoods in the weeks before the referendum, offering 150,000 bolivares (about $75) and a bag of food for a Yes vote. It is not hard to imagine that hunger would win over principles, even in a politically charged environment.

If USAID–DAI invested more than $200,000 in Petare in the months preceding the referendum and a majority of Petare residents had never even heard of the grant projects and programs allegedly taking place in their neighborhood, perhaps some of that money showed up in Carlos Oscariz's offerings to poor Petare community members.

In the end, the desired result was the same, whether via legitimate grant programs or political bribes: win the recall referendum and get rid of Chávez. In Petare, they figured out an easy way to achieve that goal: prey on poverty.

Luckily for Chávez and his supporters, they won the state of Miranda (which houses Petare) by a mere few percentage points. So the Petare losses had no serious impact on the vote outcome, though they did affect the stability of a community more than one million strong. The USAID–DAI Petare experiment suffered a further defeat at the hands of pro-Chávez forces on October 31, 2004, during regional elections: The governor of Miranda, Enrique Mendoza, lost to a pro-Chávez candidate, Diosdado Cabello, in a show of Chávez's enduring popularity there.

Witnesses in Petare say that since Mendoza lost the governorship, Primero Justicia has been suspiciously absent from their neighborhoods.

Penn, Schoen, & Berland—US Polling Firm of Choice

Despite the millions of dollars invested in the opposition to Chávez,[8] on August 15, 2004, more than 59 percent of voters ratified his mandate to keep him in office. Even though both the Carter Center and the OAS certified the official CNE referendum results, the opposition, led by the US-financed Súmate, cried fraud.

Súmate claimed it had conducted an exit poll with the US polling firm Penn, Schoen, & Berland, a firm previously used in electoral interventions in Nicaragua, Panamá, and Yugoslavia, which showed the exact opposite results, indicating that the vote to recall Chávez had exceeded 59 percent.[9] An exit poll by the right-wing anti-Chávez party and IRI counterpart, Primero Justicia, also showed the same result. All other exit polls conducted by international firms and independent observers were in line with the official CNE results. Nevertheless, Súmate and the CD claimed the vote had been fraudulently calculated and they refused to recognize the results.

A few strange things happened on the day of the referendum. The British newspaper, the *Independent*, released an article prior to the end of voting with the headline "Venezuela's Chávez on brink of referendum defeat." The article claimed that

The Venezuelan President, Hugo Chávez, looked to be losing his grip on power last night as exit polls showed him to be trailing the opposition by almost a million votes… The mid-morning results showed that the opposition, already boasting an enormous 1,758,000 votes to Chávez's 798,000, is well on its way to reaching the target of 3.76 million votes it needs to oust the authoritarian, left-wing President…

Mid-morning results? Exit polls? The *Independent* was reporting the opposition winning as of 10:49AM EST, a mere three to four hours after polls had opened. Not even the worst, most biased Venezuelan journalists reported such a "victory" before noon. The polls on August 15 were open until midnight. Per CNE regulations, release of exit poll data was prohibited before the official tally had been announced in order to avoid any disturbances or violence due to the very polarized and delicate political situation. But Súmate, along with its US counterpart, Penn, Shoen, & Berland, leaked the information on the Internet, in a clear violation of CNE rules.

The exit poll leak was part of a ploy to generate belief that the opposition was going to win. All day long, the private media gave full coverage to referendum-related events, but the stations primarily broadcast images of anti-Chávez voters at the polls. Opposition politicians and leaders were interviewed on private media news shows attesting to their belief that Chávez would lose. The private media was clearly creating an opinion matrix and they were once again censoring voices and information that disproved their claims.

At about 9:30PM, it became clear that the opposition had lost. The private channels switched from coverage of anti-Chávez voter lines to broadcasting old movies and info-mercials. Despite the ongoing miles-long lines in pro-Chávez neighborhoods that continued well into the night, the private media had decided the voting was over. They couldn't show what was really happening, that more Chavista voters were out there than the opposition had mustered up, or else the millions of Venezuelans watching television over the past few months and years would realize they had been deceived all along. No, it was best for opposition-aligned Venezuelans to go to bed watching old movies and believing that they had won the referendum. That way, they would buy the claims of fraud the opposition was prepared to present the next day once the official CNE results declared Chávez the winner.

After the polls closed around midnight, the results were fairly clear: The *No* vote had maintained approximately a twenty-point lead over the *Sí* vote throughout the day. Chávez had not been recalled. Before the official announcement could be made by the CNE directorate, the CD decided they would not accept the results. They informed the CNE of this decision, along with the Carter Center and the OAS. Though such a factor should not have altered the official determination of the CNE, the announcement was delayed. The Carter Center and the OAS had decided to hear out the CD and their claims of fraud.

Cesar Gaviria's Long Night

At about 1:00AM, there was a breakdown. Cesar Gaviria, representing the OAS in Venezuela, had taken sides with the opposition, and the OAS, per Gaviria's decision, was not going to certify the referendum results. The Carter Center, however, did not believe the claims of fraud, particularly considering the opposition had presented no evidence whatsoever of any fraud or wrongdoing during the referendum. Carter was going to certify.

In the days before the referendum, Jimmy Carter had requested a private meeting with President Chávez. In that meeting, Carter told Chávez he believed he would win the referendum. Carter felt sure that Chávez had the votes. He only asked the Venezuelan president to take the win in stride and to be reconciliatory, not reproachful.

Cesar Gaviria, on the other hand, had a history of tacitly supporting the opposition to Chávez. He considered Chávez an authoritarian and consistently pushed statements and measures against the Venezuelan government on the rest of the OAS members. Fernando Jaramillo, the representative Gaviria had chosen to lead the OAS mission in Venezuela, had been expelled from the country just a few months before, in May, for allegedly showing bias toward the opposition.

Less than one month before the referendum, Walter Moreira, the Brazilian ambassador to the OAS, had been appointed chief envoy to Venezuela. Since Gaviria had spent the greater part of the previous two years working with Venezuela, Moreira had trusted the OAS representation in the referendum observation team to him.

In the early morning hours of August 16th, Jimmy Carter and Cesar Gaviria came head to head. Gaviria was not budging. He was not going along with Carter. Had Gaviria's decision been based on solid evidence and fact, Carter probably would have joined him in rejecting the CNE's official results. But since Gaviria's last minute turnabout was due to his political alignment with the opposition, Carter was determined to convince him otherwise. Three hours of negotiations went by, and at 4:00AM Gaviria was still not going to certify the results. A middle-of-the-night call was placed to Walter Moreira, the true OAS chief in Venezuela, and he was on the first plane out of Washington the next morning.

Even when CNE President Francisco Carrasquero read the official results at 4:35AM, guaranteeing Chávez's victory, the uneasiness of Gaviria's decision echoed through Miraflores Palace. The general public, luckily, was not privy to this information, and those who supported Chávez were able to celebrate their victory.

By noon on August 16, Gaviria had come around. Moreira was in Caracas and apparently played a big part in Gaviria's change of heart. The OAS and Carter Center together gave a press conference around 1PM that day, announcing their certification of the CNE official results. With Moreira at his side, Gaviria read the OAS statement endorsing the results. His attempts to interject comments supporting opposition claims of possible fraud were thwarted by Moreira's stern glances.

To the north, the US government had not yet accepted the referendum results. Despite numerous assurances that the US would accept the Carter Center and the OAS's decision on the referendum, no official announcements were made on August 16. It took the US another day before it managed to issue a conditional acceptance of the referendum. On August 17, State Department spokesman Adam Ereli finally announced:

> We will join the group of friends of Venezuela in acknowledging the preliminary results of the referendum and noting that they show that President Chávez received the support of the majority of voters... We call on international observers to help conduct a transparent audit that will address those remaining concerns as part of a process of national reconciliation...

The US had qualified the official results as "preliminary" and called for an "audit" of votes. As Noriega had declared right before the referendum vote, "The US has invested a lot of money in this referendum." True—and they weren't going to lose sitting down.

When the audits were done with OAS and Carter Center supervision and certification, the result was the same: Chávez won, with 59 percent of the votes.

The referendum was a huge setback for the United States. For years, the US government had worked to destabilize and replace Chávez. Then, in a final push, it backed the referendum. But the results, far from having a neutral impact on the status quo, were a huge validation of Chávez; in effect, he had scored an unscheduled election victory, years before his term was set to expire.

10

CLANDESTINE STRATEGIES AND THREATS

Súmate refused to accept the referendum results. The trips to Washington increased and efforts were made to convince the world that a "mega-fraud" had taken place during the recall referendum. "Hackers were brought in from Russia to steal the votes," Súmate leaders cried. "The voting machines were rigged by the CNE," they swore. "Experts" were brought in from around the world, yet no substantive or credible evidence was ever presented.

In the meantime, the Venezuelan attorney general had charged Súmate's directors, Maria Corina Machado and Alejandro Plaz, with violation of Article 132 of the Penal Code, which makes it a crime to "conspire to destroy the government" and to "solicit international intervention in national politics" or to "incite civil war or defame the President or diplomatic representatives in the foreign press." The attorney general alleged that Súmate committed a crime by soliciting financing from the NED, an arm of the US government, in order to campaign for and lead a recall referendum against President Chávez. Furthermore, the chief prosecutor alleged that Súmate violated the Constitution by usurping functions of the electoral power through its creation of a parallel electoral registry and database used to collect and count signatures during stages of the referendum process. Two other Súmate members, Luis Enrique Palacios and Ricardo Ludwig Estévez Mazza, were also charged with aiding and abetting in the conspiracy. A preliminary hearing was scheduled in the Venezuelan courts for November 2, 2004.

When the charges were first announced against the Súmate directors in May 2004, the national prosecutor assigned to the case, Luisa Ortega Díaz, was kidnapped. Attorney Ortega Díaz was thrown into a car at gunpoint along with a companion who was with her at the time. If it hadn't been for her companion, who put up a struggle and pushed her out of the moving car, Luisa would most likely not have survived the attack. After the kidnapping, she was moved to a military base and was assigned bodyguards around the clock. She continued to preside over the matter.

The case brought against NED-grantee Súmate caused uproar in the ranks of the US State Department and the quasi-governmental NED, which is obligated to report to Congress annually on its activities and use of funds. In the weeks after the referendum, the US State Department launched a massive campaign in defense of Súmate. State Department spokesmen made repeated declarations calling for the Venezuelan government to drop the case and labeling the charges "political persecution." Maria Corina Machado became the "cover girl for democracy," jetting up to Miami, New York, and Washington at a minute's notice to host conferences, forums, and talks on the Súmate case and the political crisis in Venezuela. Her frequent visits to Washington began to raise eyebrows even within the ranks of the opposition.

The new US ambassador to Venezuela, William Brownfield, even visited Venzuelan Supreme Court Chief Justice Ivan Rincón to request he intervene to prevent the case from proceeding. Although Rincón was clear in his respect for due process and the jurisdiction of the attorney general, one of the other justices in the penal chamber of the Supreme Court decided to heed Brownfield's call. He pulled the case to review it for "clarity" and "merit" before allowing it to continue. The November 2, 2004 hearing was postponed indefinitely.

On November 8, 2004, NED President Carl Gershman made a historical visit to Venezuela with a very peculiar purpose. Gershman traveled to the South American nation to ask President Chávez to influence the outcome of the case against Súmate, despite the fact that it resided in the hands of the independent attorney general's office. But much to Gershman's surprise, no meetings had been authorized with the president or any other cabinet members and he was unable to exert the weight of the United States-backed NED over the recently re-ratified head of state. Gershman did meet with Attorney General Isaías Rodriguez and Chief Justice Rincón.

In the meeting with Rincón, Gershman threatened to prevent the issuance of a credit from the World Bank for a judicial reform program the Supreme Court had been conducting over the past few years. In return, Gershman wanted Rincón to do everything in his power to get the case against Súmate dismissed. Rincón did not bow to Gershman's threats, and sure enough, a few weeks later, the World Bank cut the credit for the Venezuelan Supreme Court.

With Attorney General Rodriguez, Gershman was more veiled. He urged the top legal authority to drop the case, hinting that its continuance could affect relations between the two nations. Rodriguez, clear on the law backing his position, refused to heed Gershman's threatening request.

Gershman's visit, the first visit by the NED president to a foreign nation to defend the organization's interests, was an apparent "last chance" offer to the Venezuelan government to stop the case or face the wrath of the US government. Even presidential candidate John Kerry got on the Súmate defense bandwagon in the days prior to the November 2004 US presidential elections, criticizing Chávez for "political persecution" and accusing him of heading toward a dictatorship. Other Súmate defenders included US Congress members Christopher Cox and Gregory Meeks, both on the NED Board of Directors, and Senator John McCain and former Secretary of State Madeline Albright, who chair the NED core grantee organizations, the IRI and the NDI, respectively. The aforementioned all wrote letters defending NED's work in Venezuela and defending its grantees, despite their notorious unconstitutional behavior during the coup and the strike.

Though NED representatives and spokespersons have time and again claimed their work in Venezuela to be "impartial" and only "promoting democracy," Gershman's declarations to the Venezuelan press showed otherwise. After being snubbed by the president, the attorney general, and the chief justice, Gershman angrily declared to the Venezuelan media that "Venezuela is neither a democracy nor a dictatorship but rather something in between." In the same breath, Gershman claimed that in Venezuela, the NED "only finances democratic groups." He also made a weak comparison between the Venezuelan government and the Chilean dictator Pinochet by claiming, "In the eighties, we were attacked by the Pinochet government, which didn't like the fact that we supported the groups that moved forward the democratic transition in Chile."

There is something deeply troubling when a representative of a group allegedly promoting democracy arrives in a country to argue against upholding that country's laws. The US has all sorts of regulations about money and elections—how much can be given, publication of the donor's name and address, and so on. For a foreign visitor to come and ask that the US not uphold such laws would widely be seen as little short of a farce.

Gershman followed through on his threats to the Venezuelan government to increase international pressure in defense of the Súmate case and to attempt to make Chávez an international "pariah" and "human rights abuser." Just 24 hours after Gershman's departure from Venezuela, a letter was released from an alleged group of 70 "international democrats" demanding that the Venezuelan president intervene in the Súmate action and prevent the attorney general from proceeding with the case.

The letter was riddled with misinformation and errors about Venezuela's legal system and laws and strangely demanded respect for democracy while asking the Venezuelan president to violate the constitutional separation of powers by intervening in a case under the authority of the attorney general. The letter called for an abandonment of the law and demanded the Súmate directors be granted "above the law" status, just because they received support from the NED and its 70 prominent "international democrats."

Although the letter was intended to look like an independent statement by 70 renowned "democrats," its ties to the NED were all too obvious. The letter was released to the public by the NED press department and of the 70 signers, more than half were linked to either the NED board of directors or had received its financial support.

In the weeks that followed, US Congressman Tom Lantos (D-CA) introduced a resolution on Capitol Hill expressing support for the NED and its work in Venezuela. The resolution also called for the Venezuelan government to drop the case against Súmate:

> 108th CONGRESS 2d Session H. RES. 867
> The House of Representatives
> (1) expresses its firm support for the efforts of the National Endowment for Democracy to promote democracy around the world;
> (2) commends all Venezuelans who have peacefully exercised the political rights which are accorded to them under Venezuela's Constitution to resolve their differences by democratic means and abhors all acts of political violence;
> (3) views charges filed against members of the Venezuelan civic organization known as Súmate of conspiring with the National Endowment for Democracy to overthrow Venezuela's government as politically motivated; and
> (4) would welcome a decision by the Government of the Bolivarian Republic of Venezuela not to prosecute Venezuelan citizens, including citizens associated with Súmate, for activities that were protected under the laws and Constitution of Venezuela when those activities were carried out.

The resolution not only applauds NED's work in Venezuela, making no mention of the hundreds of thousands of dollars given to coup leaders and instigators, but it also tacitly requests that the Venezuelan judiciary drop the legal case against members of Súmate. Following in the footsteps of Gershman and Brownfield, the Lantos resolution attempts to undermine Venezuelan law. Unfortunately for Súmate and Representative Lantos, Congress went on vacation before the resolution could be passed. But Congress did approve another piece of legislation relating to NED's activities in Venezuela. New York Congressman José Serrano (D-NY) introduced specific language into the FY2005 Omnibus Bill (the budget) that made clear NED's activities in Venezuela were questionable. The language, in the bill approving $51 million for all of NED's programs in 2005, stated:

> The Committee reaffirms the role that NED plays in strengthening democratic institutions around the world. Any perception that funds are used to directly support a particular party or candidate, or to support the removal of elected leaders through unconstitutional means, undermines the credibility and effectiveness of NED programs. The Committee expects NED to take all necessary measures to ensure that all sponsored activities adhere to the core NED principles. The Committee directs NED to provide the Committee with a comprehensive report on its activities in Venezuela from fiscal year 2001 through the present, by December 15, 2004.[10]

For the first time in history, language was inserted into legislation about NED that raised concerns about its programs and commitment to democracy. Though to this date, the required report has still not been turned in by the NED.

Miami: A Terrorist Hub

Miami is a haven for self-exiled Venezuelans seeking new ways of ousting President Chávez. In early October 2004, the Guarimba instigator Robert Alonso surfaced in Miami after a warrant had been issued for his arrest in Venezuela in connection with approximately 80 Colombian paramilitaries found on his farm outside of Caracas in May 2004— apparently implicated in a plot to assassinate Chávez. Former Venezuelan president Carlos Andrés Pérez has also taken root in Miami. From his home there, Pérez declared to *El Nacional* newspaper in July 2004 that Chávez deserved to "die like a dog" and that "violence is the only way to remove him."[11]

In October 2004, Venezuelan actor Orlando Urdaneta, also fleeing from an arrest warrant, surfaced in Miami. He appeared on a local Miami television show, *Maria Elvira Confronta* ("Maria Elvira Confronts"), on October 25, 2004, ordering the assassination of Chávez and other influential members of his government. Orlando stated:

> Of the 150,000 men in uniform in Venezuela, there must be a high percentage of honest people who, in the right moment, will rise up... But this will only happen with the physical disappearance of the "top dog" and a significant part of his pack. There is no room for doubt: there is no other way out. Physical disappearance, definitely.

When prompted by the program host to share how this would happen, Urdaneta replied, "This happens with a few men with long guns that have telescopic views, that won't fail... It's an order that I am giving right at this moment, let's go, hurry up..."[12]

Weeks later, on November 18, 2004, national prosecutor Danilo Anderson was assassinated in a car bombing in Caracas. Two charges of C4 explosive had been fixed to Anderson's car and the explosion was detonated by remote control. Anderson was the most high-profile prosecutor at the time in Venezuela. He was handling politically charged cases involving powerful interests. Danilo had just issued subpoenas to all 395 Carmona Decree signers as part of an ongoing investigation into the April 2002 coup. Though none had yet been indicted on criminal charges, several of those implicated fled to Miami.

He had also recently indicted Henry Vivos and Lazaro Forero, former metropolitan police commissioners, along with the ex-mayor of Greater Caracas, Alfredo Peña, for their involvement in the coup. Peña showed up in Miami right after the indictment was made public. Anderson had also been the prosecutor on the case against Henrique Capriles Radonsky, the former mayor who was charged with facilitating the assault on the Cuban embassy during the coup.

Anderson's assassination was the first political murder in contemporary Venezuelan history. It was meticulously planned and carried out, and was strikingly similar to the 1976 assassination of Orlando Letelier and Ronni Moffitt, which—before the World Trade Center attacks on September 11, 2001—was one of the worst terrorist acts ever carried out on US soil. Letelier had been the defense minister under Salvador Allende's democratic government, before it was overthrown in the 1973 coup at the hands of Chilean dictator Augusto Pinochet. Letelier and Moffitt were killed in a car bombing on Washington's Embassy Row, executed at the behest of Pinochet, coached by the CIA, and sanctioned by Washington.

At the end of 2004, those who ordered Anderson's murder remain unknown.

Terrorist Camps

Several ex-military officers known to have participated in the coup have also appeared in Miami, alongside Carlos Fernandez, the former Fedecámaras president and Carlos Ortega, former CTV president, who had obtained political asylum in Costa Rica, but later lost it once he clandestinely returned to Venezuela and appeared on television in a pre-referendum rally. The Venezuelan government issued arrest warrants for both Fernandez and Ortega in 2003 for their leadership of the illegal 64-day strike that caused billions of dollars in losses to Venezuela's economy. The Venezuelan government also has pending extradition requests with the US government for two military officers, German Rodolfo Varela and José Antonio Colina, alleged to be the masterminds behind the bombings of the Colombian and Spanish embassies in Caracas in fall 2003. The officers have requested political asylum and have cases pending before immigration judges in Miami.

The F-4 Comandos, an anti-Castro Cuban militia group operating in Miami, joined forces with the Junta Patriotica Venezolana (Venezuelan Patriotic Junta), run by dissident Venezuelan military official Capitan Luis Eduardo Garcia, in late 2002. The two organizations, led by professed "freedom fighters," run terrorist training camps in the greater Miami area for those seeking to overthrow both Chávez and Castro.[13]

An article in the *Wall Street Journal* entitled "Miami's Little Havana Finds New Foe in Venezuelan Leader" revealed the intentions of this Miami-based exile group:

> Capt. García says he is providing military training for some 50 members of the F-4 Commandos, 30 of them Cuban-Americans, the rest Venezuelans, in a shooting range close to the Everglades. "We are preparing for war," he says. Nevertheless, his movement opposes military coups. "Our struggle is to show the world how Chávez is the enemy of democracy."[14]

Despite requests from the Venezuelan government for the US government to investigate these camps, no action has been taken.

Future Relations

Incoming Secretary of State Condoleezza Rice set the tone for future relations with the Venezuelan government in an October 2004 statement to the press, when she declared that Chávez is a "real problem" for the region and that other nations in the hemisphere should "mobilize" to "both watch him and be vigilant about him."[15]

With more than $6 million allotted for its 2005 interventions, it was clear that the US government's job in Venezuela is not finished. But as Venezuela's Bolivarian Revolution gains strength and support around the world, one question arises: Just how far is the US government willing to go in its covert war against Chávez?

It would seem, with the re-election of Bush and the appointment of Rice as secretary of state, that the answer is almost certainly "as far as necessary." How far that would have to be is suggested by the extraordinary resilience of Chávez and Venezuela over the last few years.

In the words of President Hugo Rafael Chávez Frías, "We will not rest until we break all the chains that oppress our people, the chains of hunger, misery, and colonialism. This country will be free or we will die trying to free it."[16]

APPENDIX 1: FLOW OF US MONEY TO VENEZUELA

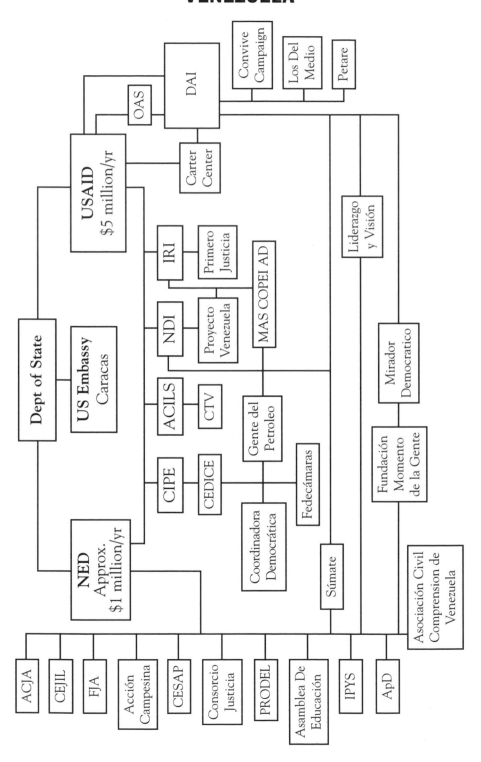

OVERALL STRUCTURE OF MONEY FLOW TO VENEZUELA

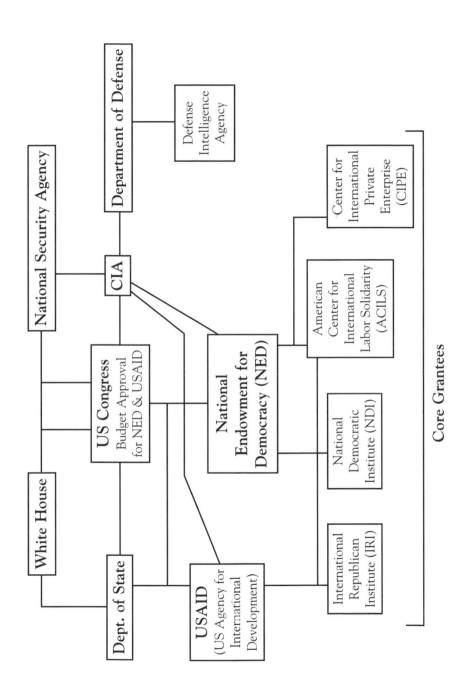

APPENDIX 2: US GOVERNMENT DOCUMENTS

NED Summary of Projects 2000

SUPPORT FOR DEMOCRATIC UNION ELECTIONS $60,084
> *Venezuela*
> The American Center for International Labor Solidarity / None

The American Center for International Labor Solidarity (ACILS) will support the efforts of the Confederation of Venezuelan Workers (CTV) to effect a process of reforms intended to reduce the influence of political parties and increase rank and file control over decision making. To this end, ACILS will conduct ten, two-day courses for regional federations of the CTV which will focus on the following topics: problems and challenges for unions in a changing world, restructuring of labor organizations, and the electoral process. 1/00

RECASTING LIBERTY: CONSTITUTIONAL REFORM

     $56,000

> *Venezuela*
> Center for International Private Enterprise /Center for the Dissemination Economic Information (CEDICE)

The Center for International Private Enterprise (CIPE) will work with CEDICE to launch a program to move the economic reform discussions toward a more participatory and democratic process that includes concrete reforms encouraging individual initiative and private enterprise. CEDICE will sponsor, in conjunction with interested business organizations and nonprofit groups, four large-scale national forums and at least six regional forums on legislation that is constitutionally required to be enacted in the National Assembly's first year of operation. Specific focus will be placed on the Organic Labor Act and the new Organic Tax Codes. Members of legislation committees, as well as national and foreign experts, and representatives of the social and economic sectors will be involved. 6/00

SUPPORT TO LOCAL GROUPS FOR ELECTION OBSERVATION $16,747
> *Venezuela*
> *Fundacion Momento de la Gente* / None

Fundacion Momento de la Gente will conduct a pre-electoral monitoring campaign, which will monitor the use of public funds in the campaign, participate in the electoral audit committee (CNE), review election materials, and conduct training for some election-day observers in various regions of the country. These activities will help promote civilian oversight and transparency in the voting and vote counting process. 6/00

FOSTERING YOUTH PARTICIPATION IN THE POLITICAL PROCESS
> *Venezuela* $50,000
> International Republican Institute / *Fundación Participación Juvenil*

The International Republican Institute (IRI) will work with Fundación Participación Juvenil to instill democratic values in Venezuelan youth so they can play an integral role in maintaining society's interest in establishing effective democratic institutions. 9/00

REGIONAL FORUM FOR DECENTRALIZATION $50,000
> *Venezuela*
> PRODEL-Venezuela / None

PRODEL-Venezuela will conduct a series of activities to establish and train a network of national and state legislators and local mayors to monitor government activity concerning decentralization and advocate for the rights and responsibilities of state and local government in Venezuela. A series of seminars and courses will be held so participants can analyze and debate pending legislation and share information about laws and policies affecting local government and decentralization 9/00

STRENGTHENING POLITICAL PARTIES $340,000
Venezuela
International Republican Institute / None

The International Republican Institute (IRI) will train national and/or local branches of existing and/or newly created political parties on such topics as party structure, management and organization; internal and external party communications; and coalition building. 1/01

CIVIL-MILITARY RELATIONS $57,820
Venezuela
Asociación Civil Comprensión de Venezuela / None

Asociación Civil Comprensión de Venezuela will organize a series of meetings, which will bring representatives of organizations from civil society together with active and retired members of the Venezuelan armed forces, to initiate a national debate on the newly changing role of the military in the country. The meetings will be held in both civilian and military institutions, under the consultation of instructors at military colleges, university professors and representatives of civil society. 1/01

STRENGTHENING CIVIL SOCIETY LINKS FOR FUNDAMENTAL POLITICAL RIGHTS
                                                                      $19,740
Venezuela
Asociación Civil Consorcio Justicia / None

Asociación Civil Consorcio Justicia will help build the capacity of civil society organizations in Venezuela to become active in the struggle against authoritarianism. *Consorcio Justicia* will host an international conference to explore examples of how civil society in countries such as Serbia and Mexico worked together to protect themselves against and defeat authoritarian regimes, as well as build a network of Venezuelan civil society organizations committed to the defense of democratic freedoms in the country. 1/01

NED Projects 2001

LEGISLATIVE MONITORING FOR PROTECTION OF POLITICAL RIGHTS$40,000
Venezuela
Momento de la Gente / None

Momento de la Gente received continued Endowment funding to organize Venezuelan civil society groups to monitor the National Assembly on key pieces of legislation pertinent to civil liberties. *Momento* will organize a series of working meetings for representatives of civil society groups to establish monitoring mechanisms and developing proposals to be submitted to congressional committees responsible for drafting the final law, with the additional aim of creating link among organizations. NED funding will also be used to cover core institutional costs. 1/01

SUPPORT FOR DEMOCRATIC UNION ACTION $154,375
Venezuela
The American Center for International Labor Solidarity /None

The American Center for International Labor Solidarity (ACILS) will support the Confederation of Venezuelan Workers' (CTV) efforts to organize disparate unions and federations into a unified national industrial unions and define a new mission and role for the union movement in the development of the nation. 9/01

RE-ENGAGING CITIZENS IN STATE-LEVEL POLITICS
$210,500

Venezuela
National Democratic Institute for International Affairs / *Momento de la Gente*

National Democratic Institute for International Affairs (NDI), in collaboration with Momento de la Gente, will assess and conduct pilot programs in up to three states to engage citizens in the policy-making process, specifically focused on government accountability and transparency. NDI will also work with state governments to include citizens' input into the decision-making process. 9/01

STRENGTHENING CIVIL SOCIETY TO PROMOTE DEMOCRATIC EDUCATION
$55,000

Venezuela
Education Assembly Civil Association /None

The Education Assembly Civil Association will organize grassroots groups to monitor education reform plans in Venezuela and formulate draft legislation for the Superior Education law, as well as create a network of parents, teachers and communities to pro-actively monitor the quality of education in the country. 9/01

NED Projects 2002

ENHANCING DEMOCRACY THROUGH ALTERNATIVE DISPUTE RESOLUTION METHODS
Venezuela

Center for International Private Enterprise / None

The Center for International Private Enterprise (CIPE) will collaborate with CEDCA, a Venezuelan non-profit group, to launch a strategic public awareness campaign and to offer a series of rigorous alternative dispute resolution (ADR) training modules. For each type of training module, CEDCA will design a training guidebook and recruit experienced instructors. 1/02

STRENGTHENING CIVIL SOCIETY LINKS FOR FUNDAMENTAL POLITICAL RIGHTS
Venezuela $84,000

Asociación Civil Consorcio Justicia / None

Asociación Civil Consorcio Justicia (Consorcio Justicia) will use Endowment funding to host a broad range of civil society groups at a working conference in late January 2002 to evaluate the situation in Venezuela and develop a policy agenda, after which Consorcio Justicia will conduct a campaign within Venezuela to improve communication and coordination among Venezuelan NGOs and to raise public awareness of their work. Finally, Consorcio Justicia will conduct a program in ten states throughout the country to educate communities on local justice issues, help organize elections to select justices of the peace and train locally elected justices. 1/02

LEGISLATIVE MONITORING AND MUNICIPAL TRAINING $64,000
Venezuela

Momento de la Gente / None

Momento de la Gente (Momento) will organize Venezuelan civil society groups to monitor the National Assembly and provide policy input on key pieces of legislation pertinent to civil liberties. Momento will also work with and help organize local elected officials to improve their ability to oversee public budgets and advocate for decentralization. Finally, Momento will maintain and strengthen its links with different civil society organizations in Venezuela and continue to work with international organizations to improve coordination and information on the political situation in Venezuela. 1/02

CONSENSUS BUILDING TO REDUCE THE INFORMAL SECTOR IN VENEZUELA
                                                                                           $66,266

Venezuela

Center for International Private Enterprise / Center for the Dissemination of Economic Information

The Center for the Dissemination of Economic Information (CEDICE) will work with several Venezuelan NGOs to develop a Pact to Rebuild Venezuela, which will include a policy paper and a series of workshops. CEDICE will also address the problem of the growing informal sector in Colombia through a series of workshops and forums that will be developed jointly with civil society groups throughout Venezuela. 3/02

NED Projects 2002

STRENGTHENING POLITICAL PARTIES $300,000
Venezuela
International Republican Institute / None

The International Republican Institute (IRI) will train national and local branches of existing and newly created political parties, both on a one-to-one basis and through group sessions. Possible training topics include party structure, management, and organization, internal and external party communications, effective constituent relations; membership and volunteer recruitment; candidate/leadership development, and coalition building. 3/02

CONSENSUS BUILDING TO REDUCE THE INFORMAL SECTOR IN VENEZUELA

$116,525
Venezuela
Center for International Private Enterprise / Center for the Dissemination of Economic Information

Through a joint effort between the Venezuelan Labor Confederation and the Citizens Assembly, a policy paper will be developed and a series of four national and ten regional workshops will be held, led by the Center for the Dissemination of Economic Information (CEDICE). CEDICE will also carry out project activities to address the problem of the growing informal sector, such as a series of workshops and forums that will be developed jointly with business groups in Zulia and Aragua States and the National Council on Commerce and Services (CONSECOMERCIO) in Caracas, as well as with the participation of other civil society groups throughout Venezuela. 6/02

MONITORING SOCIAL PROGRAMS $63,000
Venezuela
Centro al Service de la Acción Popular (CESAP) / None

The Centro al Servicio de la Accion Popular (CESAP) will monitor social expenditures, the impact of poverty-alleviation programs, and social development and change in Venezuela. The project will monitor government budgets and programs, gather data through surveys, and monitor social development indicators to develop a national picture of the state of poverty and social programs in Venezuela. CESAP will develop a network of local community groups to monitor local social programs and their implementation, and will publish a report based on its findings, which will be distributed nationally and internationally. 6/02

PROFESSIONALIZATION OF THE MEDIA $25,000
Venezuela
Instituto Prensa y Sociedad / None

The Instituto de Prensa y Sociedad (IPYS) will carry out a forum in partnership with its Venezuela-based affiliate for media owners, editors, journalists, and leaders of international media advocacy groups to reflect on the current state of freedom of expression and journalism in Venezuela. The forums' discussion will focus on analyzing the events surrounding the coup which involved the media, in addition to examining larger issues of freedom of expression in the country. The forum participants will propose recommendations for resolving issues of self-censorship, journalistic protection, and professionalization of the media. 6/02

NED Projects 2002

Venezuela $116,001

The American Center for International Labor Solidarity / None

The American Center for International Labor Solidarity (ACILS) will support the Venezuelan trade movement, represented by the CTV, in developing a program to extend organization, training, and representation to the informal sector. ACILS will also aid CTV in developing and publicizing its positions and strategies on economic and social issues as part of the development of an anti-poverty program emphasizing leadership training, articulate CTV positions more effectively with the national and international news media (including journalists union and IFJ) and on more effective use of the CTV website. 9/02

POLITICAL PARTY STRENGTHENING
Venezuela $50,000

National Democratic Institute for International Affairs / None

The National Democratic Institute for International Affairs (NDI) will conduct focus groups to detail popular perceptions of political parties and present the results to political party leaders. NDI will then use this information to encourage parties to fully embrace the need for reform and to use the results of the focus groups to shape renewal strategies. 9/02

MONITORING LAND REFORM
Venezuela $35,000

Acción Campesina / None

Acción Campesina will train monitors who will work in ten states to collect information on the effects of Venezuela's land redistribution law. The information provided by these monitors will then serve as the basis for a public information campaign. *Acción Campesina* will work with representatives of the National Assembly to communicate objective information about local disputes and conflicts generated by the law. At the end of the project, *Acción Campesina* will convene a national forum to discuss the land redistribution law and attempt to propose ways to reduce rural conflict. 9/02

CONFLICT RESOLUTION AT THE LOCAL LEVEL
Venezuela $11,000

Asociación Civil Consorcio Justicia-Occidente / None

The *Asociación Civil Consorcio Justicia-Occidente* will work with communities in the state of Táchira to promote the election of local justices of the peace and train communities and the candidates to the office of justice of the peace in conflict resolution and mediation techniques. In addition, *Consorcio Justicia-Occidente* will work with local governments and communities to improve communication and collaboration at the local level. 9/02

EDUCATION ASSEMBLY
Venezuela $57,000

Asociación Civil Asamblea de Educación / None

The *Asociación Civil Asamblea de Educación* (Education Assembly) received renewed Endowment support to monitor and distribute information on education policy issues. The Education Assembly will convene regular policy forums and press conferences to discuss education policy and their proposals and will work with the National Assembly to discuss draft legislation and reforms. Last, the Education Assembly will train local community leaders in eight states and Caracas to strengthen its national parent-teachers' network dedicated to democratic education. 9/02

CONFLICT RESOLUTION AT THE LOCAL LEVEL
Venezuela $10,000

Asociación Civil J...

NED Projects 2002–2003

The *Asociación Civil Justicia Alternativa* will conduct two workshops each in four locations in the Venezuelan state of Aragua. The workshops will train newly elected justices of the peace, local citizens and local government officials in conflict resolution, political leadership, democratic values, and the institutions and processes of the political system. Each workshop will train 15 people, with the second workshop to follow-up with participants trained in the first round. 9/02

CONFLICT RESOLUTION AT THE LOCAL LEVEL $11,000
Venezuela
Fundación Justicia de Paz del Estado Monagas / None

Fundación Justicia de Paz del Estado Monagas will work in 32 communities in the state of Monagas to create local roundtables to promote dialogue among local political actors. *Fundación Justicia de Paz* will engage in a broad public education campaign in which they will distribute information to the communities about the techniques of political dialogue and peaceful resolution of conflicts. 9/02

FY 2003

STRENGTHENING POLITICAL PARTIES AT THE LOCAL LEVEL $116,000
Venezuela
International Republican Institute / None

The International Republican Institute (IRI) will seek out local partners in the states of Zulia, Anzoátegui and Carabobo to conduct party training, and will place particular emphasis on party grassroots strengthening, external communications, and inclusion of marginalized sectors in the parties. 1/03

STRENGTHENING POLITICAL PARTIES $116,000
Venezuela
National Democratic Institute for International Affairs / None

The National Democratic Institute for International Affairs (NDI) will work with municipal leaders and governments to rebuild citizen confidence and participation in the political system and the parties through anti-corruption initiatives. NDI will also work to help renew traditional political parties, as well as assist with the building of new political parties. 1/03

POLITICAL PARTY BUILDING AT THE NATIONAL LEVEL
$299,999
Venezuela
International Republican Institute / None

The International Republican Institute (IRI) will use a combination of polling and political party training in critical areas of party reform to help Venezuela's parties establish a stronger role in the country and regain the trust of the electorate. IRI will work toward the development of detailed party platforms reflective of constituent concerns, effective two-way internal communication structures, and processes for transparent and democratic selection of party leaders. 3/03

LOCAL CIVIC EDUCATION $10,000
Venezuela
Acción para el Desarrollo / None

Acción para el Desarrollo will conduct informal civic education workshops for leaders of neighborhood associations in poor neighborhoods in and around Caracas. Acción para el Desarrollo will hold a total of 30 workshops on democratic values and conflict resolution to train presidents of neighborhood associations in seven "barrios populares." At the end of the workshops, participants will develop a plan to promote development and democratic dialogue within their communities. 3/03

STRENGTHENING THE JUDICIAL SYSTEM $54,000
Venezuela
Asociación Civil Consorcio Justicia / None

Asociación Civil Consorcio Justicia will implement a program that will monitor the status of the judicial system and its operation and work with the Congress to improve legislation and laws. Consorcio Justicia will also work with municipal officials and community leaders in the poor neighborhood of Libertador in Caracas to train local communities in the peaceful resolution of conflict and establish local mediation committees in 60 neighborhoods. 3/03

LEGISLATIVE ASSISTANCE $64,000
Venezuela
Fundación Momento de la Gente / None

The Fundación Momento de la Gente will organize Venezuelan civic groups to collaborate with the National Assembly in developing legislative initiatives and debate around three separate bills on muncipal government, electoral procedures and citizen participation. Momento will provide technical advice to assembly members, organize public seminars for the discussion of the bills, and design and propose ways of increasing public awareness of and debate on the proposed legislation. 3/03

SUPPORTING PRESS FREEDOMS $44,500
Venezuela
Instituto Prensa y Sociedad-Venezuela / None

The Instituto de Prensa y Sociedad-Venezuela (IPYS-Venezuela) will construct an alert network in Venezuela to report attacks against journalists that occur in the provinces in and around Caracas. IPYS-Venezuela will support correspondents in the provinces to monitor press conditions and investigate cases of attacks or threats, as well as offer a series of training sessions for journalists' professionalization. Finally, IPYS-Venezuela will participate in regional press advocacy meetings in order to connect with international groups and build their organizational network. 3/03

MONITORING SOCIAL PROGRAMS $65,000
Venezuela
Centro al Servicio de la Acción Popular / None

Centro al Servicio de la Acción Popular (CESAP) will monitor social expenditures, the impact of poverty alleviation programs and social development and change in Venezuela. The project will monitor government budgets and programs, gather data through surveys, and monitor social development indicators to develop a national picture of the state of poverty and social programs in Venezuela. CESAP will develop a network of local community groups to monitor local social programs and their implementation, and will publish a report based on its findings which will be distributed nationally and internationally. 6/03

NED Projects 2003

MONITORING LAND REFORM $58,000
Venezuela
Acción Campesina / None

Acción Campesina will create three local groups of promoters of farmers' rights located in highly conflict-ridden rural areas to monitor land disputes, track the needs of the rural communities, and draft proposals to reform current agrarian public policies at the state and municipal levels. Acción Campesina will also serve as a source of information to policymakers, political parties, and civil society on the implementation of national laws and its effects. 9/03

CONFLICT RESOLUTION AT THE LOCAL LEVEL $14,412
Venezuela
Asociación Civil Consorcio Justicia – Occidente / None

The Asociación Civil Consorcio Justicia – Occidente will work with communities to promote the election of local justices of the peace and train the communities and the candidates in conflict resolution and mediation techniques. 9/03

CONFLICT RESOLUTION AT THE LOCAL LEVEL $14,107
Venezuela
Asociación Civil Justicia Alternativa / None

The Asociación Civil Justicia Alternativa will conduct training on conflict resolution, human rights, the role of police and the local justice systems in conflict resolution, and police-community relations for the police and local justice officials in Giradot, in the state of Aragua. 9/03

CIVIC EDUCATION FOR POLICE $42,207
Venezuela
Asociación Civil Liderazgo y Visión / None

The Asociación Civil Liderazgo y Visión will conduct a democracy and human rights training program for officers of the Caracas metropolitan police force. To ensure the sustainability of the program, Liderazgo y Visión will train four representatives in each of the branches of the metropolitan police to serve as coordinators for follow-up and to help organize and conduct courses and informal workshops in the future. 9/03

HUMAN RIGHTS DEFENSE $83,000
Venezuela
Center for Justice and International Law / None

The Center for Justice and International Law (CEJIL) received Endowment assistance to support a staff attorney in CEJIL and two trips to Venezuela to train local human rights groups and journalists on how to prepare cases for the Inter-American system to defend freedom of expression. The staff attorney will also request and monitor the implementation of precautionary and provisional measures from the commission and the court in cases when the life of human rights defenders or journalists is in imminent danger. 9/03

NED Projects 2003

CONFLICT RESOLUTION AT THE LOCAL LEVEL $11,698
Venezuela
Fundación Justicia de Paz del Estado Monagas / None

The *Fundación Justicia de Paz del Estado Monagas* will work in 32 communities in the state of Monagas to continue to support its mediation and conflict resolution roundtables by expanding the membership of the roundtables to include representatives from local government and local, as well as state, judicial and law enforcement offices. The program will include the training of officials in mediation and conflict resolution and the establishment of a state-wide network of mediators. 9/03

ELECTIONS EDUCATION $83,400
Venezuela
Súmate / None

Súmate will develop links with other organizations in the region that work on elections, produce election-related, voter mobilization materials, and consolidate its national network of volunteers for the referendum on the president's mandate. *Súmate* will establish a coordinator in each state and train people from local organizations on the referendum process and how to conduct a get-out-the-vote campaign for the general community, in addition to developing a public information campaign on the referendum and to encourage citizens to participate in the electoral process. 9/03

NED Projects 2004

Instituto de Prensa y Sociedad – Venezuela (Press and Society Institute – Venezuela)
$72,000
To promote and defend freedom of expression. Instituto de Prensa y Sociedad – Venezuela (Press and Society Institute – Venezuela) will support an alert network, which reports attacks against journalists that occur in the provinces and in Caracas. Training workshops to strengthen the investigative reporting skills of journalists will also be held.

Asociación Civil Consorcio Justicia (Justice Consortium)
$67,000
To monitor the judicial system and its operation and work with the Congress to improve legislation and laws. The Asociación Civil Consorcio Justicia (Justice Consortium) will work with local organizations outside Caracas and with Ecuadorian and Peruvian NGOs to share information and programs and establish a regional judicial observatory. In addition, the Justice Consortium will work with the Peruvian NGO, Institute for Legal Defense to establish a democratic leadership training program that will train local and community leaders in the interior of Venezuela.

Acción para el Desarrollo (Action for Development)
$12,420
To conduct civic education in conflict resolution and community leadership. Acción para el Desarrollo (Action for Development) will conduct workshops for leaders of local "neighborhood associations" in poor neighborhoods in and around Caracas. The workshops will focus on the themes of democratic values, the role of civil society and community organizations in democracy, how to negotiate and mediate local conflicts, the Bolivarian Constitution and the rights of Venezuelans, and how to address the violation of political and human rights.

International Republican Institute
$285,000
To promote the development of responsive, democratic political parties. IRI will focus its efforts on long-term party strengthening in the following areas: political platform development; internal and external communications; strengthening party structure; coalition building; and youth involvement in the parties. IRI will offer trainings to all of the major political parties across the ideological spectrum. IRI will work to expand party outreach to marginalized groups through trainings of local party officials.

Center for International Private Enterprise
$92,488
To promote democratic mechanisms of participation for entrepreneurs that are currently left out of the policymaking process and help forge solutions to structural problems underlying informal commerce. CIPE and its Venezuelan partner Center for the Dissemination of Economic Knowledge (CEDICE) will conduct a survey of the informal sector in Sucre and Baruta; conduct outreach initiatives including workshops, fora, and publication of an informational brochure; and promote debate and discussion on the informal sector among government leaders at the local and national levels.

Centro al Servicio de la Acción Popular (Center at the Service of Popular Action)
$60,000

To monitor social expenditures, the impact of poverty-alleviation programs and social development and change in Venezuela. CESAP will develop a network of local community groups to monitor local social programs and their implementation, and will publish a report based on its findings which will be distributed nationally and internationally. The report will serve as the basis for a public education campaign on social development in Venezuela and how to improve social programs to better address Venezuelan poverty.

Center for International Private Enterprise
$33,006

To promote a debate on the relationship between institutions and economic growth. CIPE and its local partner Center for the Dissemination of Economic Knowledge will conduct a two-day international conference to bring together in Caracas leading scholars, businessmen and women, political leaders, university student leaders and representatives of think tanks throughout the Americas to discuss how to promote institutional reform, economic growth and the role of a liberal society in that process.

Acción Campesina (Farmers in Action)
$65,000

To promote farmers' rights at the national and local levels through policy reform on agriculture and land redistribution. *Acción Campesina* will serve as a source of information to policy makers, political parties and civil society on the implementation of national laws and its effects on the rural sector and on small farmers.

Asociación Civil Consorcio Justicia – Occidente (Civil Association "Justice Consortium" – West)
$16,000

To strengthen community leadership and peaceful resolution of conflict. *Consorcio Justicia-Occidente* will work with local community organizations in four municipalities in the state of Táchira, on the border of Colombia, to train over 100 community leaders in democratic rights, community organization and techniques of conciliation and negotiation. *Consorcio Justicia-Occidente* will then work with these leaders in their communities to help them carry out projects to develop strategies for addressing local problems.

Asociación Civil Justicia Alternativa (Civil Association "Alternative Justice")
$13,980

To promote conflict resolution and participation at the local level. *Justicia Alternativa* will train community leaders and elected officials in the city of Girardot in Aragua state. Through the training and follow-up, *Justicia Alternativa* will bring together community representatives and locally elected officials to initiate a dialogue for the development of communities and neighborhoods.

Asociación Civil Liderazgo y Visión (Civil Association "Leadership and Vision")
$56,000

To conduct a human rights and democracy training program for officers of the Caracas metropolitan police force. *Liderazgo y Visión* will conduct 60 training courses in the Caracas police academy, training a total of 1,800 members of the metropolitan force. In addition,

NED Projects 2004

Liderazgo y Visión will train a total of twelve representatives in each of the branches of the metropolitan police to serve as coordinators for follow-up and to help organize and conduct courses and informal workshops in the future.

Center for Justice and International Law
$90,000

To promote and defend human rights in Venezuela. CEJIL will continue to present and litigate cases before the Inter-American System (IAS), train human rights activists, journalists, and young leaders in international human rights standards and the use of the IAS, and support and encourage Venezuelan NGOs and civil society organizations in their efforts to defend human rights and promote reasoned discourse and dialogue over the future of human rights and democracy in their country.

Fundación Justicia de Paz del Estado Monagas (Justice of Peace of Monagas State Foundation)
$11,490

To promote women's leadership and conflict resolution at the local level. *Fundación Justicia de Paz* will work with community organizations throughout the state of Monagas to train local women leaders and female judicial officials in peaceful resolution of conflict, constitutional rights, and state judicial institutions.

NED grant to CIPE-CEDICE 2002–2003 "Plan Consensus"

PROJECT ACTIVITIES

Project Advisory Committee

The project advisory committee will consist of the following individuals and organizations:

Hugo Fonseca Viso	Fedecámaras
Jorge Botti	Fedecámaras
Jesus Urbieta	Confederación de Trabajadores Venezolanos
Nelson Landáez	Confederación de Trabajadores Venezolanos
Maxim Ross	Citizens Assembly
Marisol Fuentes	Sol Communications
William Echeverría	Radio Caracas
Jorge Reyes	Sinergía
Tiziana Polesel	CEDICE
Luis Eduardo Rodriguez	CEDICE
Aurelio Concheso	CEDICE
Mikel De Viana, SJ	Catholic Church

Meetings with Civil Society Groups

Four meetings will be organized with Fedecámaras, CTV, as well as civil society groups in Venezuela. The business and labor sectors, the media, the church, and other non-profit groups will gather to discuss and develop a broad consensus on a National Agenda—the specific economic policies that Venezuela should adopt in order to resolve the urgent crisis that the country currently faces in the economic as well as political and social arenas.

In addition, four members of CEDICE's academic group and two representatives of the Citizens Assembly will conduct a study to investigate the causes of the current economic crisis as well as to identify measures for both sustainable economic development as well as social improvement.

Development and Dissemination of a Policy Paper

Based on the collaborative analysis and consensus from the four meetings and the research study described above, the groups will develop a National Agenda document to describe their economic policy recommendations. To present and promote the results to the public at large, the groups will work with the media (*El Nacional*, *El Universal*, and Globo Visión) to design and implement a dissemination strategy.

Regional Workshops and National Forums

"Plan Consensus" (cont.)

Organization	Representative
Asamblea de Ciudadanos (civil association)	Mr. Axel Capriles
Abriendo Caminos (political movement)	Mr. Pedro Penzini
Alianza Bravo Pueblo (political party)	Mr. Antonio Ledezma
Fundación Raúl Leoni/Acción Democrática (political party)	Mr. Ramón Rangel
Gente de Petróleo (civil association)	Mr. Nelson Benitez
Instituto Altos Estudios Sindicales/CTV (workers' union)	Mr. Alfredo Padilla
Alianza Cívica de la Sociedad Civil (civil association)	Mr. Elias Santana
Ifedec-Copei (political party)	Mr. Eduardo Fernández
Liderazgo y Visión (civil association)	Mr. Alonso E. Domínguez
Proyecto Venezuela (political party)	Mrs. María Isabel Canales
Red Democrática Universitaria (civil association)	Mr. Tomás Páez
Visión Emergente (political party)	Mr. Cipriano Heredia
Un Solo Pueblo (political party)	Mr. William Ojeda
Bandera Roja (left political party)	Mr. Carlos Hermoso
Resistencia Civil (civil association)	Mr. Domingo A. Rangel
Democratic Coordinator (opposition umbrella organization)	Mr. Diego B. Urbaneja
Fedecámaras (strategic committee) (business association)	Mrs. Albis Muñoz Mr. Fedor Saldivia

State Department cable, September 2001

UNCLASSIFIED   PTO9054

PAGE 01   CARACA   02839   272141Z   RELEASED IN FULL
ACTION EB-00

```
INFO  LOG-00   AIT-03   CEA-01   CIAE-00  CTME-00  DODE-00  ITCE-00
      WHA-00   SRPP-00  EXME-00  E-00     UTED-00  VC-00    FRB-00
      H-01     TEDE-00  INR-00   ITC-01   L-00     VCE-00   AC-01
      NSAE-00  NSCE-00  OES-01   OMB-01   OPIC-01  ACE-00   SP-00
      SSO-00   SS-00    STR-00   TEST-00  TRSE-00  USIE-00  FMP-00
      EPAE-00  DRL-02   G-00     NFAT-00  SAS-00    /012W
                --------------265FBA  272141Z /38
```

R 272125Z SEP 01
FM AMEMBASSY CARACAS
TO SECSTATE WASHDC 3380
USDOC WASHDC
INFO DEPT OF COMMERCE WASHDC
DEPT OF ENERGY WASHDC

UNCLAS CARACAS 002839

STATE FOR EB, H, WHA/AND
USDOC FOR 4331/MAC/TWELCH; 3134/USFCS/OIO/WH/DLUTTER

E.O. 12958: N/A
TAGS: EFIN, ETRD, WTO, VE
SUBJECT: VENEZUELA-U.S. BUSINESS COUNCIL REQUESTS WASHINGTON
MEETINGS

1. ACTION REQUEST; SEE PARAGRAPH 5.

2. SENIOR OFFICERS OF THE VENEZUELA-U.S. BUSINESS COUNCIL (CEVEU)
                      UNCLASSIFIED

PAGE 02   CARACA   02839   272141Z
PLAN TO VISIT WASHINGTON D.C. FROM NOVEMBER 1-2, 2001 AND WISH TO
MEET WITH SENIOR GOVERNMENT OFFICIALS IN THE DEPARTMENT, OFFICE OF
U.S. TRADE REPRESENTATIVE, DEPARTMENT OF COMMERCE, DEPARTMENT OF
ENERGY, AND SELECTED MEMBERS OF CONGRESS. CEVEU (CONSEJO DE
EMPRESARIOS VENEZUELA-ESTADOS UNIDOS) IS A HIGHLY RESPECTED
BUSINESS AND TRADE ASSOCIATION THAT HAS TAKEN THE LEAD IN
PROMOTING INITIATIVES THAT CLOSELY MIRROR U.S. POSITIONS. THIS
VISIT IS AN EXCELLENT OPPORTUNITY FOR SENIOR U.S. OFFICIALS TO
HEAR ABOUT PENDING U.S.-VENEZUELAN TRADE ISSUES FROM THE
VENEZUELAN PRIVATE SECTOR PERSPECTIVE. CEVEU PARTICULARLY LOOKS
FORWARD TO AN EXCHANGE OF VIEWS ON FTAA, THE PROPOSED BILATERAL
INVESTMENT TREATY, THE PROPOSED NEW ROUND OF WTO NEGOTIATIONS, AND
THE POSSIBLE INCLUSION OF VENEZUELA IN THE ANDEAN TRADE
PREFERENCES ACT (ATPA).

September 2001 cable (cont.)

Current Class: UNCLASSIFIED
Current Handling: n/a

3. THE CEVEU DELEGATION WILL CONSIST OF GUSTAVO MARTURET,
PRESIDENT OF CEVEU AND CHIEF EXECUTIVE OFFICER OF BANCO MERCANTIL;
LOPE MENDOZA, PRESIDENT OF CONINDUSTRIA (COUNCIL OF INDUSTRIES);
DR. PEDRO CARMONA, PRESIDENT OF FEDECAMERAS (NATIONAL COUNCIL OF
CHAMBERS OF BUSINESS); ALEJANDRO REYES, VICE PRESIDENT OF CEVEU;
ANA TERESA WALLIS, EXECUTIVE DIRECTOR OF CEVEU; LUIS ENRIQUE BALL,
CEVEU DIRECTOR AND CEO OF THE PRIVATE FIRM EUROCIENCIA; AND
TENTATIVELY, DR. GUSTAVO JULIO VOLLMER, CEVEU DIRECTOR AND
PRESIDENT OF THE PRIVATE FIRM CORPALMAR.

4. THE CEVEU REPRESENTATIVES HAVE REQUESTED MEETINGS WITH GRANT
D. ALDONAS, UNDER SECRETARY OF COMMERCE FOR INTERNATIONAL TRADE;
VICKY BAILEY, ASSISTANT SECRETARY FOR POLICY AND INTERNATIONAL
AFFAIRS, DEPARTMENT OF ENERGY; ANTHONY WAYNE, ASSISTANT SECRETARY
OF STATE FOR ECONOMIC AND BUSINESS AFFAIRS; AND REGINA VARGO, U.S.
TRADE REPRESENTATIVE FOR LATIN AMERICA. THEY HAVE ALSO REQUESTED
UNCLASSIFIED

PAGE 03   CARACA 02839 272141Z
APPOINTMENTS WITH U.S. REPRESENTATIVE CASS BALLENGER, U.S.
REPRESENTATIVE GREGORY MEEKS, U.S. REPRESENTATIVE MARK SOUDER, ALL
OF WHO HAVE RECENTLY VISITED VENEZUELA AND SHARE AN ACTIVE
INTEREST IN IMPROVED BILATERAL RELATIONS. LASTLY, THEY WISH TO
MEET WITH U.S. SENATOR BOB GRAHAM AND U.S. REPRESENTATIVE PHILIP
CRANE, WHO ARE SPONSORING RECENTLY INTRODUCED ATPA LEGISLATION IN
THE SENATE AND HOUSE OF REPRESENTATIVES, RESPECTIVELY.

5. EMBASSY CARACAS STRONGLY SUPPORTS THIS REQUEST FROM CEVEU.
THE MEMBERS OF THE CEVEU DELEGATION ARE HIGHLY REGARDED AND
INFLUENTIAL BUSINESS LEADERS WHO HAVE CONSISTENTLY PLAYED A
CRITICAL ROLE IN ADVANCING U.S. COMMERCIAL INTERESTS IN VENEZUELA.
EMBASSY REQUESTS THE DEPARTMENT AND OTHER AGENCIES ASSISTANCE IN
ARRANGING THESE MEETINGS.

HRINAK

UNCLASSIFIED

<< END OF DOCUMENT >>

Current Class: UNCLASSIFIED

UNCLASSIFIED

Current Class: UNCLASSIFIED
Current Handling: n/a

CONFRONTATION OF IDEAS, NOT A CONFRONTATION IN THE STREETS.
END SUMMARY.

STATESMAN-LIKE CARMONA STRESSES NON-VIOLENCE
----

2. CARMONA ADDRESSED THE VENEZUELAN-AMERICAN CHAMBER OF
COMMERCE (VENAMCHAM) DECEMBER 6, AND GAVE A WIDELY COVERED
PRESS CONFERENCE ON DECEMBER 7. IN BOTH APPEARANCES,
CARMONA DELIVERED CALM AND STATESMAN-LIKE SPEECHES
EXPLAINING THE WORK STOPPAGE WILL NOT BE VIOLENT, BUT WILL
BE ONLY A QCONFRONTATION OF IDEAS.Q FEDECAMARAS HAS NOT
PLANNED ANY PUBLIC DEMONSTRATION FOR DECEMBER 10, BUT SAID
IT SHOULD BE A DAY TO QSTAY HOME FROM WORK.Q

3. AT THE VENAMCHAM EVENT, CARMONA RECEIVED AN EXTENDED
UNCLASSIFIED

PAGE 03   CARACA 03606 01 OF 02 080156Z
STANDING OVATION, AND WAS INTRODUCED AS QTHE RIGHT MAN FOR
THE RIGHT TIME IN VENEZUELA.Q AS WITH ALL OF HIS RECENT
PUBLIC APPEARANCES, THE PRESS SWARMED CARMONA, GIVING HIM AT
LEAST THE AURA OF A POLITICAL FIGURE AND PROVIDING SOME
FOCUS TO WHAT WERE DISPARATE OPPOSITION VOICES.

SUPPORT FOR THE SHUTDOWN
----

4. THE CONFEDERATION OF VENEZUELAN WORKERS (CTV) ANNOUNCED
THAT THEY SUPPORT THE DECEMBER 10 SHUTDOWN, BUT WOULD NOT
HOLD ANY PUBLIC MARCH OR DEMONSTRATION ON DECEMBER 10.
HOWEVER, CTV SAID IF THE GOV DOES NOT LISTEN TO THEIR
CONCERNS THEY WILL CONSIDER FURTHER NATIONAL STRIKES.

5. THE TRANSPORTATION WORKERS, BANK EMPLOYEES, AND HEALTH
WORKERS ALSO ANNOUNCED SUPPORT FOR THE SHUTDOWN. LOCAL
GASOLINE SERVICE STATIONS HAVE NOT DECIDED IF THEY WILL
CLOSE. ALTHOUGH THE GOV ANNOUNCED THE CARACAS METRO WILL
REMAIN OPEN, SUPPORT FROM THE TRANSPORTATION SECTOR
(REPRESENTING TAXIS AND BUSES) COULD GUARANTEE A TRUE
SHUTDOWN OF CARACAS AND OTHER METROPOLITAN AREAS.

6. U.S. CORPORATIONS CONTACTED BY POST REPORTED A MIX OF
PLANNED ACTIONS. SOME WILL CLOSE AND OTHERS WILL OPEN BUT
MONITOR THE SITUATION. THE U.S. CORPORATIONS POINTED TO
SECURITY CONCERNS AND TRANSPORTATION DIFFICULTIES FOR
WORKERS AS REASONS FOR CLOSING. CITING CONCERN FOR
INVOLVEMENT IN DOMESTIC POLITICS, THOSE THAT EXPECT TO BE

Current Class: UNCLASSIFIED

State Department cable, March 2002

UNCLASSIFIED

UNCLASSIFIED   PTQ6780

PAGE 01   CARACA 00546 01 OF 02 052201Z   RELEASED IN FULL
ACTION INR-00

INFO LOG-00   NP-00   ACQ-00   DODE-00   WHA-00   DS-00   UTED-00
      VC-00   TEDE-00   VCE-00   AC-01   NSAE-00   ACE-00   IRM-00
      TEST-00   DSCC-00   DRL-02   NFAT-00   SAS-00   /003W
      ------------------6FF49F 052202Z /38
R 052151Z MAR 02
FM AMEMBASSY CARACAS
TO SECSTATE WASHDC 4949
INFO CIA WASHDC
DIA WASHDC
NSC WASHDC
USCINCSO MIAMI FL
AMEMBASSY BOGOTA
AMEMBASSY BRASILIA
AMEMBASSY GEORGETOWN
AMEMBASSY LIMA
AMEMBASSY LA PAZ
AMEMBASSY QUITO
USINT HAVANA

UNCLAS SECTION 01 OF 02 CARACAS 000546

INR FOR COZART
NSC FOR AMBASSADOR MAISTO
USCINCSO FOR POLAD

SENSITIVE

UNCLASSIFIED

PAGE 02   CARACA 00546 01 OF 02 052201Z
E.O. 12958: NA
TAGS: PREL, PGOV, VE
SUBJ: LABOR, BUSINESS AND CHURCH ANNOUNCE TRANSITION
PACT

1. (SBU) SUMMARY: WITH MUCH FANFARE, THE VENEZUELAN GREAT
AND GOOD ASSEMBLED ON MARCH 5 TO HEAR REPRESENTATIVES OF
THE CONFEDERATION OF VENEZUELAN WORKERS, THE FEDERATION OF
BUSINESS CHAMBERS, AND THE CATHOLIC CHURCH PRESENT THEIR
"BASES FOR A DEMOCRATIC ACCORD," TEN PRINCIPLES ON WHICH TO
GUIDE A TRANSITIONAL GOVERNMENT. INITIALLY INTERPRETED IN
THE PRESS AND SOME CIRCLES AS PERHAPS A BASIS OF DIALOGUE
WITH THE CHAVEZ GOVERNMENT--THE DOCUMENT WAS ANNOUNCED, BUT
NOT RELEASED, LAST WEEK--THIS ACCORD WAS CLEARLY INTENDED
FOR THE OPPOSITION FORCES' EXCLUSIVE USE. IT WAS

UNCLASSIFIED

March 2002 cable (cont.)

Current Class: UNCLASSIFIED
Current Handling: n/a

ENTHUSIASTICALLY RECEIVED BY THE ASSEMBLED "ESCUALIDOS,"
WHO INTERRUPTED THE SPEAKERS OFTEN WITH ANTI-CHAVEZ CHANTS.
THIS ACCORD REPRESENTS AN IMPORTANT STEP FOR THE
OPPOSITION, WHICH HAS BEEN QUICK TO CONDEMN CHAVEZ BUT HAD
SO FAR OFFERED NO VISION OF ITS OWN. END SUMMARY.

TEN POINTS FOR A DEMOCRATIC ACCORD
----

2. (U) WITH MUCH FANFARE, THE VENEZUELAN GREAT AND GOOD
ASSEMBLED ON MARCH 5 IN CARACAS'S ESMERALDA AUDITORIUM TO
HEAR REPRESENTATIVES OF THE CONFEDERATION OF VENEZUELAN
WORKERS (CTV), THE FEDERATION OF BUSINESS CHAMBERS
(FEDECAMARAS), AND THE CATHOLIC CHURCH PRESENT THEIR "BASES
FOR A DEMOCRATIC ACCORD"--TEN PRINCIPLES ON WHICH TO GUIDE
UNCLASSIFIED

PAGE 03   CARACA 00546 01 OF 02 052201Z
A TRANSITIONAL GOVERNMENT. THE EXISTENCE OF THIS ACCORD
WAS ANNOUNCED LAST WEEK AND HAS SINCE DRAWN MUCH
SPECULATION ABOUT WHETHER IT WAS INTENDED AS THE BASIS FOR
A POST-CHAVEZ GOVERNMENT OR AS A LAST-DITCH EFFORT TO
PROMOTE A DIALOGUE WITH THE GOVERNMENT. IN HIS COMBATIVE
CENTERPIECE ADDRESS, CTV PRESIDENT CARLOS ORTEGA DISPELLED
ANY REMAINING DOUBTS; THIS ACCORD IS "A PACT FOR US," HE
EMPHASIZED, TO GUIDE US THROUGH THE TRANSITION AND TO
ESTABLISH A "GOVERNMENT OF DEMOCRATIC UNITY." THE CROWD
GREETED THESE REMARKS WITH ROUSING ANTI-CHAVEZ CHANTS.

3. (U) BESIDES ATTRACTING EXTENSIVE MEDIA COVERAGE, THE
SPEECHES ON THE ACCORD WERE BEING BROADCAST, WE WERE TOLD,
BY ALL NON-GOVERNMENTAL TV STATIONS. FR. LUIS UGALDE,
S.J., RECTOR OF THE CATHOLIC UNIVERSITY OF ANDRES BELLO,
EXPLAINED HOW THIS ACCORD BEGAN WITH CONFERENCES BETWEEN
BUSINESS AND LABOR HOSTED BY THE CATHOLIC EPISCOPAL
CONFERENCE LAST DECEMBER. JESUS URBIETA, FORMER CTV
INTERIM PRESIDENT AND HEAD OF THE CONFEDERATION'S THINK
TANK, READ THE MAIN POINTS, WHICH CAN BE SUMMARIZED
BRIEFLY:

--OVERCOMING POVERTY BY PROVIDING MORE ECONOMIC
OPPORTUNITIES. THIS INCLUDES "FIGHTING POPULIST VISIONS
THAT FOOL THE POPULAR SECTORS WITH MESSIANIC OR ERRONEOUS
VISIONS OF THE REALITY OF THE COUNTRY."

--FORGING NATIONAL UNITY THAT INCLUDES EVERYONE IN THE
DEMOCRATIC PROCESS AND INFORMAL SECTORS IN THE NATIONAL
ECONOMY.

Current Class: UNCLASSIFIED

UNCLASSIFIED

Current Class: UNCLASSIFIED
Current Handling: n/a

UNCLAS SECTION 02 OF 02 CARACAS 000546

INR FOR COZART
NSC FOR AMBASSADOR MAISTO
USCINCSO FOR POLAD

SENSITIVE

UNCLASSIFIED

PAGE 02   CARACA 00546 02 OF 02 052201Z

E.O. 12958: NA
TAGS: PREL, PGOV, VE
SUBJ: LABOR, BUSINESS AND CHURCH ANNOUNCE TRANSITION
PACT

FUNCTION.

--PROMOTING COOPERATION BETWEEN LABOR AND CAPITAL, AND THE
RIGHT OF CONSUMERS, TOO.

--RECUPERATING THE INTERNATIONAL IMAGE OF VENEZUELA.

--STRIVING AGAINST CORRUPTION--"WE NEED MORAL LEADERSHIP
THAT PREACHES BY EXAMPLE AND WITH ITS ACTIONS"--AND
PROMOTING "PUBLIC AUSTERITY" TO PREVENT THE SQUANDERING OF
RESOURCES.

4. (U) FOR THE MOST PART, THE SPEAKERS AVOIDED DISCUSSING
THE POLITICS OF THE MOMENT, AND THEY HAD NO NEED TO POINT
OUT HOW THEIR POINTS CONTRAST WITH THE ACTUAL
CHARACTERISTICS OF THE CHAVEZ GOVERNMENT. FEDECAMARAS
PRESIDENT PEDRO CARMONA DID CALL FOR THE RESIGNATION OF THE
PDVSA'S BOARD OF DIRECTORS, AND AT ONE POINT ORTEGA
DENOUNCED CHAVEZ BY NAME. OTHERWISE, THE SPEAKERS
EMPHASIZED THEIR ACCORD AS "A SHARED VISION" AND "A SIGNAL
OF HOPE" FOR VENEZUELANS PREOCCUPIED WITH WHAT WAS DEEMED
"A TRUE NATIONAL EMERGENCY."

- -
COMMENT: ANOTHER PIECE FALLS INTO PLACE
                    UNCLASSIFIED

PAGE 03   CARACA 00546 02 OF 02 052201Z
- -

5. (SBU) THIS ACCORD REPRESENTS AN IMPORTANT STEP FOR THE
OPPOSITION, WHICH HAS BEEN ALWAYS QUICK TO CONDEMN CHAVEZ
BUT HAD SO FAR OFFERED NO COMPREHENSIVE VISION OF ITS OWN.
BUT ONCE AGAIN, IN THE ABSENCE OF A SINGLE OPPOSITION PARTY

Current Class: UNCLASSIFIED

March 2002 cable (cont.)

Current Class: UNCLASSIFIED
Current Handling: n/a

OR FIGURE THAT CAN RALLY PUBLIC SENTIMENT, BUSINESS AND
LABOR LEADERS, WITH THE SUPPORT OF THE CATHOLIC CHURCH,
HAVE STEPPED INTO THE BREACH. THE OPPOSITION PARTIES NOW
WILL CERTAINLY HASTEN TO ENDORSE THIS ACCORD, WHICH, THOUGH
SOMEWHAT VAGUE AND FEEL-GOODY, MAY WELL FORM THE FRAME OF
REFERENCE AND CODE OF CONDUCT FOR A TRANSITIONAL
GOVERNMENT. THEY MAY FIND IT DIFFICULT, HOWEVER, TO
RECAPTURE THE SPOTLIGHT FROM ORTEGA AND CARMONA, THE TWO
UNLIKELY ALLIES BUT INDISPENSABLE LEADERS OF THE ANTI-
CHAVISTA OPPOSITION.

COOK

UNCLASSIFIED

<< END OF DOCUMENT >>

Current Class: UNCLASSIFIED

Senior Executive Intelligence Brief

(b)(1)
(b)(3)

The SEIB must be returned to CIA within 5 working days

Monday, 11 March 2002

National Security Information

Unauthorized Disclosure Subject to Criminal Sanctions
Reproduction of this Document Prohibited

CIA PASS   SEIB 02-457CHX

TOP SECRET

~~TOP SECRET~~

Key Current Warning Issues

The DCI Strategic Warning Committee considers the following the most critical warning issues during the next few weeks.

Venezuela. There are increased signs that Venezuelan business leaders and military officers are becoming dissatisfied with President Chavez, and he clearly is concerned and is trying to tone down his rhetoric. The opposition has yet to organize itself into a united front. If the situation further deteriorates and demonstrations become even more violent or if Chavez attempts an unconstitutional move to add to his powers, the military may move to overthrow him.

The DCI Strategic Warning Committee, chaired by the National Intelligence Officer for Warning, comprises representatives from the Directors of the National Security Agency, the Defense Intelligence Agency, and the National Imagery and Mapping Agency; the Assistant Secretary of State for Intelligence and Research; and the Deputy Director for Intelligence, Central Intelligence Agency.

TOP SECRET

11 March 2002

CIA SEIB Brief, 6 April 2002

TOP SECRET

Venezuela:

Conditions Ripening for Coup Attempt

Dissident military factions, including some disgruntled senior officers and a group of radical junior officers, are stepping up efforts to organize a coup against President Chavez, possibly as early as this month, The level of detail in the reported plans— targets Chavez and 10 other senior officials for arrest—lends credence to the information, but military and civilian contacts note that neither group appears ready to lead a successful coup and may bungle the attempt by moving too quickly.

— Civilian groups opposed to Chavez's policies, including the Catholic Church, business groups, and labor, are backing away from efforts to involve them in the plotting, probably to avoid being tainted by an extraconstitutional move and fear that a failed attempt could strengthen Chavez's hand.

Prospects for a successful coup at this point are limited. The plotters still lack the political cover to stage a coup, Chavez's core support base among poor Venezuelans remains intact, and repeated warnings that the US will not support any extraconstitutional moves to oust Chavez probably have given pause to the plotters.

— Chavez is monitoring opponents inside and outside the military,

To provoke military action, the plotters may try to exploit unrest stemming from opposition demonstrations slated for later this month or ongoing strikes at the state-owned oil company PDVSA. White-collar oil workers began striking on Thursday at facilities in 11 of 23 states as part of an escalating protest against Chavez's efforts to politicize PDVSA.

— Protracted strikes, particularly if they have the support of the blue-collar oil workers' union, could trigger a confrontation.

State Department cable, 9 April 2002

Current Class: CONFIDENTIAL   UNCLASSIFIED
Current Handling: n/a

LAST NIGHT - BIG PARTY AT PDVSA AND LOUD CACEROLAZOS
----

8. (SBU) A JUBILANT CROWD, ESTIMATED BY ECONOFF TO BE FIVE
TO SEVEN THOUSAND STRONG, GATHERED AT PDVSA HEADQUARTERS
UNTIL LATE LAST NIGHT LISTENING TO A MYRIAD OF OPPOSITION
SPEAKERS AND GENERALLY CELEBRATING WHAT THEY PERCEIVED TO BE
THEIR GATHERING MOMENTUM.   VIRTUALLY ALL PROMINENT
OPPOSITION FIGURES INCLUDING PEDRO CARMONA, ALFREDO PENA,
AND CARLOS ORTEGA GAVE IMPROMPTU SPEECHES. CARMONA SEEMED
PARTICULARLY ENERGIZED BY THE SIZE AND MOOD OF THE CROWD
                    CONFIDENTIAL

PAGE 05   CARACA 00966 01 OF 03 111109Z

                    CONFIDENTIAL

               CONFIDENTIAL   PTQ8421

PAGE 01   CARACA 00966 02 OF 03 111110Z
ACTION WHA-00

INFO LOG-00   NP-00   AID-00   ACQ-00   CEA-01   CIAE-00   COME-00
      CTME-00 DINT-00 DODE-00 DOEE-00 DOTE-00 PERC-00   SRPP-00
      DS-00   EB-00   EXIM-01 E-00   FAAE-00 VC-00   FRB-00
      H-01   TEDE-00 INR-00   ITC-01   LAB-01   L-00   VCE-00
      AC-01   NSAE-00 NSCE-00 OES-01   OMB-01   OPIC-01   PA-00
      PM-00   PRS-00   ACE-00   P-00   SP-00   IRM-00   SSO-00
      STR-00   TRSE-00 USIE-00 PMB-00   DSCC-00 DRL-02   G-00
      NFAT-00 SAS-00   /011W
               ------------------8279D0 111145Z /38

O 111048Z APR 02
FM AMEMBASSY CARACAS

Current Class: CONFIDENTIAL

Current Class: CONFIDENTIAL UNCLASSIFIED
Current Handling: n/a

TO SECSTATE WASHDC IMMEDIATE 5429
INFO OPEC COLLECTIVE IMMEDIATE
AMEMBASSY BOGOTA
AMEMBASSY QUITO
AMEMBASSY LA PAZ
AMEMBASSY LIMA
USCINCSO MIAMI FL

C O N F I D E N T I A L SECTION 02 OF 03 CARACAS 000966

NSC FOR AMB MAISTO
USCINSCO FOR POLAD

E.O. 12958: DECL: 1.6X1
                    CONFIDENTIAL

PAGE 02   CARACA   00966   02 OF 03   111110Z
TAGS: ECON, PGOV, PREL, EPET, ETRD, VE
SUBJECT: "PARO" UPDATE/GENERAL STRIKE ANNOUNCED

AFTER APPEARING LESS THAN ENTHUSIASTIC ABOUT CONTINUING
OPPOSITION ACTIONS DURING THE DAY.

9. (SBU) THROUGHOUT CARACAS, "CACEROLAZOS" WERE CONSTANT AND
LOUD.   MANY PARTS OF CARACAS WERE FILLED WITH PEOPLE
GATHERED ON STREET CORNERS, CARS DRIVING WITH LIGHTS
BLINKING AND HORNS SOUNDING.   IT WAS A CELEBRATORY
ATMOSPHERE NOT UNLIKE AFTER VENEZUELA DEFEATED PARAGUAY IN
WORLD CUP QUALIFYING.   TELEVISION REPORTED SIMILAR EVENTS IN
MANY OTHER PARTS OF VENEZUELA.

CADENA BATTLE
----

10. (SBU) THE BATTLE OVER THE GOV ORDERED CADENAS CONTINUED
LAST NIGHT WITH ALL STATIONS USING A SPLIT-SCREEN WITH THE
OFFICIAL CADENA ON ONE SIDE AND COVERAGE OF OPPOSITION
EVENTS ON THE OTHER.   (NON-NEWS CHANNELS ALSO TOOK ADVANTAGE
OF THE SPLIT-SCREEN AS A SPORTS ONLY CHANNEL CONTINUED
SPORTS COVERAGE ON ONE HALF OF THE SCREEN).

11. (SBU) THROUGHOUT THE DAY TODAY, THE GOV HAD NO CADENAS.
MVR SOURCES SAID THAT CHAVEZ HAD MADE A DECISION TO BACK
DOWN.   HE WAS DESCRIBED AS A "BOXER WHO MADE A TACTICAL
RETREAT."   INSTEAD, THE GOV LEADERS SPOKE THROUGH TELEVISION
INTERVIEWS THROUGHOUT THE DAY WHICH WERE COVERED AS ORDINARY
NEWS EVENTS BY THE TELEVISION STATIONS.

                    CONFIDENTIAL

Current Class: CONFIDENTIAL

State Department cable, 11 April 2002

UNCLASSIFIED   PTQ0954

PAGE 01   CARACA 00985 01 OF 02 120403Z
ACTION DS-00

INFO LOG-00 MFA-00 NP-00   AMAD-00 ACQ-00 CIAE-00 COME-00
      DODE-00 DOTE-00 WHA-00 EB-00   FAAE-00 UTED-00 VC-00
      TEDE-00 INR-00 VCE-00 AC-01   NSAE-00 NSCE-00 PER-00
      ACE-00 IRM-00 SSO-00 SS-00   TEST-00 EPAE-00 DSCC-00
      DRL-02 NFAT-00 SAS-00   /003W
      ------------------8512E6 120403Z /38

O 120341Z APR 02   RELEASED IN PART
FM AMEMBASSY CARACAS
TO SECSTATE WASHDC IMMEDIATE 5455   B6, B1, 1.4(D)
INFO DEPT OF TREASURY WASHDC//OASIA//
AMEMBASSY BOGOTA
AMEMBASSY LA PAZ
AMEMBASSY LIMA
AMEMBASSY QUITO
USCINCSO MIAMI FL//POLAD//

UNCLAS SECTION 01 OF 02 CARACAS 000985

NSC FOR AMB MAISTO
STATE FOR DS/OP/WHA, S/ES-O_DS/OP/CC

SENSITIVE

E.O. 12958: N/A
TAGS: ASEC, ECON, PGOV, PREL, VE
SUBJECT: TALE OF TWO CITIES - THE MARCH ON MIRAFLORES PALACE

UNCLASSIFIED

PAGE 02   CARACA 00985 01 OF 02 120403Z
SENSITIVE BUT UNCLASSIFIED, PLEASE HANDLE ACCORDINGLY.

REF: CARACAS 000965

- - - - - - -
SUMMARY
- - - - - - -

1. (SBU) MEETING ON THE MORNING OF APRIL 11TH, THE OPPOSITION'S
"COORDINATING COMMITTEE FOR DEMOCRACY AND LIBERTY" DECIDED TO GO
FOR BROKE - TO SEEK THE IMMEDIATE DEPARTURE OF PRESIDENT CHAVEZ BY
POPULAR ACCLAMATION. SEVERAL PARTICIPANTS VOICED UNEASE OVER THE
GROWING PRESSURE TO MARCH ON THE MIRAFLORES PRESIDENTIAL PALACE.
THE FOLLOWING OPPOSITION RALLY HELD IN FRONT OF PDVSA HEADQUARTERS
IN CHACAO WAS AN OVERWHELMING SUCCESS. THE CTV AND FEDECAMARAS

UNCLASSIFIED .

Current Class: UNCLASSIFIED
Current Handling: SBU

LEADERS WERE SWEPT INTO THE SPONTANEOUS MARCH ON MIRAFLORES'. WHEN
THE PEACEFUL MARCHERS CAME TO WITHIN ONE BLOCK OF THE PALACE,
TROOPS FROM THE PRESIDENTIAL GUARD SHOT DOZENS OF TEAR GAS
CANISTERS TO KEEP THEM AT BAY. TENS OF THOUSANDS OF DEMONSTRATORS
REMAINED IN THE AREA THROUGHOUT THE AFTERNOON. END SUMMARY.

OPPOSITION'S STRONG DISPLAY OF RESOLVE AND UNITY
----

2. (SBU) THE OPPOSITION'S "COORDINATING COMMITTEE" MET AT
FEDECAMARAS FOR TWO HOURS TO DISCUSS AND REACH AGREEMENT ON
STRATEGY FOR THE MORNING'S UPCOMING MARCH FROM PARQUE DEL ESTE TO
PDVSA HEADQUARTERS IN CHACAO. IT WAS CLEAR THAT THERE WAS GROWING
SUPPORT TO CONTINUE THE MARCH FROM PDVSA ON TO MIRAFLORES.
SEVERAL ATTENDEES URGED CAUTION AND EXPRESSED THE BELIEF THE
                    UNCLASSIFIED

PAGE 03   CARACA 00985 01 OF 02 120403Z
OPPOSITION WAS NOT YET READY FOR THAT STEP. OTHERS STRONGLY
MAINTAINED THAT IT WAS TIME TO DIRECTLY CONFRONT THE EXECUTIVE AND
DEMAND THAT THE PRESIDENT AND HIS MINISTERS RESIGN. BY UNANIMOUS
·VOICE VOTE, THE COMMITTEE DECIDED TO LET FEDECAMARAS PRESIDENT
PEDRO CARMONA AND CTV PRESIDENT CARLOS ORTEGA MAKE THE DECISION
REGARDING THE MARCH AT THE PDVSA RALLY -- TO ALLOW THEM TO GAUGE
THE TEMPERAMENT OF THE CROWD. THE 80 PLUS PARTICIPANTS BROKE UP
THE MEETING IN HIGH SPIRITS AND HEADED OUT TO CHACAO.

THE ROAR OF THE CROWD...
----

3. (SBU) BY 11:00AM, THE AREA SURROUNDING PDVSA HEADQUARTERS WAS A
SEA OF HUMANITY -- MEN, WOMEN, CHILDREN. FROM THE PRESS GALLERY
LOCATED ON A PEDESTRIAN BRIDGE OVER THE MAIN PLAZA, ECONOFFS
LOOKED OUT OVER A TIGHTLY PACKED CROWD STRETCHING FOR SEVERAL
BLOCKS IN ALL DIRECTIONS. WHEN THE FIRST SPEAKER WAS INTRODUCED,
THE ROAR OF APPROVAL WAS REMARKABLE - AND IT BUILT FROM THERE. BY
THE TIME PEDRO CARMONA SPOKE, IT HAD BECOME A FOREGONE CONCLUSION:
ON TO MIRAFLORES. WITH CARMONA, ORTEGA, AND FORMER PDVSA
PRESIDENT GUAICAIPURO LAMEDA IN THE VANGUARD, THE MULTITUDE SURGED
ONTO THE AUTOPISTA FOR THE FOUR-MILE MARCH DOWNTOWN.

4. (SBU) [   ]
[   ] THE COMMITTEE WAS HURRIEDLY PUTTING THE
FINAL TOUCHES ON A DOCUMENT DEMANDING THE RESIGNATION OF PRESIDENT
CHAVEZ -- BY POPULAR ACCLAMATION. [   ] THE DOCUMENT
WOULD BE DELIVERED TO CHAVEZ BY THE COMMITTEE'S LEADERSHIP WHEN
THE MARCH REACHED MIRAFLORES.

Current Class: UNCLASSIFIED

UNCLASSIFIED

Current Class: UNCLASSIFIED
Current Handling: SBU

UNCLASSIFIED

PAGE 04   CARACA 00985 01 OF 02 120403Z
5. (U) ALONG THE MARCH ROUTE, THE PARTICIPANTS -- NUMBERING EASILY
IN THE TENS OF THOUSANDS -- WERE IN A FESTIVE AND EXPECTANT MOOD,
SINGING THE NATIONAL ANTHEM AND CHANTING "NOT ONE STEP BACK!"
"CHAVEZ - JUST LEAVE!" THERE WERE NO WEAPONS, ONLY MEN AND WOMEN
OF ALL AGES AND SOCIAL CLASSES. THE OVERRIDING SENTIMENT
EXPRESSED BY MANY PARTICIPANTS WAS ONE OF DISBELIEF - OVER THE
OBJECTIVE AND THE SIZE OF THE CROWD. A PHALANX OF METROPOLITAN
POLICE MOTORCYCLES RODE ALONG AT THE HEAD OF THE MARCH, CLEARING
THE STREETS OF TRAFFIC.

PRESIDENTIAL GUARD OVERREACTS
----

5. (U) AS THE MARCHERS TURNED THE FINAL CORNER AT ROUGHLY 2:00PM
AND APPROACHED THE LONG DRIVE LEADING UP TO THE PRESIDENTIAL
PALACE, IT APPEARED THEY WOULD REACH THEIR OBJECTIVE AND THE NOISE
FROM HORNS, WHISTLES, CLAXONS, AND SHOUTS REACHED A CRESCENDO.
LESS THAN A BLOCK FROM THE PALACE GATES, APPROXIMATELY A DOZEN
TEAR GAS CANISTERS WERE LAUNCHED FROM BEHIND THE PALACE WALLS AND
FELL AMONG THE LEAD ELEMENTS. AMID CRIES OF SURPRISE AND SOME
FEAR, THE CROWD TURNED AND FLED BACK TO THE CROSSROADS AT THE

UNCLASSIFIED

UNCLASSIFIED   PTQ0955

PAGE 01   CARACA 00985 02 OF 02 120403Z
ACTION DS-00

INFO   LOG-00   MFA-00   NP-00   AMAD-00   ACQ-00   CIAE-00   COME-00
       DODE-00 DOTE-00   WHA-00   EB-00   FAAE-00   UTED-00   VC-00
       TEDE-00 INR-00   VCE-00   AC-01   NSAE-00   NSCE-00   ACE-00
       IRM-00   SSO-00   SS-00   TEST-00   ASDS-01   EPAE-00   DSCC-00
       DRL-02   NFAT-00   SAS-00   /004W
                    ------------------8512EA 120403Z /38
O 120341Z APR 02
FM AMEMBASSY CARACAS
TO SECSTATE WASHDC IMMEDIATE 5456
INFO DEPT OF TREASURY WASHDC//OASIA//
AMEMBASSY BOGOTA
AMEMBASSY LA PAZ
AMEMBASSY LIMA
AMEMBASSY QUITO
USCINCSO MIAMI FL//POLAD//

UNCLAS SECTION 02 OF 02 CARACAS 000985

Current Class: UNCLASSIFIED

11 April 2002 cable (cont.)

Current Class: UNCLASSIFIED   UNCLASSIFIED
Current Handling: SBU

NSC FOR AMB MAISTO
STATE FOR DS/OP/WHA, S/ES-O_DS/OP/CC

SENSITIVE

E.O. 12958: N/A
TAGS: ASEC, ECON, PGOV, PREL, VE
SUBJECT: TALE OF TWO CITIES - THE MARCH ON MIRAFLORES PALACE

UNCLASSIFIED

PAGE 02   CARACA   00985   02 OF 02   120403Z
BOTTOM OF THE DRIVE.

6. (U) WITH THE CONTINUOUS ARRIVAL OF MORE MARCHERS, THE LEAD
SECTIONS TRIED ONCE AGAIN TO APPROACH THE PALACE APPROXIMATELY 20
MINUTES LATER. THIS TIME THEY ADVANCED EVEN CLOSER, BUT BY NOW
THE PRESIDENTIAL GUARD HAD FORMED UP IN SOLID RANKS JUST BELOW THE
PALACE GATES. THIS TIME A BARRAGE OF ROUGHLY 20 GAS CANISTERS
RAINED DOWN ON THE MARCHERS -- THE CROWD RAN AND STARTED TO PANIC.
THEY REGROUPED AT THE CROSSROADS AND A NEARBY PLAZA, BUT NEVER
AGAIN ATTEMPTED TO APPROACH MIRAFLORES.

7. (SBU) FOR THE NEXT TWO HOURS (3-5PM) THE CROWD MILLED AROUND A
LATE-ARRIVING SOUND TRUCK AND CHEERED A PROGRESSION OF SECONDARY
SPEAKERS. FEW FEDECAMARAS OR CTV LEADERS ARRIVED AND THE CROWD
GREW INCREASINGLY UNCERTAIN OF WHAT WOULD NEXT TRANSPIRE. TOWARD
5.00PM, ECONOFF OBSERVED INCREASING VIOLENCE IN THE NEARBY
STREETS. PARTICULARLY ON THE NEXT THOROUGHFARE, AVENIDA BARALT, A
SMALL CONTINGENT OF THE MARCH BECAME THE TARGET OF STEADY ROCK AND
BOTTLE THROWING BY CHAVISTAS AND REPEATED BARRAGES OF TEAR GAS
CANISTERS FIRED BY THE NATIONAL GUARD. THE DISTINCT SOUNDS OF
GUNFIRE ERUPTED AROUND 5:30PM IN THE SURROUNDING STREETS AND THE
REMAINING CROWD QUICKLY BROKE UP AND RETREATED TOWARD EASTERN
CARACAS ALONG AVENIDA BOLIVAR.

Current Class: UNCLASSIFIED

```
Current Class: CONFIDENTIAL       UNCLASSIFIED
Current Handling: n/a
```

CONFIDENTIAL   PTQ4212

PAGE 01   CARACA   00995   01 OF 02   122049Z
ACTION WHA-00

```
INFO  LOG-00  NP-00    AID-00   CEA-01   CIAE-00  CTME-00  DINT-00
      DODE-00 DOTE-00  PERC-00  SRPP-00  EB-00    EXIM-01  E-00
      FAAE-00 VC-00    FRB-00   H-01    ·TEDE-00  INR-00   ITC-01
      L-00    VCE-00   AC-01    NSAE-00  NSCE-00  OES-01   OMB-01
      OPIC-01 PM-00    PRS-00   ACE-00   SP-00    IRM-00   SSO-00
      SS-00   STR-00   TRSE-00  USIE-00  EPAE-00  PMB-00   DRL-02
      G-00    NFAT-00  SAS-00    /010W
      -----------------859814   122049Z /38
```

O 122027Z APR 02
FM AMEMBASSY CARACAS
TO SECSTATE WASHDC IMMEDIATE 5466
INFO USDOC WASHDC
DOE WASHDC
USINT HAVANA
AMEMBASSY MEXICO
AMEMBASSY PORT OF SPAIN
AMEMBASSY BRASILIA
AMEMBASSY QUITO
AMEMBASSY LIMA
AMEMBASSY BOGOTA
OPEC COLLECTIVE

RELEASED IN PART
B1, 1.4(D)

C O N F I D E N T I A L SECTION 01 OF 02 CARACAS 000995

E.O. 12958: DECL: 4/11/12
TAGS: ECON, EPET, ENRG, VE
SUBJECT: PDVSA: BACK TO NORMAL
                    CONFIDENTIAL

PAGE 02   CARACA   00995   01 OF 02   122049Z

1. CLASSIFIED BY AMBASSADOR CHARLES S. SHAPIRO FOR REASONS
1.5 (B) AND (D).

2. (C) SUMMARY: TELEVISED SCENES OF JOY HAVE MARKED THE
RETURN OF PETROLEOS DE VENEZUELA (PDVSA) EMPLOYEES TO THEIR
LA CAMPINA HEADQUARTERS BUILDING. FIRED EMPLOYEES HAVE
BEEN REINSTATED. FORMER VICE PRESIDENTS KARL MAZEIKA,
EDUARDO PRASELJ AND VICENZO PAGLIONE WILL ACT AS
COORDINATORS IN THE SELECTION OF A NEW BOARD. PDVSA
EXECUTIVES UNDERLINE THAT THE COMPANY SHOULD RETURN TO
NORMAL OPERATIONS BY EARLY NEXT WEEK. SHIPMENTS ARE
EXPECTED TO RESUME TODAY. PDVSA SPOKESPERSON STATED
PUBLICLY THAT NO OIL WILL BE SENT TO CUBA

UNCLASSIFIED

Current Class: CONFIDENTIAL UNCLASSIFIED
Current Handling: n/a

END SUMMARY.

PDVSA GOVERNABILITY
----

3. (U) THE PARRA BOARD RESIGNED ON APRIL 11 IN WHAT MANY
HERE DESCRIBE AS EX-PRESIDENT CHAVEZ'S LAST DITCH SCHEME TO
DEFUSE THE CRISIS BY TRYING FINALLY TO NEGOTIATE WITH THE
PDVSA DISSIDENTS. IN VIRTUALLY HIS FIRST ACT AS INTERIM
PRESIDENT, PEDRO CARMONA ESTANGA REINSTATED THE
FIRED/RETIRED/REMOVED EXECUTIVES TO THEIR POSITIONS. KARL
MAZEIKA, EDUARDO PRASELJ AND VICENZO PAGLIONE, THREE OF THE
FOUR VICE PRESIDENTS ON THE LAMEDA BOARD, WERE TAPPED TO
FORM A HIGH LEVEL COORDINATING COMMITTEE UNTIL THE
DESIGNATION OF A NEW PDVSA PRESIDENT AND BOARD. SOME HAVE
SUGGESTED THAT GENERAL LAMEDA MIGHT BE RE-APPOINTED AS
                    CONFIDENTIAL

PAGE 03   CARACA 00995 01 OF 02 122049Z
PRESIDENT BUT HE IS ALSO BEING MENTIONED AS A POSSIBLE
"MILITARY" PERSON ON THE TRANSITION TEAM. LUIS GIUSTI, NOW
ON HIS WAY TO CARACAS, IS ALSO SURE TO HAVE A ROLE IN
DECIDING VENEZUELA'S FUTURE ENERGY POLICIES.

4. (U) EDGAR PAREDES, EXECUTIVE DIRECTOR, REFINING SUPPLY
AND TRADING, (SUSPENDED ON APRIL 5) RESUMED THE ROLE HE HAS
PLAYED AS SPOKESPERSON FOR THE PAST SIX WEEKS, AND
ADDRESSED A NOON PRESS CONFERENCE. PAREDES UNDERLINED THAT
PDVSA EMPLOYEES HAVE BEEN WORKING SINCE THE NIGHT OF APRIL
11 TO RESTORE NORMAL OPERATIONS. HE NOTED THAT THE
DOMESTIC MARKET IS NOW GUARANTEED WHILE VENEZUELA'S EXPORT
PARTNERS ARE ON THEIR WAY TO BEING FULLY SUPPLIED AS WELL.
FULL OPERABILITY IS EXPECTED BY EARLY NEXT WEEK. PAREDES
ALSO CALLED FOR TOLERANCE IN DEALING WITH PDVSA EMPLOYEES
WHO DID NOT STRIKE.

CUBA CONNECTION TO END?
----

5. (C) PAREDES ALSO SAID, "WE NOT GOING TO SEND EVEN ONE
BARREL OF OIL TO CUBA," WHICH DREW THUNDEROUS APPLAUSE.

Current Class: CONFIDENTIAL

Current Class: CONFIDENTIAL   UNCLASSIFIED
Current Handling: n/a

END SUMMARY.

COLOMBIAN GOVERNMENT SUPPORTS
NEW HEAD OF VENEZUELAN GOVERNMENT

----

2. (U) IN A TELEVISED INTERVIEW, ACTING COLOMBIAN
FOREIGN MINISTER CLEMENCIA FERERO SPOKE WARMLY ABOUT
VENEZUELAN INTERIM PRESIDENT PEDRO CARMONA. FERERO SAID
CONFIDENTIAL

PAGE 03   BOGOTA   03355   01 OF 02   122307Z
SHE HAS KNOWN CARMONA FOR MANY YEARS, THAT CARMONA IS
WELL KNOWN TO THE COLOMBIAN BUSINESS COMMUNITY, IS
COMMITTED TO REGIONAL INTEGRATION, AND IS A GREAT
FRIEND OF COLOMBIA. TRADE MINISTER OROSCO TOLD THE
AMBASSADOR THE SAME: CARMONA IS WELL-KNOWN TO THE GOC
AND HAS WORKED CLOSELY WITH THEM ON A NUMBER OF ISSUES.

Current Class: CONFIDENTIAL

State Department cable, 13 April 2002

Current Class: UNCLASSIFIED
Current Handling: SBU

SENSITIVE BUT UNCLASSIFIED, PLEASE HANDLE ACCORDINGLY.

NEW GOVERNMENT SWORN IN

1.(SBU) ON THE EVENING FRIDAY, APRIL 12, PEDRO CARMONA
ESTANGA WAS SWORN IN AS INTERIM PRESIDENT OF
VENEZUELA. THOSE WHO SIGNED THE TEXT OF THE SWEARING
IN INCLUDED REPRESENTATIVES FROM VARIOUS SECTORS OF
CIVIL SOCIETY. THESE INCLUDED: THE CATHOLIC CHURCH
(CARDINAL JOSE IGNACIO VELASCO); THE BUSINESS
COMMUNITY (LUIS ENRIQUE PONS ZULOAGA); THE POLITICAL
PARTIES (JOSE CURIEL); NGOS (ROCIO GUIJARRO); MEDIA
(MIGUEL ANGEL MARTINEZ); REGIONAL GOVERNORS (MANUEL
ROSALES, GOVERNOR OF ZULIA STATE); INDUSTRY AND
                         UNCLASSIFIED

PAGE 03   CARACA 00996   01 OF 02   031745Z
COMMERCE (CARLOS FERNANDEZ, VICE PRESIDENT OF
FEDECAMARAS AND JULIO BRAZON, OF CONSECOMERCIO); AND
BANKING (IGNACIO SALVATIERRA).

NATIONAL ASSEMBLY DISSOLVED
----

2. (SBU) AFTER HIS SWEARING IN, CARMONA ANNOUNCED BY DECREE
THAT THE NATIONAL ASSEMBLY WOULD BE DISSOLVED, AND
THAT NEW NATIONAL ASSEMBLY ELECTIONS WOULD TAKE PLACE
NO LATER THAN DECEMBER OF THIS YEAR.   PRESIDENTIAL
ELECTIONS WOULD TAKE PLACE IN NO LATER THAN 365 DAYS.
HE ALSO ANNOUNCED THAT "BOLIVARIAN" WOULD BE REMOVED
FROM THE OFFICIAL NAME OF THE COUNTRY, RETURNING IT TO
THE REPUBLIC OF VENEZUELA.

3. (SBU) THE DECREE ALSO ANNOUNCED THAT A CONSULTATIVE
COUNCIL WOULD BE FORMED, MADE UP OF 35 INDIVIDUALS
REPRESENTING VARIOUS SECTORS OF DEMOCRATIC SOCIETY.
IT IS UNCLEAR WHO THESE PEOPLE WILL BE, OR HOW THEY
WILL BE CHOSEN TO PARTICIPATE.

4. (SBU) ADDITIONALLY, CARMONA ANNOUNCED THAT THE 48
DECREES ANNOUNCED BY PRESIDENT CHAVEZ IN NOVEMBER OF
2001 WOULD BE SUSPENDED, AND THAT A COMMISSION
REPRESENTING DIFFERENT SECTORS OF SOCIETY WOULD BE
FORMED TO REVIEW AND REVISE THEM.

5. (SBU) CARMONA ALSO ANNOUNCED THAT PDVSA WORKERS WHO WERE
FIRED, SUSPENDED, OR FORCED INTO RETIREMENT WOULD BE

Current Class: UNCLASSIFIED

UNCLASSIFIED

Current Class: UNCLASSIFIED
Current Handling: SBU

UNCLASSIFIED

PAGE 04   CARACA 00996 01 OF 02 031745Z
REINSTATED.

6. (SBU) FINALLY, CARMONA ASKED THE INTERNATIONAL COMMUNITY
TO HAVE PATIENCE WITH HIS NEW GOVERNMENT, AND
EXPLAINED THAT IN THE FIRST FEW HOURS, UNDESIREABLE
EVENTS COULD OCCUR, BUT THAT HE AND HIS GOVERNMENT
WERE AGAINST HATE AND RETALIATION. HE SAID THAT ALL
VENEZUELANS HAVE THE OBLIGATION TO CONTROL THEIR
PASSIONS AND KEEP EVENTS UNDER CONTROL.

NEW CABINET

7.(SBU) CARMONA'S NEW CABINET APPOINTMENTS INCLUDE:

MINISTER OF THE INTERIOR: RAFAEL DAMIAN BUSTILLOS
MINISTER OF THE EXTERIOR: JOSE RODRIGUEZ ITURBE
MINISTER OF FINANCE: LEOPOLDO MARTINEZ
MINISTER OF AGRICULTURE: RAUL.DE ARMAS
MINSTER OF LABOR: CESAR AUGUSTO CARBALLO
MINISTER OF PLANNING AND DEVELOPMENT: LEON ARISMENDI
MINISTER OF DEFENSE: HECTOR RAMIREZ PEREZ
MINISTER OF HEALTH: RAFAEL ARREAZA
MINISTER OF THE SECRETARY: JESUS ENRIQUE BRICENO
PROSECUTOR GENERAL: DANIEL ROMERO
PRESIDENT OF PDVSA: GUAICAIPURO LAMEDA

ARRESTS AND DETENTIONS

UNCLASSIFIED

PAGE 05   CARACA 00996 01 OF 02 031745Z

UNCLASSIFIED

UNCLASSIFIED   PTQ8948

PAGE 01   ·   CARACA 00996 02 OF 02 031748Z
ACTION DS-00

INFO LOG-00   COR-01   MFA-00   NP-00   AID-00   AMAD-00 A-00
      ACQ-00   CA-01   CCO-00   CEA-01   CIAE-00 COME-00 CTME-00
      INL-00   DINT-00 DODE-00 DOEE-00 ITCE-00 DOTE-00 WHA-00
      SRPP-00 EB-00   EXME-00 E-00   FAAE-00 UTED-00 VC-00
      FRB-00   OBO-00   H-01   TEDE-00 INR-00   IO-00   ITC-01

Current Class: UNCLASSIFIED

UNCLASSIFIED

Current Class: UNCLASSIFIED
Current Handling: SBU

LAB-01	L-00	VCE-00	M-00	AC-01	NSAE-00	NSCE-00
OCS-03	OES-01	OMB-01	OPIC-01	OPR-01	PA-00	PM-00
PRS-00	ACE-00	P-00	SCT-00	SP-00	IRM-00	SSO-00
SS-00	STR-00	TEST-00	TRSE-00	USIE-00	USSS-00	ASDS-01
EPAE-00	ECA-00	IIP-00	PMB-00	DSCC-00	DRL-02	G-00
NFAT-00	SAS-00	/017W				

------------------A9CB03 031753Z /38

O 131803Z APR 02
FM AMEMBASSY CARACAS
TO SECSTATE WASHDC IMMEDIATE 5469
INFO OPEC COLLECTIVE PRIORITY
AMEMBASSY BOGOTA PRIORITY
AMEMBASSY QUITO
AMEMBASSY LA PAZ
AMEMBASSY LIMA
AMEMBASSY PANAMA
USCINCSO MIAMI FL

UNCLAS SECTION 02 OF 02 CARACAS 000996

SENSITIVE

UNCLASSIFIED

PAGE 02   CARACA 00996 02 OF 02 031748Z
C O R R E C T E D C O P Y - CAPTION AND PARA MARKINGS ADDED

NSC FOR AMB MAISTO
USCINSCO FOR POLAD
DEPT CA FOR MARY A. RYAN AND DS/OP/WHA AND S/ES-
ODS/OP/CC

E.O. 12958: N/A
TAGS: ECON, PGOV, PREL, EPET, ASEC, CASC, VE
SUBJECT: SITREP: SATURDAY APRIL 13

8. (SBU) TO DATE, SEVERAL MEMBERS OF CHAVEZ'S MVR PARTY
HAVE BEEN DETAINED BY POLICE FORCES. THESE INCLUDE
MVR DEPUTY WILLIAM TAREK SAAB AND FORMER INTERIOR
MINISTER RODRIGUEZ CHACIN. WE HAVE ALSO HEARD REPORTS
THAT TACHIRA GOVERNOR RONALD BLANCO LA CRUZ AND MERIDA
GOVERNOR FLORENCIO PORRAS, BOTH OF MVR, WERE BEING
HELD. WE DO NOT KNOW WHAT CHARGES, IF ANY, HAVE BEEN
FILED AGAINST THEM. TAREK WILLIAM SAAB HAS REPORTEDLY
BEEN RELEASED AS OF APRIL 13.

CONGDRN DXPRDGODD

Current Class: UNCLASSIFIED

13 April 2002 cable (cont.)

Current Class: UNCLASSIFIED
Current Handling: SBU

9. (SBU) POLOFF HAS RECEIVED SEVERAL PHONE CALLS FROM PARTY
MEMBERS WHO ARE CONCERNED ABOUT THE NEW GOVERNMENT'S
COURSE OF ACTION, ESPECIALLY THE DISSOLUTION OF
CONGRESS. THEY RESENT NOT BEING INCLUDED IN THE NEW
GOVERNMENT, AND FEAR THAT THE CARMONA GOVERNMENT IS
PROCEEDING UNDEMOCRATICALLY. ALTHOUGH MANY PARTY
                        UNCLASSIFIED

PAGE 03   CARACA 00996 02 OF 02 031748Z
REPRESENTATIVES WERE INVOLVED IN THE DECISION TO NAME
CARMONA INTERIM PRESIDENT, THE PARTY REPRESENTATIVES
WHO ARE NOW EXPRESSING CONCERN SAY THAT THE PARTY
LEADERS THEMSELVES WERE NOT CONSULTED.

10. (SBU) THE NGO COMMUNITY HAS ALSO EXPRESSED CONCERN
ABOUT THE NEW CARMONA GOVERNMENT. THEY ARE ESPECIALLY
CONCERNED THAT THE INDEPENDENT BRANCHES OF THE
GOVERNMENT THAT MAKE UP THE "PODER CIUDADANO," THE
FISCALIA GENERAL (ATTORNEY GENERAL'S OFFICE), THE
DEFENSORIA DEL PUEBLO (HUMAN RIGHTS OMBUDSMAN), AND
THE CONTROLARIA GENERAL (CONTROLLER GENERAL), ARE NO
LONGER FUNCTIONING.

DISTURBANCES NOT REPORTED
----

11. (SBU) THERE HAVE BEEN REPORTS THAT SPORADIC VIOLENCE
HAS TAKEN PLACE IN VARIOUS AREAS OF CARACAS. THE
NIGHT OF APRIL 12, WE RECEIVED WORD THAT THERE WERE
DISTURBANCES IN NEIGHBORHOOD OF PETARE, GUARENAS, 23
DE ENERO, EL VALLE, AND CATIA LA MAR. THE ROAD FROM
CARACAS TO MAIQUETIA AIRPORT WAS CLOSED BY THE
NATIONAL GUARD AFTER REPORTS OF SHOOTING. THESE
EVENTS HAVE NOT/NOT BEEN REPORTED BY LOCAL MEDIA.
ACCORDING TO PAS CONTACTS, THE MEDIA BELIEVED THAT THE
DISTURBANCES WERE PLANNED TO INCITE PANIC, AND FELT
THAT COVERAGE WOULD ADD TO THAT PANIC.

12. (SBU) THIS AFTERNOON, WE HAVE RECEIVED WORD THAT AT
                        UNCLASSIFIED

PAGE 04   CARACA 00996 02 OF 02 031748Z
LEAST TWO SHOPPING CENTERS HAVE BEEN CLOSED BY GUARDS
AND EVACUATED, PERHAPS TO PREVENT LOOTING. AS OF
MIDDAY, AN EMBASSY CONTACT REPORTED THAT METRO HAS
BEEN CLOSED, AND THAT GUNFIRE COULD BE HEARD DOWNTOWN.
TEAR GAS IS ALSO REPORTEDLY BEING USED. NO LOCAL NEWS
CHANNELS ARE REPORTING THESE EVENTS.

Current Class: UNCLASSIFIED

CIA Document, 14 April 2002

TIER

SECRET/[redacted]

DIRECTORATE OF INTELLIGENCE

SPOT COMMENTARY

14 April 2002
02:00 EDT
Spot Com 4

CIADI _ _ _ _ _ _SPOTCOMM 020414-0200

Venezuela: Counter-Coup Paves Way for Chavez's Return [redacted]

(b)(1)
(b)(3)

Escalating public protests and signs that his military support was flagging prompted interim President Pedro Carmona to resign late Saturday night. Chavez's vice president, Diosdado Cabello, was sworn in as the new interim president, and plans are currently being made to bring Chavez back to Caracas to resume office.

- Media reports indicate that tens of thousands of protestors began surrounding the presidential palace late Saturday demanding Chavez's return. Chavez's exact whereabouts are unknown at this time, but some reports indicate he is being ushered back from his residence in Orchila—a small island 100 kilometers off the coast of Venezuela—to Caracas.

- Chavez's supporters have taken over the government-owned television station and claim that they have full-control of military headquarters at Fort Tiuna, and that Chavez will return before dawn. [redacted]

Carmona's support unraveled quickly yesterday as political parties, labor unions, and the military sensed he was moving too quickly and without their consultation. Disbanding Congress and scrapping the constitution left Carmona operating without a legal framework and ruling by decree—a move condemned by many regional leaders and the international community.

- Chavez's political and military allies have begun to reclaim their positions in the Cabello-led government. Former Commander of the Armed Services General Rincon and former Defense Minister Rangel reportedly have been reinstated. [redacted]

The military—an institution that in general cherishes its apolitical status—will likely be forced to play a greater role in this new transition government. Acting President Cabello and other hard-line Chavez supporters may have the legal pretext to govern that Carmona lacked, but they lack broad popular support and almost certainly will not be able to unite the now sharply polarized society.

Bringing Chavez back into the scene will only deepen the current political crisis. If the ousted leader does return to office as is rumored, anti-Chavez protestors—a group that has dwarfed his supporters in previous protests, but is less likely to instigate a confrontation— might take to the streets again, escalating the potential for sustained violence. [redacted]

State Department cable, 14 April 2002

UNCLASSIFIED

(E28)

RELEASED IN PART

CONFIDENTIAL   PTO4159

B1, 1.4(D)

PAGE 01   CARACA 01009 141012Z
ACTION DS-00

INFO   LOG-00   MFA-00   NP-00   AID-00   ACQ-00   CA-01   CEA-01
       CIAE-00 COME-00 CTME-00 INL-00   DINT-00 DODE-00 DOEE-00
       DOTE-00 WHA-00   PERC-00 SRPP-00 EB-00   EXIM-01 E-00
       FAAE-00 VC-00   FRB-00   H-01   TEDE-00 INR-00   ITC-01
       LAB-01   L-00   VCE-00   AC-01   NSAE-00 NSCE-00 OCS-03
       OES-01   OMB-01   OPIC-01 PA-00   PM-00   PRS-00   ACE-00
       P-00   SCT-00   SP-00   IRM-00   SSO-00   SS-00   STR-00
       TRSE-00 USIE-00 ASDS-01 IIP-00   PMB-00   DSCC-00 DRL-02
       G-00   NFAT-00 SAS-00   /016W
                -----------------85EC05 141015Z /38

O 140950Z APR 02
FM AMEMBASSY CARACAS
TO SECSTATE WASHDC IMMEDIATE 5484
INFO OPEC COLLECTIVE PRIORITY
AMEMBASSY BOGOTA PRIORITY
AMEMBASSY QUITO
AMEMBASSY LA PAZ
AMEMBASSY LIMA
USCINCSO MIAMI FL

C O N F I D E N T I A L CARACAS 001009

NSC FOR AMB MAISTO
USCINSCO FOR POLAD

DEPT CA FOR MARY A. RYAN
                    CONFIDENTIAL

PAGE 02   CARACA 01009 141012Z
DEPT ALSO FOR DS/OP/WHA AND S/ES-ODS/OP/CC

E.O. 12958: DECL: 04/14/12
TAGS: ECON, PGOV, PREL, EPET, ASEC, CASC VE
SUBJECT: VENEZUELA SITREP AS OF 4:00AM APRIL 14 - CHAVEZ RETURNS

REF: A.CARACAS 1002 B.1001 C.1000 D.00998 E.00996 F.00984 G.00980
H.00974 I.00973 J.00966 K.00948

CLASSIFIED BY AMBASSADOR CHARLES S. SHAPIRO. REASON
1.5 (B) AND (D).

TRIUMPHANT RETURN OF CHAVEZ
----
1. (SBU) AT 2:50AM APRIL 14, HUGO CHAVEZ ARRIVED AT MIRAFLORES
PALACE AND WAS GREETED BY A LARGE CROWD OF CELEBRATING SUPPORTERS.

UNCLASSIFIED

Current Class: CONFIDENTIAL   UNCLASSIFIED
Current Handling: n/a

OFFICIAL TELEVISION REPORTED THAT CHAVEZ FLEW BY HELICOPTER FROM
ORCHILA ISLAND TO A MILITARY FACILITY IN MARACAY, AND THEN ON TO
MIRAFLORES IN CARACAS. THEREAFTER, OFFICIAL TELEVISION SHOWED
CHAVEZ GOVERNMENT MINISTERS AND MILITARY SUPPORTERS ARRIVING
INSIDE MIRAFLORES GATES.

2. (SBU) CHAVEZ APPEARED INSIDE OF MIRAFLORES, FLANKED BY WILLIAM
LARA, ISAIS RODRIGUEZ, DIASDADO CABELLO AND JOSE VICENTE RANGEL,
AND DELIVERED AN HOUR LONG ADDRESS WHICH STARTED AT 4:30AM APRIL
14. CHAVEZ IMMEDIATELY CALLED FOR CALM AND SAID EVERYONE SHOULD
GO HOME "TO YOUR HOUSE, TO YOUR FAMILY." HE PROMISED THAT THERE
WILL BE NO REVENGE OR PERSECUTION OF HIS OPPONENTS, BUT OBLIQUELY
NOTED THAT CHANGES HAVE TO BE MADE. HE REFERENCED THAT HE HAD
ACCEPTED THE RESIGNATION OF THE PDVSA BOARD OF DIRECTORS
(APPARENTLY TENDERED BY PRESIDENT GASTON PARRA ON APRIL 11), AND
                         CONFIDENTIAL

PAGE 03   CARACA .01009 141012Z
WILL WORK TO CONSTITUTE A NEW BOARD. HE ALSO ISSUED A CALL TO
FORM ROUNDTABLES FOR NATIONAL DIALOGUE. CHAVEZ EXPLAINED THAT HE
WAS NOT MISTREATED WHILE IN CUSTODY, AND FIRMLY DECLARED THAT HE
DID NOT RESIGN AT ANY TIME.

LOCAL TV COVERAGE
----
4. (SBU) ALL LOCAL TELEVISION CHANNELS (AND AT LEAST TWO
INTERNATIONAL CHANNELS) COVERED CHAVEZ'S ADDRESS LIVE, APPARENTLY
THROUGH A FEED FROM VENEZOLANA DE TELEVISION, THE STATE CONTROLLED
CHANNEL. EARLIER, LOCAL TELEVISION CHANNELS CARRIED FEEDS FROM
THE STATE-CONTROLLED CHANNEL IN WHICH CHAVEZ SUPPORTERS TALKED
FROM INSIDE THE STUDIO, OR CARRIED REGULAR ENTERTAINMENT. THERE
HAS BEEN NO INDEPENDENT LOCAL TELEVISION REPORTING THROUGHOUT THE
NIGHT.

CARMONA'S ILL-FATED DECLARATION

                         CONFIDENTIAL

Current Class: CONFIDENTIAL

State Department cable, 14 April 2002 (Otto Reich)

```
Current Class: CONFIDENTIAL      UNCLASSIFIED
Current Handling: n/a


                      CONFIDENTIAL      PTO5001


PAGE 01          STATE    070877  150111Z    RELEASED IN PART
ORIGIN WHA-00                                B1, 1.4(D)

INFO  LOG-00   NP-00    AMAD-00  ACQ-00  CIAE-00 INL-00  DS-00
      EUR-00   VC-00    TEDE-00  INR-00  IO-00   JUSE-00 LAB-01
      L-00     VCE-00   NSAE-00  OIC-02  P-00    SP-00   SS-00
      R-00     DSCC-00  DRL-02   NFAT-00 SAS-00          /005R

070877
SOURCE: DISKETTE.020728
DRAFTED BY: WHA/AND:BRNARANJO:BRN -- 04/14/02 X74216ANDVE02/CABLES/RAL
APPROVED BY: WHA:OJREICH
WHA:JCSTRUBLE   WHA/AND:JDFARRAR   D:KBUE    P:TLENDERKING
WHA/USOAS:RNORIEGA
                 ------------------8612CD  150112Z /38

O 150107Z APR 02
FM SECSTATE WASHDC
TO WESTERN HEMISPHERIC AFFAIRS DIPL POSTS IMMEDIATE
INFO NSC WASHDC IMMEDIATE 0000
JOINT STAFF WASHDC IMMEDIATE 0000
SECDEF WASHDC IMMEDIATE 0000
USSOUTHCOM MIAMI FL IMMEDIATE
USMISSION USUN NEW YORK IMMEDIATE
AMEMBASSY VATICAN IMMEDIATE
AMEMBASSY MADRID IMMEDIATE
AMEMBASSY LONDON IMMEDIATE
USMISSION GENEVA IMMEDIATE

C O N F I D E N T I A L STATE 070877

E.O. 12958: DECL: 04/14/12
                    CONFIDENTIAL

PAGE 02          STATE    070877  150111Z
TAGS: PREL, PGOV, PHUM, KDEM, VE
SUBJECT: RALLYING INTERNATIONAL SUPPORT FOR VENEZUELAN
DEMOCRACY

1.  (U)  CLASSIFIED BY ASSISTANT SECRETARY FOR WESTERN
HEMISPHERE AFFAIRS OTTO J. REICH.  REASONS:  1.5(B) AND
(D).
```

Current Class: CONFIDENTIAL

UNCLASSIFIED

Current Class: CONFIDENTIAL   UNCLASSIFIED
Current Handling: n/a

BACKGROUND
----

3. (U) ON APRIL 11, HUNDREDS OF THOUSANDS OF VENEZUELANS
GATHERED TO SEEK REDRESS OF THEIR GRIEVANCES. CHAVEZ
SUPPORTERS FIRED ON ANTI-GOVERNMENT PROTESTORS RESULTING
IN MORE THAN 100 WOUNDED OR KILLED. VENEZUELAN MILITARY
AND POLICE REFUSED GOVERNMENT ORDERS TO FIRE ON
DEMONSTRATORS. THE GOVERNMENT PREVENTED FIVE INDEPENDENT
TELEVISION STATIONS FROM REPORTING ON EVENTS. AFTER
MEETING WITH SENIOR MILITARY OFFICERS, CHAVEZ ALLEGEDLY
RESIGNED THE PRESIDENCY. A PROVISIONAL CIVILIAN
GOVERNMENT, LED BY PEDRO CARMONA, ASSUMED POWER AND
PROMISED EARLY ELECTIONS.

4. (U) ON APRIL 12, PEDRO CARMONA WAS SWORN IN AS
PROVISIONAL PRESIDENT. THE PROVISIONAL GOVERNMENT
ANNOUNCED THE DISSOLUTION OF VENEZUELA'S NATIONAL ASSEMBLY
AND SUPREME TRIBUNAL OF JUSTICE. SUBSEQUENTLY, ON APRIL

Current Class: CONFIDENTIAL

Current Class: CONFIDENTIAL UNCLASSIFIED
Current Handling: n/a

13, CARMONA, WHO HAD BEEN UNDER INTENSE U.S.,
CONFIDENTIAL

PAGE 04   STATE   070877 150111Z
INTERNATIONAL, AND DOMESTIC PRESSURE TO MAINTAIN
CONSTITUTIONAL CONTINUITY, REVERSED COURSE AND REINSTATED
THE NATIONAL ASSEMBLY AND CHARGED IT WITH SELECTING A
PROVISIONAL PRESIDENT.

5. (U) THROUGHOUT APRIL 13, HOWEVER, PRO-CHAVEZ FORCES
MADE A CONCERTED EFFORT TO RESTORE CHAVEZ TO THE
PRESIDENCY. PRO-CHAVEZ FORCES SEIZED THE MIRAFLORES
PRESIDENTIAL PALACE, SWORE IN CHAVEZ VICE PRESIDENT
DIOSDADO CABELLO AS ACTING PRESIDENT, AND SEIZED OR FORCED
THE EVACUATION OF ALL MEDIA OUTLETS. FINALLY, TROOPS
LOYAL TO CHAVEZ SEIZED CONTROL OF FUERTE TIUNA, HOME OF
VENEZUELA'S MINISTRY OF DEFENSE, AND ARRESTED CARMONA AND
HIS MILITARY HIGH COMMAND. CHAVEZ RETURNED TO CARACAS AND
RESUMED HIS PRESIDENCY.

6. (U) PRESIDENT CHAVEZ ADDRESSED THE NATION EARLY IN
THE MORNING ON APRIL 14. IN HIS ADDRESS, CHAVEZ:
PROMISED HE WOULD NOT RETALIATE AGAINST OR PERSECUTE HIS
OPPONENTS, SAID HE WOULD REFLECT ON HIS ACTIONS AND URGED
OTHERS TO DO SO AS WELL, ISSUED A CALL FOR NATIONAL
ROUNTABLES OF DIALOGUE TO BEGIN ON APRIL 18, SAID HE HAD
NOT BEEN MISTREATED, AND STATED THAT HE HAD NEVER
RESIGNED.

U.S. POSITION ON EVENTS IN VENEZUELA
----

7. (U) BEGIN TEXT OF WHITE HOUSE STATEMENT:

CONFIDENTIAL

PAGE 05   STATE   070877 150111Z
THE WHITE HOUSE
OFFICE OF THE PRESS SECRETARY

FOR IMMEDIATE RELEASE   APRIL 14, 2002

STATEMENT BY THE PRESS SECRETARY

THE UNITED STATES IS MONITORING THE SITUATION IN VENEZUELA
WITH GREAT CONCERN. WE DEEPLY REGRET THE VIOLENCE AND
LOSS OF LIFE, AND CALL ON ALL VENEZUELANS TO WORK
PEACEFULLY TO RESOLVE THIS CRISIS.

Current Class: CONFIDENTIAL

UNCLASSIFIED

Current Class: CONFIDENTIAL
Current Handling: n/a

WE WELCOME AND SUPPORT THE DECISION BY THE ORGANIZATION OF
AMERICAN STATES TO SEND IMMEDIATELY A FACT-FINDING MISSION
HEADED BY SECRETARY GENERAL CESAR GAVIRIA TO VENEZUELA TO
SUPPORT THE RE-ESTABLISHMENT OF FULL DEMOCRACY, WITH
GUARANTEES FOR CITIZENS AND RESPECT FOR FUNDAMENTAL
FREEDOMS, WITHIN THE FRAMEWORK OF THE INTER-AMERICAN
DEMOCRATIC CHARTER.

THE PEOPLE OF VENEZUELA HAVE SENT A CLEAR MESSAGE TO
PRESIDENT CHAVEZ THAT THEY WANT BOTH DEMOCRACY AND REFORM.
THE CHAVEZ ADMINISTRATION HAS AN OPPORTUNITY TO RESPOND TO
THIS MESSAGE BY CORRECTING ITS COURSE AND GOVERNING IN A
FULLY DEMOCRATIC MANNER.

PRESIDENT CHAVEZ HAS NOW CALLED FOR NATIONAL REFLECTION
AND DIALOGUE. HE NEEDS TO SEIZE THIS OPPORTUNITY TO
ENSURE LEGITIMACY BY REACHING OUT TO THE POLITICAL
OPPOSITION, CIVIL SOCIETY, AND TO ALL DEMOCRATIC FORCES IN
VENEZUELA.

                    CONFIDENTIAL

PAGE 06   STATE   070877   150111Z

THE UNITED STATES AND THE WORLD COMMUNITY OF DEMOCRACIES
WILL BE CLOSELY FOLLOWING EVENTS IN VENEZUELA. PRESIDENT
CHAVEZ BEARS PARTICULAR RESPONSIBILITY TO PRESERVE THE
PEACE, TO PROTECT HUMAN RIGHTS AND DEMOCRATIC FREEDOMS,
AND TO CREATE THE CONDITIONS NECESSARY FOR A NATIONAL
DIALOGUE. WE CALL ON HIM TO WORK WITH ALL VENEZUELANS AND
WITH THE ORGANIZATION OF AMERICAN STATES TOWARD THIS END.

END TEXT OF WHITE HOUSE STATEMENT.
POWELL

                    CONFIDENTIAL

<< END OF DOCUMENT >>

Current Class: CONFIDENTIAL

State Department press guide, 16 April 2002

ALL POSTS FOR PAO, USSOCOM FOR POLAD

E.O. 12958: N/A
TAGS: OPRC, KPAO
SUBJECT: WHA GUIDANCE, APRIL 16, 2002

SUMMARY OF CONTENTS:
WHA PRESS GUIDANCE, APRIL 16 (VENEZUELA)
END SUMMARY.

WHA PRESS GUIDANCE, APRIL 16, 2002:

-- VENEZUELA: MEETINGS, U.S. INVOLVEMENT, LEGITIMACY,
REACTION TO CHAVEZ SPEECH, ARRESTS OF CARMONA ET AL --

Q: DID U.S. OFFICIALS MEET WITH VENEZUELAN OPPOSITION
OFFICIALS PRIOR TO THE APRIL 11 REMOVAL OF PRESIDENT CHAVEZ
UNCLASSIFIED

PAGE 03   STATE   072430   162107Z
FROM POWER?

A: U.S. OFFICIALS HAVE MET WITH A BROAD SPECTRUM OF
VENEZUELANS OVER THE PAST SEVERAL MONTHS BOTH IN CARACAS AND
IN WASHINGTON. U.S. OFFICIALS MET WITH BUSINESS COMMUNITY
REPRESENTATIVES, LABOR UNION OFFICIALS, CATHOLIC CHURCH
LEADERS, OPPOSITION POLITICAL LEADERS, AND A WIDE ARRAY OF
VENEZUELAN GOVERNMENT OFFICIALS.

IF ASKED:

IN THE COURSE OF NORMAL DIPLOMATIC CONTACTS, U.S. OFFICIALS
MET WITH PEDRO CARMONA, THE PRESIDENT OF THE VENEZUELAN
FEDERATION OF CHAMBERS OF COMMERCE (FEDECAMARAS).

OUR MESSAGE TO ALL VENEZUELAN CONTACTS HAS BEEN CONSISTENT.
THE POLITICAL SITUATION IN VENEZUELA IS ONE FOR VENEZUELANS
TO RESOLVE PEACEFULLY, DEMOCRATICALLY AND CONSTITUTIONALLY.
WE EXPLICITLY TOLD ALL OF OUR VENEZUELAN INTERLOCUTORS ON
NUMEROUS OCCASIONS AND AT MANY LEVELS THAT UNDER NO
CIRCUMSTANCES WOULD THE UNITED STATES SUPPORT ANY
UNCONSTITUTIONAL, UNDEMOCRATIC EFFORT, SUCH AS COUP, TO
REMOVE PRESIDENT CHAVEZ FROM POWER.

Q: WAS THE UNITED STATES INVOLVED IN THE EFFORT TO REMOVE
VENEZUELAN PRESIDENT CHAVEZ FROM POWER?

A: ABSOLUTELY NOT.

16 April 2002 press guide (cont.)

Q: WHY THEN DID THE U.S. NOT CONDEMN THE REMOVAL OF
PRESIDENT CHAVEZ FROM POWER ON FRIDAY, APRIL 12 AND CALL FOR
UNCLASSIFIED

PAGE 04   STATE   072430   162107Z
HIS IMMEDIATE REINSTATEMENT?

A: OUR RESPONSE TO THE SITUATION IN VENEZUELA ON APRIL 12
LAID OUT THE FACTS AS WE KNEW THEM TO BE DURING A VERY
CONFUSING TIME.   THOSE FACTS WERE THAT HUNDREDS OF THOUSANDS
OF VENEZUELANS DEMONSTRATED PEACEFULLY AGAINST THE CHAVEZ
GOVERNMENT, THAT THE CHAVEZ GOVERNMENT RESPONDED WITH A
CRACK-DOWN AGAINST PROTESTORS AND THE INDEPENDENT MEDIA, THAT
PRESIDENT CHAVEZ WAS REPORTED TO HAVE DISMISSED HIS VICE
PRESIDENT AND CABINET AND RESIGNED, AND THAT A TRANSITIONAL
GOVERNMENT HAD ASSUMED POWERS AND CALLED FOR NEW ELECTIONS.

OUR POSITION WAS THAT THIS SITUATION SHOULD BE RESOLVED
PEACEFULLY AND DEMOCRATICALLY, AND IN ACCORDANCE WITH THE
INTER-AMERICAN DEMOCRATIC CHARTER.

WE FOLLOWED THIS STATEMENT BY HELPING TO DRAFT A RESOLUTION
AT THE ORGANIZATION OF AMERICAN STATES (OAS) INVOKING ARTICLE
20 OF THE INTER-AMERICAN DEMOCRATIC CHARTER.   ARTICLE 20
ALLOWS FOR ANY OAS MEMBER STATE (OR THE SECRETARY GENERAL) TO
CONVOKE THE OAS PERMANENT COUNCIL TO UNDERTAKE A "COLLECTIVE
ASSESSMENT OF THE SITUATION" WHEN THERE HAS BEEN "AN
UNCONSTITUTIONAL ALTERATION OF THE CONSTITUTIONAL REGIME THAT
SERIOUSLY IMPAIRS THE DEMOCRATIC ORDER IN A MEMBER STATE."
WITH THAT OBJECTIVE, OUR REPRESENTATIVE TO THE OAS CLEARLY
STATED THAT THE SO-CALLED "PROVISIONAL GOVERNMENT" HAD YET TO
DEMONSTRATE THAT THEY ARE THE "LEGALLY CONSTITUTED CIVILIAN
AUTHORITY."   OUR DELEGATION ALSO SAID THAT THE OAS MUST
RIGOROUSLY INSIST THAT VENEZUELAN AUTHORITIES RESPECT THE
ESSENTIAL ELEMENTS OF DEMOCRACY.

UNCLASSIFIED

PAGE 05   STATE   072430   162107Z
WE JOINED THE CONSENSUS TO SUPPORT THE OAS RESOLUTION OF
APRIL 13 THAT CONDEMNED THE "ALTERATION OF CONSTITUTIONAL
ORDER," CALLED FOR THE "NORMALIZATION OF THE DEMOCRATIC
INSTITUTIONAL FRAMEWORK IN VENEZUELA, WITHIN THE CONTEXT OF
THE INTER-AMERICAN DEMOCRATIC CHARTER," AND CALLED FOR THE
OAS SECRETARY GENERAL TO CONDUCT A FACT-FINDING MISSION TO
VENEZUELA.

WE ARE PLEASED THAT THE HEMISPHERE IS ENGAGED IN SUPPORTING
DEMOCRACY IN VENEZUELA.   WE TRUST THAT OUR HEMISPHERIC
PARTNERS WILL CONTINUE THIS ENGAGEMENT TO ENSURE THAT

UNCLASSIFIED

Current Class: UNCLASSIFIED
Current Handling: n/a

VENEZUELA RESPECTS DEMOCRATIC INSTITUTIONS AND PROCESSES AND
FOLLOWS THROUGH ON ITS COMMITMENTS FOR NATIONAL DIALOGUE AND
RECONCILIATION.

Q: IS THE GOVERNMENT OF VENEZUELAN PRESIDENT HUGO CHAVEZ
LEGITIMATE?

A: YES. THE VENEZUELAN PEOPLE FREELY AND FAIRLY ELECTED
HUGO CHAVEZ TO BE PRESIDENT OF VENEZUELA IN DEMOCRATIC
ELECTIONS IN DECEMBER 1998 AND JULY 2000. LEGITIMACY EARNED
THROUGH ELECTIONS MUST BE MAINTAINED AND NURTURED THROUGH
DEMOCRATIC GOVERNANCE THAT RESPECTS THE ESSENTIAL ELEMENTS OF
DEMOCRACY. PRESIDENT CHAVEZ'S CALL FOR NATIONAL DIALOGUE AND
RECONCILIATION IS A WELCOME INITIAL INITIATIVE TOWARD FULLY
RESTORING THE ESSENTIAL ELEMENTS OF DEMOCRACY.

Q: DO YOU HAVE ANY REACTION TO PRESIDENT CHAVEZ'S APRIL 15
SPEECH?

A: WE WELCOME PRESIDENT CHAVEZ'S CALLS FOR ROUNDTABLES OF
UNCLASSIFIED

PAGE 06   STATE   072430 162107Z
NATIONAL DIALOGUE AND RECONCILIATION. THIS IS AN IMPORTANT
FIRST STEP IN RECLAIMING VENEZUELA'S DEMOCRACY. WE URGE THE
VENEZUELAN GOVERNMENT TO SUPPORT FULLY THE ORGANIZATION OF
AMERICAN STATES (OAS) SECRETARY GENERAL'S FACT-FINDING
MISSION TO VENEZUELA. THROUGH ITS GOOD OFFICES, THE OAS CAN
PLAY AN IMPORTANT ROLE BY SUPPORTING A BROAD AND INCLUSIVE
NATIONAL DIALOGUE THAT PROMOTES RECONCILIATION AND
STRENGTHENING THE ESSENTIAL ELEMENTS OF DEMOCRACY IN
VENEZUELA.

Q: DO YOU HAVE ANY COMMENT REGARDING THE DETENTION OF
PROVISIONAL PRESIDENT PEDRO CARMONA AND THE MILITARY OFFICERS
THAT SUPPORTED HIS GOVERNMENT?

A: IT IS OUR UNDERSTANDING THAT PEDRO CARMONA, INDIVIDUALS
WHO WORKED WITH CARMONA, AND MILITARY LEADERS THAT SUPPORTED
CARMONA HAVE BEEN DETAINED. AS WE WOULD WITH ANY VENEZUELAN
CITIZEN, WE URGE THE VENEZUELAN GOVERNMENT TO RESPECT THE
HUMAN RIGHTS OF THESE INDIVIDUALS AND TO HANDLE THEIR CASES
IN ACCORDANCE WITH THE FUNDAMENTAL PRINCIPLES OF JUSTICE.
PRESIDENT CHAVEZ HAS PROMISED TO RESPECT THE HUMAN RIGHTS OF
THOSE PERSONS WHO WERE DETAINED. WE WELCOME THIS PROMISE,
AND TRUST THAT PRESIDENT CHAVEZ WILL FOLLOW THROUGH ON IT.
POWELL

UNCLASSIFIED

Current Class: UNCLASSIFIED

State Department press guide, 17 April 2002

Current Class: UNCLASSIFIED
Current Handling: n/a

TAGS: OPRC, KPAO
SUBJECT: WHA GUIDANCE, APRIL 17, 2002

SUMMARY OF CONTENTS:
WHA PRESS GUIDANCE, APRIL 17 (VENEZUELA)
END SUMMARY.

WHA PRESS GUIDANCE, APRIL 17, 2002

-- VENEZUELA: REICH CALL TO PEDRO CARMONA --

QUESTION: DID ASSISTANT SECRETARY OF STATE REICH SPEAK WITH
VENEZUELA'S THEN INTERIM PRESIDENT ON FRIDAY APRIL 12 TO
ADVISE HIM TO NOT DISSOLVE THE NATIONAL ASSEMBLY?

                    UNCLASSIFIED

PAGE 03   STATE   073182   172107Z
A: CONTRARY TO A REPORT IN THE NEW YORK TIMES, ASSISTANT
SECRETARY REICH DID NOT SPEAK WITH THEN-INTERIM PRESIDENT
PEDRO CARMONA ON FRIDAY APRIL 12 OR AT ANY OTHER TIME DURING
VENEZUELA'S CRISIS LAST WEEK.

THROUGH OUR EMBASSY IN CARACAS, AMBASSADOR REICH DID CONVEY
THE EXPECTATIONS OF THE U.S. GOVERNMENT THAT THE INTERIM
GOVERNMENT WOULD RESPECT THE INSTITUTIONS AND PRACTICES OF
DEMOCRACY IN VENEZUELA, INCLUDING THE CONTINUED FUNCTIONING
OF ALL BRANCHES OF GOVERNMENT.

IF PRESSED: OVER THE COURSE OF FRIDAY AND SATURDAY,
AMBASSADOR SHAPIRO SPOKE WITH A NUMBER OF VENEZUELANS
INVOLVED IN THE EVENTS THERE, INCLUDING THEN INTERIM
PRESIDENT CARMONA.

THE ASSERTION THAT THE UNITED STATES SOUGHT TO "STAGE MANAGE"
THE SITUATION IN VENEZUELA, IS FLATLY INCORRECT. OUR
DIPLOMATIC EFFORTS, LIKE THOSE OF OUR DEMOCRATIC ALLIES, WERE
FOCUSED ON HELPING VENEZUELANS RESOLVE THEIR CRISIS
PEACEFULLY AND DEMOCRATICALLY.

THROUGH REGULAR DIPLOMATIC CONTACTS BOTH IN WASHINGTON AND IN
CARACAS, WE MADE CLEAR OUR REJECTION OF ANY UNCONSTITUTIONAL,
UNDEMOCRATIC EFFORT BY ANY PARTY IN VENEZUELA.
POWELL

                    UNCLASSIFIED

<< END OF DOCUMENT >>

Current Class: UNCLASSIFIED

State Department press guide, 19 April 2002

Q: WHAT ABOUT ASSERTIONS THAT U.S. OFFICIALS HAVE BEEN TOO
CLOSE TO THOSE VENEZUELANS WHO WERE INVOLVED IN THE EVENTS OF

APRIL 11-13?

A: U.S. OFFICIALS HAVE MET WITH A BROAD SPECTRUM OF
VENEZUELANS OVER THE PAST SEVERAL MONTHS BOTH IN CARACAS AND
IN WASHINGTON. U.S. OFFICIALS MET WITH BUSINESS COMMUNITY
REPRESENTATIVES, LABOR UNION OFFICIALS, CATHOLIC CHURCH
LEADERS, OPPOSITION POLITICAL LEADERS, PRO-CHAVEZ
LEGISLATORS, AND A WIDE ARRAY OF VENEZUELAN GOVERNMENT
OFFICIALS. IN THE COURSE OF NORMAL DIPLOMATIC CONTACTS, U.S.
OFFICIALS MET WITH PEDRO CARMONA, THE PRESIDENT OF THE
VENEZUELAN FEDERATION OF CHAMBERS OF COMMERCE (FEDECAMARAS).

OUR MESSAGE TO ALL VENEZUELAN CONTACTS HAS BEEN CONSISTENT.
THE POLITICAL SITUATION IN VENEZUELA IS ONE FOR VENEZUELANS
TO RESOLVE PEACEFULLY, DEMOCRATICALLY AND CONSTITUTIONALLY.
WE EXPLICITLY TOLD ALL OF OUR VENEZUELAN INTERLOCUTORS ON
NUMEROUS OCCASIONS AND AT MANY LEVELS THAT UNDER NO
CIRCUMSTANCES WOULD THE UNITED STATES SUPPORT ANY
UNCONSTITUTIONAL, UNDEMOCRATIC EFFORT, SUCH AS A COUP.

Q: WHAT ABOUT THE STATEMENT OF A DIPLOMAT PRESENT AT A
FEBRUARY 12 MEETING AT THE DEPARTMENT OF STATE THAT
DEPARTMENT OFFICIALS WERE QUICK TO POINT OUT THAT CHAVEZ HAD
RESIGNED?

A: OUR RESPONSE TO THE SITUATION IN VENEZUELA ON APRIL 12
LAID OUT THE FACTS AS WE KNEW THEM TO BE DURING A VERY
CONFUSING TIME. THOSE FACTS WERE THAT: (1) HUNDREDS OF
THOUSANDS OF VENEZUELANS DEMONSTRATED PEACEFULLY AGAINST THE
CHAVEZ GOVERNMENT, (2) THE CHAVEZ GOVERNMENT RESPONDED WITH A
BLOODY CRACK-DOWN AGAINST PROTESTORS AND THE INDEPENDENT

MEDIA, (3) PRESIDENT CHAVEZ HAD DISMISSED HIS VICE PRESIDENT
AND CABINET AND RESIGNED, AND (4) A TRANSITIONAL GOVERNMENT
WOULD ASSUME POWER AND CALL FOR NEW ELECTIONS.

IN ALL OF OUR STATEMENTS, WE EMPHASIZED THAT VENEZUELANS
NEEDED TO RESOLVE THIS SITUATION PEACEFULLY, DEMOCRATICALLY,
AND CONSITUTIONALLY IN ACCORDANCE WITH THE INTER-AMERICAN
DEMOCRATIC CHARTER. AS STATED BEFORE, IT WAS OUR
UNDERSTANDING THAT PRESIDENT CHAVEZ HAD RESIGNED AND THAT
THERE WAS NO SUCCESSOR. IT WAS UP TO VENEZUELANS TO DECIDE
HOW TO RESOLVE THIS SUCCESSION CRISIS. ONCE VENEZUELANS HAD

State Department press guide, 22 April 2002

ALL POSTS FOR PAO, USSOCOM FOR POLAD

E.O. 12958: N/A
TAGS: OPRC, KPAO
SUBJECT: WHA GUIDANCE, APRIL 22, 2002

SUMMARY OF CONTENTS:
1. WHA PRESS GUIDANCE, APRIL 22 (VENEZUELA)
2. WHA PRESS GUIDANCE, APRIL 19 (CUBA)
3. S/CT PRESS GUIDANCE, APRIL 19 (ECUADOR)
4. TAKEN QUESTIONS, APRIL 19 (CANADA, VENEZEULA)
END SUMMARY.

----
1. WHA PRESS GUIDANCE, APRIL 22, 2002

-- VENEZUELA: AMBASSADOR SHAPIRO MEETING WITH
CARMONA/ASSERTIONS U.S. TOO CLOSE TO OPPOSITION --
UNCLASSIFIED

PAGE 03   STATE   075817   222122Z

Q: WHAT DID AMBASSADOR SHAPIRO SAY TO PEDRO CARMONA?

A: AMBASSADOR SHAPIRO SPOKE WITH PEDRO CARMONA TWICE IN THE
IMMEDIATE AFTERMATH OF APRIL 11. FIRST, ON APRIL 12 BEFORE
CARMONA SWORE HIMSELF IN, AMBASSADOR SHAPIRO PHONED CARMONA
AND TOLD HIM THAT ANY POLITICAL TRANSITION PROCESS HAD TO BE
CONSTITUTIONAL AND DEMOCRATIC AND URGED HIM NOT TO DISSOLVE
THE NATIONAL ASSEMBLY. ON APRIL 13, AFTER CARMONA HAD SWORN
HIMSELF IN AS THE &INTERIM PROVISIONAL PRESIDENT8 AND HAD
DISSOLVED THE NATIONAL ASSEMBLY, AMBASSADOR SHAPIRO MET WITH
CARMONA (AT MIRAFLORES PALACE) AND PROVIDED HIM A COPY OF THE
INTER-AMERICAN DEMOCRATIC CHARTER, URGED HIM TO RE-ESTABLISH
THE NATIONAL ASSEMBLY, TO MOVE TO ELECTIONS AS SOON AS
POSSIBLE, AND TO CONTACT THE ORGANIZATION OF AMERICAN STATES
(OAS) SECRETARY GENERAL TO WELCOME AN OAS DELEGATION.

DURING HIS MEETING WITH INTERIM PRESIDENT CARMONA, AMBASSADOR
SHAPIRO URGED CARMONA TO IMMEDIATELY RESTORE CONSTITUTIONAL
ORDER AND NORMALIZE DEMOCRATIC RULE IN VENEZUELA.

OUR MESSAGE TO ALL VENEZUELAN CONTACTS HAS BEEN CONSISTENT:
THE POLITICAL SITUATION IN VENEZUELA IS ONE FOR VENEZUELANS
TO RESOLVE PEACEFULLY, DEMOCRATICALLY AND CONSTITUTIONALLY.
WE EXPLICITLY TOLD ALL OF OUR VENEZUELAN INTERLOCUTORS ON
NUMEROUS OCCASIONS AND AT MANY LEVELS THAT UNDER NO
CIRCUMSTANCES WOULD THE UNITED STATES SUPPORT ANY
UNCONSTITUTIONAL, UNDEMOCRATIC EFFORT, SUCH AS A COUP.

Current Class: UNCLASSIFIED

NED trip report, 16–25 June 2002

To: Carl, Barbara, Sandra, and Taryn
From: Chris Sabatini
RE: Trip Report Venezuela, June 16-25

1.   General political situation

Complicated. It's the word you always hear when you ask people to explain what's happening in Venezuela. They say it with a sense of despair and defeat. The political agendas of different actors and alliances are complicated and obscure (What is the end-game of the ex-chavistas, such as Luis Miquilena, who are now backing a plan to remove Chavez? Does Chavez know about the political conspiracies that are swirling around him, according to some, within his own inner circle? Is he planning to use them to his own advantage?) The role of the military and their intentions are complicated. (The military has become factionalized, and it's unclear who backs whom and why.) And for these reasons, it's difficult, if not impossible, to predict what will happen in the future. (The lines are clearly drawn between Chavistas and anti-Chavistas,with the anti-Chavez groups—military and civilian—hatching numerous and conflicting plans to remove the president and Chavez publicly and aggresively proclaiming his intention to defend the revolution, in a phrase borrowed from Fidel Castro, "to the death.") In the midst of this polarized, political muddle two things become clear: first, the border that once divided military and civilian politics has been broken, perhaps irrevocably and second Venezuelan politics are locked in a confrontation for which it appears there is no consensus exit, and which admits very little room for outside mediation. Since April 11th, the government and the opposition have become locked in a zero-sum game, while much of the population waits to see its outcome. In the meantime, the economy continues to deteriorate, with some observers predicting a collapse of the financial and public sector within months.

Venezuelan politics have become a dizzying swirl of plots, counterplots and hidden agendas. Members of the traditional opposition (the CTV, the business community, and opposition parties) continue to mobilize protest marches to call for Chavez's resignation. Shortly before I arrived, the opposition had organized a march to the presidential palace. At the march, one opposition party, *Acción Democrática*, declared that it would remain in front of the palace until Chavez resigned. (They later decamped, unvictorious.) In the same march, several of the more political civil society groups (led by Elias Santana of *Queremos Elegir*) called for mass protest against the government by refusing to pay taxes--a plan which is actually unworkable since most Venezuelan taxes are based on sales tax which is automatically calculated in the charge when you make a purchase. For many of these groups, the goal is to mobilize sufficient public pressure and protest to force the resignation of the government. There are a number of politicized civil society groups (among them *Queremos Elegir* and *Red de Veedores*) that have joined in this call for immediate resignation. Many had hoped that the march planned for July 11th, the third anniversary of April 11th, would bring the full force of popular opposition against the government and force the president to step down. But even then, many people claimed—as they have been saying for years—that Chavez wouldn't last that long—that the military will attempt to remove him before then. At the same time, Chavez has stepped up his political attacks against his opponents and has allegedly increased his distribution of arms to the Bolivarian Circles.

One of the more active groups that has been plotting Chavez's removal is a group of ex-Chavistas, named *Solidaridad*, led by ex-interior minister Luis Miquilena. In collaboration with a number of groups, *Solidaridad* has initiated several judicial cases against the president. In all, there have been 61 cases brought against the President, the most important of these include allegation of mis-appropriation of state funds (FIEM) derived from the oil windfall of the last three years, campaign finance violations in which the president allegedly did not declare $1.5 million in funds received from the *Banco de Vizcaya*, and charges stemming from the shooting on April 11th. The plan to prosecute Chavez for any of these charges was given a boost the week I was in Venezuela when the supreme court ruled that plaintiffs in cases against the government could bring the cases directly to the Supreme Court, rather than through the Prosecutor General. The Prosecutor General, Isais Rodriguez, is an avowed Chavista who has openly voiced his continued support for the president. (The Supreme Court's decision was actually a violation of the recently approved criminal procedures code, which removed justices from prosecution and established a more U.S.-style adversarial system.) Many people credit the supreme court's decision to the machinations of Miquilena, who, as interior minister under Chavez, had named a number of the justices to the court. The decision and the cases that will result represent the opposition's more "institutionalist" route for removing Chavez.

But while the more democratic path to changing the government signals a greater intent by some sectors of the opposition to use state channels to force a change of government, the opposition's enthusiasm for Miquilena's actions is curious. Only months before, when he was in government, many people deeply distrusted Miquilena, believing him to be the sinister, ideological puppeteer of the charismatic Chavez. The belief was that the 84 year-old Miquilena was using Chavez as the charismatic public face for his ideological master plan. Now he has become the architect and dealmaker in support of the opposition. There are also rumors that he maintains close contact with several people in the administration and some sectors of the military.

The military's role in all of this is unclear. It is clearly factionalized, among units and between officer classes. There are strong rumors of conspiracies being hatched by the military and dissident officer groups. But the extent to which these individuals and groups command loyalty among the ranks is unclear. First there is the COMACATE, a group of dissident junior officers (commanders, captains, majors and lieutenant colonels). A week before I arrived they issued a public declaration denouncing the government as illegitimate. Another faction includes retired military officers, which held a march to protest the Chavez government. There are also rumors that different civilian leaders are maintaining regular contact with various elements in military, and that the opposition to Chavez within the military extends to the inner circle of military hierarchy around the President. The big event was to have come July 5th when the president announced a new round of military promotions. While the much-anticipated uprising never occurred, many believe that this leapfrogging of promotion (in a military that has always prided itself—though not always followed it—on its merit-based system) and the government's alleged support for the FARC in Colombia will ultimately provoke a coup by disaffected officers.

In all of this, military officers are assuming a greater political role. They now have an audience and pockets of support for their opposition to the government, and there is a sense that some military officers are enjoying this public role. There is a notable increase in their pronouncements and their general presence in the public debate. The military has now become a part and a victim of the political polarization within Venezuela. After the events of April 11th and the public reaction to them, however, there is a notable reluctance of civil society and civilian politicians (at least publicly) to embrace the military too closely. In contrast to the situation before April 11th, civil society leaders are less enthusiastic about military officers now declaring their opposition to the government, which they do with increasing frequency. The events of April 11th demonstrated the deep divisions within the military. Many fear that the next military coup would result in bloodshed. A coup d'etat now would likely provoke a confrontation between units and officers still loyal to the President and the rebellious officers. The Chavez government would also certainly unleash its "*Circulos Bolivarianos*"--which Chavez has continued to arm and incite to support the revolution. There are also claims that should the sectors of the military move against the government, its strategy would be one of "take no prisoners" and one which may also seek to exclude some of the more moderate and/or leftist civilian politicians from any future government.

For his part, Chavez has done little to demonstrate his good faith or desire for a mediated solution and has continued to inflame popular passions and class tensions. The events of April 11th appear to have only hardened its position. There are rumors—fairly common, if that's any indication of their veracity, but in this situation who knows?—that the government has distributed Uzi's to the Bolivarian circles. The person in charge of organizing the Bolivarian Circles has an office in the presidential palace and the arms are apparently financed by the state. The government has also installed anti-aircraft missiles on the roofs of several buildings around the city, allegedly in anticipation of the July 11th march. Statements by the President have inflamed the situation and appear to be preparing the country for a conflict. In a speech, delivered in a shantytown on the same day of the march of the retired-military officers, the President, encircled by mid-level officers and dressed in an orange jumpsuit, asked his followers "not to be unaware" of what was going on and to be ready to "defend the revolution" against those who are trying to undermine it. The verbal assaults against his opponents continue daily, on the radio, on t.v, in press conferences, and in public speeches. The intention obviously is to prepare his followers (he has supposedly at least 20% core support in the population) to back him—violently if necessary—against any attempts to remove him. As a result, middle and upper classes feel extremely insecure and fear for their lives and property. Contingency plans have been developed in middle and upper class neighborhoods for residents to defend themselves in the event that private groups armed by the government attack.

State Department press guide, 12–13 August 2002

UNCLASSIFIED

Current Class: UNCLASSIFIED
Current Handling: n/a

ALL POSTS FOR PAO, USSOCOM FOR POLAD

E.O. 12958: N/A
TAGS: OPRC, KPAO
SUBJECT: WHA GUIDANCE, AUGUST 13, 2002

SUMMARY OF CONTENTS:
1. TAKEN QUESTION, AUGUST 12 (VENEZUELA)
2. WHA PRESS GUIDANCE, AUGUST 12 (VENEZUELA)
3. WHA PRESS GUIDANCE, AUGUST 13 (CUBA, COLOMBIA, MEXICO)
END SUMMARY.

----
1. TAKEN QUESTION - WHA PRESS GUIDANCE, AUGUST 12, 2002:

-- VENEZUELA: VISIT OF FOREIGN MINISTER ROY CHADERTON
(TQ FROM 8-12-02 DAILY PRESS BRIEFING) --
                    UNCLASSIFIED

PAGE 03   STATE   155266   141703Z

QUESTION: IS A MEETING BETWEEN DEPUTY SECRETARY ARMITAGE AND
VENEZUELAN FOREIGN MINISTER ROY CHADERTON SCHEDULED? IF SO,
WHEN?

ANSWER: THE DEPUTY SECRETARY WILL MEET WITH VENEZUELAN
FOREIGN MINISTER ROY CHADERTON ON TUESDAY, AUGUST 20.

QUESTION: WILL THE SUBJECT OF THE VENEZUELAN SUPREME COURT'S
DELIBERATIONS ON THE QUESTION OF WHETHER TO CHARGE WITH
REBELLION FOUR SENIOR MILITARY OFFICERS BE ON THE AGENDA?
WHAT ELSE WILL BE INCLUDED ON THE AGENDA?

ANSWER: THE DEPUTY SECRETARY AND THE FOREIGN MINISTER
CHADERTON WILL DISCUSS A WIDE VARIETY OF ISSUES INCLUDING THE
CURRENT POLITICAL SITUATION IN VENEZUELA AND ISSUES OF MUTUAL
INTEREST TO OUR BILATERAL RELATIONSHIP.

----
2. WHA PRESS GUIDANCE, AUGUST 12, 2002:

-- VENEZUELA: REVOCATION OF VISAS --

Q: CAN YOU CONFIRM THAT PEDRO CARMONA AND MOLINA TAMAYO'S US
VISAS WERE REVOKED?

A: MESSRS. CARMONA AND TAMAYO'S VISAS WERE REVOKED UNDER
SECTION 214(B) OF THE IMMIGRATION AND NATIONALITY ACT, WHICH

Current Class: UNCLASSIFIED

UNCLASSIFIED

Current Class: UNCLASSIFIED
Current Handling: n/a

PROVIDES THAT FOREIGN NATIONALS ARE PRESUMED TO BE INTENDING
UNCLASSIFIED

PAGE 04   STATE   155266   141703Z
IMMIGRANTS AND THEREFORE INELIGIBLE FOR A NONIMMIGRANT VISA
UNLESS THEY CAN ESTABLISH THEY QUALIFY FOR NONIMMIGRANT
CLASSIFICATION.

Q. WHAT WAS THE BASIS FOR THE DETERMINATION THAT THEY DIDN'T
QUALIFY FOR VISAS ANY LONGER UNDER SECTION 214(B).

A: VISA RECORDS ARE CONFIDENTIAL UNDER U.S. LAW, AND I
CAN,T PROVIDE ANY DETAILS ON THE UNDERLYING FACTUAL BASIS
FOR THE INELIGIBILITY FINDINGS.

----
3. WHA PRESS GUIDANCE, AUGUST 13, 2002:

-- CUBA: FORMER UN AMBASSADOR IN DEPARTMENT --

Q: WILL FORMER UN AMBASSADOR TO CUBA JORGE ALCIBIADES
HIDALGO BASULTO BE MEETING WITH ANYONE IN THE DEPARTMENT?

A: FORMER UN AMBASSADOR TO CUBA JORGE ALCIBIADES HIDALGO
BASULTO WILL MEET WITH STATE DEPARTMENT OFFICIALS, INCLUDING
ASSISTANT SECRETARY FOR WESTERN HEMISPHERE AFFAIRS OTTO J.
REICH. WE LOOK FORWARD TO HEARING HIDALGO'S FIRST-HAND
ASSESSMENT OF THE SITUATION ON THE ISLAND.

-- COLOMBIA: "STATE OF INTERNAL DISTURBANCE" DECLARED --

UNCLASSIFIED

PAGE 05   STATE   155266   141703Z
QUESTION: DO YOU HAVE ANY COMMENT ON THE PRESIDENT URIBE,S
DECLARATION OF A STATE OF INTERNAL DISTURBANCE? WHAT IS THE
STATUS OF THE EMBASSY? AMERICAN COMMUNITY? ADDITIONAL
TRAVEL WARNINGS ANTICIPATED?

A: PRESIDENT URIBE DECLARED A "STATE OF INTERNAL
DISTURBANCE" EARLY AUGUST 12, AS PROVIDED FOR UNDER THE 1991
CONSTITUTION. A "STATE OF INTERNAL DISTURBANCE" MAY LAST A
MAXIMUM OF 270 DAYS, AND ALLOWS FOR THE PRESIDENT TO ISSUE
DECREE LAWS, DECLARE CURFEWS MAKE SEARCHES WITHOUT WARRANT,
WHILE PROMISING THE PROTECTION OF HUMAN RIGHTS AND CIVIL
LIBERTIES. A RANGE OF COLOMBIAN POLITICAL LEADERS HAVE
SPOKEN OUT IN FAVOR OF THE DECREE.

WE ARE UNAWARE OF SPECIFIC NEW THREATS AGAINST EITHER THE

Current Class: UNCLASSIFIED

UNCLASSIFIED

USAID $10 million grant to DAI for Venezuela program

AWARD/CONTRACT	1. THIS CONTRACT IS RATED ORDER UNDER DPAS (15 CFR 350)	RATING N/A	PAGE 1	OF	PAGES 49

2. CONTRACT NO. (Proc. Inst. Ident.) HDA-C-00-02-00179	3. EFFECTIVE DATE 08-30-2002	4. REQUISITION/PURCHASE REQUEST/PROJECT NO. 12506-0129

5. ISSUED BY CODE	6. ADMINISTERED BY (If other than Item 5) CODE
U.S. Agency for Intl. Development M/OP/HRAM/DATI 1300 Pennsylvania Avenue, NW Room 7.10.15, RRB Washington DC 20523-7100	

7. NAME AND ADDRESS OF CONTRACTOR (No., street, city, county, State and ZIP Code)	8. DELIVERY
Development Alternatives, Inc. 7250 Woodmont Ave., Suite 200 Bethesda MD 20814	☐ FOB ORIGIN ☒ OTHER (See below)
	9. DISCOUNT FOR PROMPT PAYMENT N/A
	10. SUBMIT INVOICES (4 copies unless otherwise specified) ITEM Sect G.3
	TO THE ADDRESS SHOWN IN:

CODE	FACILITY CODE

11. SHIP TO/MARK FOR CODE	12. PAYMENT WILL BE MADE BY CODE
	U.S. Agency for Intl. Development M/FM/CMP/DCB-Room 7.07-133 1300 Pennsylvania Avenue, NW Washington DC 20523-7100

13. AUTHORITY FOR USING OTHER THAN FULL AND OPEN COMPETITION:	14. ACCOUNTING AND APPROPRIATION DATA See Sect G.6.
☐ 10 U.S.C. 2304(c)( ) ☒ 41 U.S.C. 253(c)(5)	

15A. ITEM NO.	15B. SUPPLIES/SERVICES	15C. QUANTITY	15D. UNIT	15E. UNIT PRICE	15F. AMOUNT
001 - 005	Basic - Year 1 : 08/30/02 - 08/29/03 - $5,200,607	1			
006 - 010	Option - Year 2 : 08/30/03 - 08/29/04 - $4,861,255	1			
	TOTAL ESTIMATED COST: $10,061,862				
			15G. TOTAL AMOUNT OF CONTRACT		$10,061,862.00

16. TABLE OF CONTENTS
See Attached Table of Contents

(X)	SEC.	DESCRIPTION	PAGE(S)	(X)	SEC.	DESCRIPTION	PAGE(S)
		PART I - THE SCHEDULE				PART II - CONTRACT CLAUSES	
x	A	SOLICITATION/CONTRACT FORM	1-3	x	I	CONTRACT CLAUSES	38-48
x	B	SUPPLIES OR SERVICES AND PRICES/COSTS	4-6			PART III - LIST OF DOCUMENTS, EXHIBITS AND OTHER ATTACH.	
x	C	DESCRIPTION/SPECS/WORK STATEMENT	7-21	x	J	LIST OF ATTACHMENTS	49
x	D	PACKAGING AND MARKING	22			PART IV - REPRESENTATIONS AND INSTRUCTIONS	
x	E	INSPECTION AND ACCEPTANCE	23				
x	F	DELIVERIES OR PERFORMANCE	24-26		K	REPRESENTATIONS, CERTIFICATIONS AND OTHER STATEMENTS OF OFFERORS	
x	G	CONTRACT ADMINISTRATION DATA	27-31		L	INSTRS., CONDS. AND NOTICES TO OFFER	
x	H	SPECIAL CONTRACT REQUIREMENTS	32-38		M	EVALUATION FACTORS FOR AWARD	

CONTRACTING OFFICER WILL COMPLETE ITEM 17 OR 18 AS APPLICABLE

17. ☐ CONTRACTOR'S NEGOTIATED AGREEMENT (Contractor is required to sign this document and return ____ copies to issuing office.) Contractor agrees to furnish and deliver all items or perform all the services set forth or otherwise identified above and on any continuation sheets for the consideration stated herein. The rights and obligations of the parties to this contract shall be subject to and governed by the following documents: (a) this award/contract, (b) the solicitation, if any, and (c) such provisions, representations, certifications, and specifications, as are attached or incorporated by reference herein. (Attachments are listed herein.)	18. ☒ AWARD (Contractor is not required to sign this document.) Your offer on Solicitation Number M/OP-02-1364 , including the additions or changes made by you which additions or changes are set forth in full above, is hereby accepted as to the items listed above and on any continuation sheets. This award consummates the contract which consists of the following documents: (a) the Government's solicitation and your offer, and (b) this award/contract. No further contractual document is necessary.
19A. NAME AND TITLE OF SIGNER Anna Marie Scott Director of Contracts and Grants	20A. NAME OF CONTRACTING OFFICER Mercedes Eugenia (cb)
19B. NAME OF CONTRACTOR BY (Signature of person authorized to sign)	19C. DATE SIGNED 30 Aug 02	20B. UNITED STATES OF AMERICA BY (Signature of Contracting Officer)	20C. DATE SIGNED 30 Aug 02

STANDARD FORM 26 REV (4-88)

AUG-30-2002 16:46   96%   P.02

USAID $10 million grant to DAI (cont.)

SECTION C - DESCRIPTION/SPECIFICATIONS/STATEMENT OF WORK

C.1 STATEMENT OF WORK - VENEZUELA STATEMENT OF WORK
SPECIFICATIONS

1. BACKGROUND

USAID's Office of Transition Initiatives (OTI) was established in 1994 to respond to countries experiencing a significant and sometimes rapid political transition, which may or may not be accompanied by a social and/or economic crisis. OTI assesses designs and implements programs that have characteristics of being fast, flexible, innovative, tangible, targeted, catalytic and overtly political, focusing on the root causes of the crisis.

A political transition may occur as a result of military intervention like in Kosovo or Haiti; a change in presidency like in Indonesia or Peru; a peace agreement like in Guatemala or Mindanao, Philippines; or in support for peaceful resolution to political strife as in Colombia. OTI is often engaged in the most sensitive political issues of the US government's priority and high profile countries. It operates on the premise that fast, flexible, targeted, catalytic and overt political transition assistance can assist countries in moving away from crisis or other "at risk" situations to stability. Operating under the special authorities of the International Disaster Assistance (IDA) account funding, OTI's initial responses and set-up are rapid; its operations decentralized and streamlined, and its programs brief - normally about two years. Therefore, time is always of the essence in each phase of its program: assessment, deployment, operations set-up, grant making and phase-out or hand-off. With this OTI must have the ability to change, reorient or otherwise refocus its programs and/or respond to new crises in the country or region.

In the field, OTI works with organizations of various political dimensions, including indigenous groups; cooperatives; associations; informal groups; local, regional and national governments; private voluntary organizations (PVO's); student groups; media; international organizations; private sector and coalitions of these entities. Activities may include efforts to: promote reconciliation, conflict resolution and prevention; advance an economic recovery with employment and vocational training; promote independent media with journalist training and law reform; demobilize and reintegrate ex-combatants; increased land access with determining efforts; provide nation-wide training to regional and local elected officials; promote national messages using television, radio and newsprint; reactivate critical NGO's with start-up grants; promote governance with elections support; develop a strong civil society; and initiate rural infrastructure rehabilitation projects with community participation.

OTI frequently uses small grants (from $500 to under $100,000) with defined goals, objectives, deliverables, and reporting, to undertake these initiatives. The prototype grant involves some or all of the following:

USAID $10 million grant to DAI (cont.)

broad and diverse community participation in the grant's design and implementation; community grant counterpart (e.g. in labor or materials); catalytic nature; near-term, high-impact; a media component to amplify the results; tangible visible benefits; and in-kind procurement. The types of grants may vary, but they focus on the root causes of the crisis. Because the grant aims to "advance peaceful democratic change," these grants may focus on issues of higher risk and/or activities not currently being funded by others. These grants are usually (or primarily) "disbursed" in-kind, but cash or cash advances are sometimes more cost effective and efficient depending on the country situation, grantee, grant amount and grant type. Depending on the country and program focus, in-kind assistance may include, but not limited to office equipment, printing materials, conference/seminar venues, agricultural equipment or building supplies.

While the Cognizant Technical Officer (CTO) is Washington-based, one or more U.S. Personal Services Contractors (PSC's) will be assigned in the field to manage, oversee and make day-to-day decisions regarding the contract management and implementation of OTI's country program. The senior OTI field representative (a USPSC) will provide overall programmatic focus, direction, and grant approval. The senior OTI field representative will also determine the types or range of organizations or grantees that will be funded. The country representative will make these decisions based upon U.S. foreign policy interests and in close collaboration with the U.S. Embassy.

Field staffing and administrative structures may also vary according to the demands of each country program and area. There may be one or more OTI regional offices, possibly with a coordinating office in the capital, US Embassy or USAID Mission. In addition OTI may be required to establish a regional program to respond to a crisis. For each program the number of offices and location of offices will be determined by the senior OTI field representative in consideration of the programmatic focus and cost effectiveness and efficiency. Although the country context may vary, OTI works closely in the design and implementation of programs, with the US Embassy, the USAID Mission and the Office of Foreign Disaster Assistance (when present in the country).

OTI often needs a contractor to provide support for all phases of the program. Depending on the program, the contractor will be responsible for administrative, logistics, procurement and finance aspects of the program. More specifically, the contractor will set up offices; purchase office equipment and vehicles; locate and hire staff; establish communications systems; develop and maintain a procurement and financial system; determine grant worthiness; develop and maintain the database; and monitor grant effectiveness and impact. The contractor will be expected to provide varying amounts of funds on short notice and in countries where there are no or limited banking institutions.

Contracting partners are critical to the success of OTI programs because they are expected to overcome the significant challenges posed by "war torn" or otherwise unstable countries in which OTI operates.

2. CONTRACT DURATION

The contract will be for a one-year period, with an option to renew for an additional year at the end of the first year. A six-day workweek is authorized for the first six months, thereafter, with advanced CTO approval.

3. COUNTRY BACKGROUND - VENEZUELA

Venezuela has operated as a functioning, although imperfect, democracy since 1958. Under an arrangement known as punto fijo, the country's two most influential political parties, the social democratic AD (Accion Democratica) and the Christian democratic COPEI, agreed on means to share and control power. Low petroleum prices in the late 1980s produced national financial crises and economic measures that resulted in public outcry over the problems the country faced and the government's inability to mend the situation. The economic stress and the government's sometimes-repressive response to public reaction marked the acceleration of increasingly widespread dissatisfaction with puntofijismo and a weakening of already fragile democratic institutions.

In 1998, Hugo Chavez was elected by an overwhelming majority of voters on a platform to address the problems of the poor and address corruption, which had become a hallmark of the puntofijismo. In recent months, his popularity has waned and political tensions have risen dramatically as President Chavez has attempted to implement several controversial reforms. The tensions came to a head on April when several protesters were shot outside the presidential palace.

Support for democracy remains the top foreign policy priority in the hemisphere for the United States and the United States has a strong interest in ensuring that it endures in Venezuela. For democracy to remain viable, support is needed for the institutions that provide for checks and balances, and ensure the protection of human rights and the free expression of ideas, including, at both the national and local levels, by the media, civil society, political parties, and government institutions.

Venezuela is at a critical juncture in its democratic history and targeted, flexible assistance aimed at supporting democracy could make a difference. A pillar of USAID's strategy is conflict mitigation, and OTI through the contractor chosen through this scope of work will specifically focus on program areas that seek to restore democratic balance and ease societal tensions. The timing for an OTI program is perhaps more relevant today than when the initial assessment was conducted.

4. PROGRAM DESCRIPTION

The contractor will establish a flexible, quick-disbursing small grant fund, able to respond to the rapidly evolving political situation in Venezuela. For the base year the value of the grants to be disbursed will be $3,500,000. If the option is exercised, the value of the grants to be disbursed for the option year will be $3,500,000. This fund will be managed by an OTI field representative reporting to the U.S. Ambassador in Venezuela and supported by the incumbent contractor or cooperating agency. The field representative will maintain close collaboration with other Embassy offices in identifying opportunities, selecting partners, and ensuring the program remains consistent with U.S. foreign policy. The OTI field representative will approve grants under $100,000. The contractor shall develop grant formats that are subject to prior approval by the Office of Procurement/Contracting Officer for each type of proposed grant under this contract (i.e. PIOs, U.S. Organizations, and local, regional and national governments). The contractor will develop a field grant guide and provide trained and experienced grants

USAID $10 million grant to DAI (cont.)

managers for grants under contracts, and more specifically where grants will be provided to U.S. Organizations, PIOs, and local, regional and national governments. In accordance with OTI's approved Grants Under Contracts deviation, dated 1/7/02, grants under this contract are authorized as follows:
1) **U.S. Organizations:** The OTI field representative shall approve grants to U.S. organizations up to $100,000. The Contracting Officer must approve any such grants over $100,000.
2) **Public International Organizations (PIOs):** The OTI field representative shall approve grants to PIOs as defined in ADS 308.7, up to $100,000. The Contracting Officer must approve such grants over $100,000.
3) **Local, Regional and National Government Organizations:** The OTI field representative shall approve grants to local, regional and national government organizations, up to $100,000. Any such grants over $100,000 require prior approval of the Cognizant Technical Officer (CTO).

The minimum criteria for grant selection and approval will include, but not be limited to:

- Consistent with US interests and objectives.
- Consistent with the OTI program areas (some of which are outlined below).
- Demonstrate potential for short-term impact, i.e., less than 6 months.
- Significant counterpart contribution.

The current situation augers strongly for rapid U.S. government engagement. OTI, through its contractor, will act quickly to initiate non-partisan programs that promote pluralism and a democratic society. It will include the participation of all groups that seek to promote an inclusive democracy in Venezuela. OTI will not provide assistance to any groups seeking to unconstitutionally alter the political order. The OTI program will be part of a coordinated approach by the U.S. government supporting democracy.

OTI is already working closely with the USAID's Latin America and Caribbean (LAC) Bureau to ensure a successful handoff of the program. OTI anticipates an initial focus on the following two program areas:

1) **Preserve Democratic Institutions and Processes** - OTI will work with democratically oriented elements in labor, business, political organizations, government and civil society to strengthen democratic institutions and processes. OTI will also work with media institutions through journalist training and other means to ensure balanced coverage of events and political matters in Venezuela.

2) **Enhance Dialogue/Reconciliation/Conflict Mediation** - Deprived of effective democratic means of expressing dissent, the opposition has been forced to implement work stoppages and marches to express its grievances; the most recent iteration ended in violence with over a dozen people killed and many more wounded. President Chavez has promised to institute round-tables and promote general dialogue among various societal groups to reduce tension. OTI will work with NGOs that seek to promote dialogue on an inclusive social and political agenda for Venezuela and open avenues of dialogue currently closed due to the polarization of the population. Through public debates, town hall meetings, and university sponsored conferences, for example, OTI will

USAID-DAI grant for TV commercials, 9 December 2002

Development Alternatives, Inc.
Calle Guaicaipuro con Calle Mohedano
Torre Hener, Piso 2. Oficina 2-B,
Urb. El Rosal 1060-Caracas, Venezuela

Venezuela: Iniciative para la
Construción de Confianza

$(b)(6)$

Ref: Grant agreement between Development Alternatives, Inc. (DAI) and   *(b)(6)*
                (b)(6)
                Grant Number G-3822-101-008

Ref: USAID Contract No. HDA-C-00-02-00179 VICC
                Venezuelan Confidence Building Initiative

Dear   *(b)(6)*

In response to your proposal dated 11/01/2002, Development Alternatives, Inc (hereinafter, simply VICC/DAI") is pleased to award   *(b)(6)*
, or "the Beneficiary"), with a grant, **in kind**, of up to $US 9946.85 to be paid in local currency, in support of its project **Diálogo Social y Formación de Ciudadanía** for the period between 12/09/2002 and 02/07/2003.

The grant is financed by the United States Agency for International Development (USAID) through contract # HAD-C-00-02-00179 with DAI. This grant is to support the activities of the project, according to the attached Program Description (Annex 1), Program Budget (Annex 2) and Standard Provisions (Annex 3). The final proposal, budget and standard provisions (Annexes 1, 2 & 3) are considered integral parts of this Grant Agreement.

All acquisitions made by DAI on behalf of the Beneficiary will be in accordance with USAID procurement regulations. The Chief of Party or designated Program Development Officer (PDO) will make the necessary decisions about any dispute arising from or related to this grant.

All materials produced under the terms of this agreement -- written, graphic, film, magnetic tape, or otherwise -- shall remain the property of both the Grantee and DAI. Both the Grantee and DAI retain rights to publish or disseminate in all language reports arising from such materials, unless otherwise specified in this agreement. The rights and duties provided for in this paragraph shall continue, notwithstanding the termination of the contract or the execution of its other provisions. The Grantee shall acknowledge the support of USAID in any report, audio or video materials, presentation, or document based in whole or in part on work performed under this Agreement. Such acknowledgments shall be as follows:

"This workshop program, documents, radio advertisement,etc. *was prepared with funds provided by Development Alternatives, Inc., with financing from the U.S. Agency for International Development under Contract Number HDA-C-00-02-00179 Venezuela Confidence Building Initiative Project (VICC)."*

The party receiving the grant has full responsibility for executing the project or activity being supported by the grant and for complying with the award conditions. Although the receiving party is encouraged to ask for the opinion and support of VICC/DAI about any specific problems that may arise, this suggestion does not diminish the responsibility of the party receiving the grant. The latter party must apply solid technical and administrative criteria. The grant award does not imply that the responsibility for operative decisions has been transferred to VICC/DAI. The party receiving the grant has the responsibility of notifying VICC/DAI about any significant problems associated with the administrative or financial aspects of the grant award. All information and documents pertaining to this grant must be made available for **three** years following the termination of this grant.

Final Report: The Beneficiary will present the Final Project Progress Report before **02/10/2003** or within fifteen days after the finalization of the last activity of the program should any delay occur during the implementation. The final report will include the accomplishment of the grant benchmarks or milestones for which the grant was awarded. The final report will consist of a technical report and a financial report.

The Beneficiary will send all reports to the designated Program Development Officer, (b)(6) VICC/DAI **Calle Guaicaipuro con Calle Mohedano, Torre Hener, Piso 2. Oficina 2-B, Urb. El Rosal 1060-Caracas, Venezuela.**

Sincerely,

John H. Mc Carty Dec. 6, 2002   Date: 12/06/2002

Jack McCarthy, Director/DAI

Acknowledgement of receipt: (b)(6)

Signed by: _____ (b)(6) _____   Date: 12/06/2002

Department of Defense, 12 December 2002

SUBJ: ██████████████ ▬ CUBAN TROOPS AND
REVOLUTIONARY ARMED FORCES OF COLOMBIA GUERRILLAS IN
VENEZUELA TO SUPPORT CHAVEZ (U)

WARNING: (U) THIS IS AN INFORMATION REPORT, NOT
FINALLY EVALUATED INTELLIGENCE. REPORT CLASSIFIED
S E C R E T - REL UK AUS CAN.

DEPARTMENT OF DEFENSE

DOI: (U) 20021212.

REQS: (U) ████████████████████████

PAGE 4 RUEPMDA1131 S E C R E T REL CAN REL AUS REL UK

SOURCE: (U) //████████████████████

SUMMARY: (S/REL UK AUS CAN) ████████████████████

TEXT: 1 (S/REL UK AUS CAN) ████████████████████

2. (S/REL UK AUS CAN) T

PAGE 5 RUEPMDA1131 S E C R E T REL CAN REL AUS REL UK

3. (S/REL UK AUS CAN) ON 12 DECEMBER, CHAVEZ ORDERED
THE DESTRUCTION OF **TELEVISION** STATIONS OF GLOBOVISION,
TELEVEN, CANAL DOS, AND POSSIBLY OTHER MEDIA OUTLETS.
THESE ATTACKS ARE SCHEDULED TO TAKE PLACE ON THE EVENING
OF 12 DECEMBER.

NATIONAL ENDOWMENT FOR DEMOCRACY

Grant Agreement No. 2003-548.0
between

Grantor: National Endowment for Democracy
1101 15ᵗʰ Street, NW, Suite 700
Washington, DC 20005

Grantee: Súmate, A.C.
Centro Empresarial Los Palos Grandes, piso 7
Av. Andres Bello, Los Palos Grandes, Chacao
Estado Miranda
Caracas, Venezuela

1.   AUTHORITY

This Grant is awarded in accordance with the authority contained in P.L. 98-164, as amended (hereafter referred to as the "Act") and Grant No. S-LMAQM-03-GR-001 between the United States Department of State and the National Endowment for Democracy (hereafter referred to as "the Endowment").

2.   PURPOSE

The purpose of this Grant is to enable the Grantee to carry out the project objectives shown in Attachment A, Program Description, which are consistent with the purposes stated in Section 502(b) of the Act.

3.   GRANT AMOUNT AND BUDGET

The amount obligated under this Grant is $53.400, which is to be expended according to the Grant Budget shown in Attachment B.

The Grantee shall not use funds designated for Program Costs to pay Administrative Costs, nor vice versa, without prior written approval of the Endowment. The Grantee shall also obtain written approval from the Endowment prior to making an expenditure which would increase costs in a major budget category within either the Program or Administrative Costs budget by more than 15 percent or $5,000 (whichever amount is larger) above the amount budgeted for that category. Adjustments among budget categories shall not result in an increase in the total amount of the Grant. The Endowment will not fund costs in excess of the Grant amount shown above.

4.   GRANT PERIOD

The effective date of this Grant is September 12, 2003.
The expiration date of this Grant is September 30, 2004.

All expenditures from Grant funds must be either for authorized activities that take place or for authorized obligations that are incurred during this Grant Period, unless otherwise stated in the Grant. Expenditures for costs incurred prior to the effective date or after the expiration date will be disallowed. Payments made after the expiration date for expenses incurred within the Grant Period are allowable.

If the Grant Period is insufficient for satisfactory completion of the project objectives, the Agreement may be amended to extend the period. The Grantee must request the extension in writing prior to the current expiration date, explaining the circumstances which warrant the extension. Requests for amendments may

CIA letter to Jeremy Bigwood about Súmate, 30 March 2004

Central Intelligence Agency

Washington, D.C. 20505

MAR 3 0 2004

Mr. Jeremy Bigwood
3200 16th Street, N.W., #806
Washington, D.C. 20010

Reference: F-2004-00521

Dear Mr. Bigwood:

This is in response to your letter dated 31 December 2003 in which you appealed the 24 December 2003 determination of this Agency in response to your 5 December 2003 Freedom of Information Act request for records pertaining to "the Venezuelan organization called Sumate (also called SÚMATE) from January 2000 until the present."

Specifically, you appealed our determination to neither confirm nor deny the existence or nonexistence of records pertaining to these records.

The Agency Release Panel has considered your appeal and has determined that the Agency can neither confirm nor deny the existence or nonexistence of records responsive to your request on the basis of Freedom of Information Act exemptions (b)(1) and (b)(3). Therefore, in accordance with Agency regulations, the Agency Release Panel has denied your appeal. For your information, Agency regulations are set forth in part 1900 of title 32 of the Code of Federal Regulations.

In accordance with the provisions of the Freedom of Information Act, you have the right to seek judicial review of this determination in a United States district court.

We appreciate your patience while your appeal was being considered.

Sincerely,

Robert T. Herman

Robert T. Herman
Executive Secretary
Agency Release Panel

NOTES

A note that information is available at "venezuelafoia" means that a document was obtained from the US government by the author or Jeremy Bigwood under the Freedom of Information Act (FOIA) and may be found on the author's website at www.venezuelafoia.info. Note also that "embassy" refers to the US embassy in Caracas.

INTRODUCTION

[1] *Ultimas Noticias* 4 May 2003

[2] Interview with Philip Agee, ex-CIA official.

[3] See US Supreme Court decision in Zadvydas v. Davis.

CHAPTER 1: CHILE AND NICARAGUA: THE COUP COOKBOOK

[1] George Miller (D-CA) cited the figure: "We are going into this election process [spending] $1 billion dollars. We funded the Contras, we have destroyed [Nicaragua's] economy, we have taken Mrs. Chamorro and we pay for her newspaper to run, we funded her entire operation, and now we are going to provide her the very best election that America can buy." *Congressional Record* (House) 4 October 1989, H6642.

[2] See *The Church Report*, 94th Congress, 1st session. "On Covert Action in Chile 1963–1973."

[3] "National Endowment for Democracy: A Foreign Policy Branch Gone Awry," a policy report by the Council on Hemispheric Affairs and the Inter-Hemispheric Education Resource Center, 1990. Today, Republican Senator John McCain and Democrat Madeline Albright oversee the International Republican Institute (IRI) and National Democratic Institute (NDI), respectively.

[4] See William Robinson, *A Faustian Bargain: US Intervention in the Nicaraguan Elections and American Foreign Policy in the Post-Cold War Era* (Boulder, CO: Westview Press) 93. On a side note, Beatríz Rángel currently works with the Cisneros Group in New York and Miami, which is the multinational corporation owned by media mogul Gustavo Cisneros, a Cuban-Venezuelan

involved in the April 2002 coup attempt against President Chávez. Up until mid-2004, Rángel was also a board member of the Inter-American Dialogue, a Washington, DC, think tank that has been highly critical of the Chávez administration.

[5] The CTV continues to be one of the NED's major recipients in Venezuela, as well as a clear instrument of US policy, evident through the union's key role in the 2002 coup d'état against President Chávez and the subsequent illegal oil industry strike in the winter of 2002–2003.

[6] The US government did not use *La Prensa* as its only conduit of information. It also provided funding through the NED, USAID, and the US Information Agency (USIA) to finance radio stations and local television outlets in Nicaragua.

[7] The US government accomplished this by promising not to covertly finance the opposition through the CIA. This promise, however, was promptly broken.

[8] See William Blum, *Killing Hope: US Military and CIA Interventions Since World War II* (Monroe, ME: Common Courage Press, 2004) 163–172.

CHAPTER 2: CHÁVEZ'S RISE TO POWER SPURS VISA DENIAL

[1] See Noam Chomsky and Edward S. Herman, *The Washington Connection and Third World Fascism: The Political Economy of Human Rights, Vol. I* (Boston: South End Press, 1979).

[2] Richard Gott, *In the Shadow of the Liberator: The Impact of Hugo Chávez on Venezuela and Latin America* (London: Verso, 2000).

[3] NACLA Report on the Americas XXVII.5 (March/April 1994) "Report on Venezuela."

[4] See the NACLA report and Gott.

[5] After Chávez's 56 percent, the vote was split as follows: Henrique Salas Römer, 39 percent; Irene Sáez, 4 percent; Alfaro Ucero, less than 2 percent.

[6] "...*los Estados Unidos que parecen destinados por la Providencia para plagar la América de miserias a nombre de la Libertad?*..." Simón Bolívar, *Guayaquil*, 5 August 1829.

Chapter 3: From Tragedy in Vargas to Premonitions of a Coup

[1] Embassy cable from January 2000, available at venezuelafoia.

Chapter 4: US Taxpayer Dollars Create Primero Justicia

[1] See Appendix or venezuelafoia.

[2] IRI-NED grant available at venezuelafoia.

[3] Document mentioning IRI training with Mike Collins available at venezuelafoia.

[4] Information about Collins' session with CEDICE for local journalists available at venezuelafoia.

[5] www.emperors-clothes.com/analysis/iri-ven.htm

[6] Joshua Kurlantzick, "The Coup Connection: How an Organization Financed by the US Government has been Promoting the Overthrow of Elected Leaders Abroad" *Mother Jones* November 2004; also available at www.globalpolicy.org/empire/intervention/2004/coupconnection1104.htm

Chapter 5: Decoding Venezuela

[1] GOV is Government of Venezuela.

[2] Embassy Cable 003392, November 1, available at venezuelafoia.

[3] On February 13, 2002, Carlos Ortega met with Otto Reich in Washington, DC. See www.state.gov/r/pa/prs/dpb/2002/8034.htm.

[4] United States Department of State and the Broadcasting Board of Governors Office of Inspector General, "A Review of US Policy Toward Venezuela: November 2001—April 2002," Report Number 02-OIG-003, July 2002. Redacted for public use.

Chapter 6: A Coup by Any Other Name

[1] E-mail from Lourdes Kistler at ACILS to Mary Sullivan at the Department of State, confirming the Ortega delegation visit and meeting with Otto Reich on February 11, 2002. Available at venezuelafoia.

[2] Intelligence assessment, 20 March 2002, US Southern Command, Joint Intelligence Center. Available at venezuelafoia.

[3] SEIB of 5 March 2002, available at venezuelafoia.

[4] Embassy cable March 2002, available at venezuelafoia.

[5] SEIB of 11 March 2002, available at venezuelafoia.

[6] SEIB of 1 April 2002, available at venezuelafoia.

[7] SEIB of 6 April 2002, available at venezuelafoia.

[8] See David Corn, "Our Gang in Venezuela?," *Nation* 5 August 2002.

[9] Embassy cable April 2002, available at venezuelafoia.

[10] See the documentary film, *Crónica de un Golpe de Estado*, Venezolana de Televisión, 2002.

[11] See *Panorama* 31 August 2003.

[12] Embassy cable 11 April 2002, available at venezuelafoia.

[13] Embassy cable 11–12 April 2002, available at venezuelafoia.

[14] See the documentary footage from the 2003 film *The Revolution Will Not Be Televised*, which captured this television broadcast in which the hosts thank Venevisión, Globovisión, and RCTV for the success of the coup.

[15] www.whitehouse.gov/news/releases/2002/04/20020412-1.html

[16] On November 23, 2004, Spain's foreign minister, Miguel Angel Moratinos, declared that the previous Spanish ambassador in Venezuela received instructions from his foreign minister to support the coup against President Chávez. Just a few days later, Mexico's ex-foreign minister, Jorge Casteñeda, accused the ex-presidents of El Salvador and Colombia of backing the coup against Chávez. Casteñeda affirmed that at the Rio Summit on April 12, 2002, Spain and the US tried to convince the other nations to back the Carmona government. When that proposal was rejected, El Salvador and Colombia spearheaded another.

[17] For NED–IRI funding see venezuelafoia.

[18] Embassy cable 13 April 2002, available at venezuelafoia.

[19] Fairness in Accuracy and Reporting (FAIR) issued a media advisory on April 18, 2002 entitled, "US Papers Hail Venezuelan Coup as Pro-Democracy Move," explaining that papers such as the *New York Times* triumphantly declared that "Chávez's 'resignation' meant that 'Venezuelan democracy is no longer threatened by a would-be dictator.'" The *New York Times* went so far as to blindly write that Chávez "stepped down after the military intervened and handed power to a respected business leader." After Chávez was returned to power on April 13–14, the *Times* ran a second editorial on 16 April 2002, seemingly apologizing for their April 13 celebratory tone: "In his three years in office, Mr. Chávez has been such a divisive and demagogic leader that his forced

departure last week drew applause at home and in Washington. That reaction, which we shared, overlooked the undemocratic manner in which he was removed. Forcibly unseating a democratically elected leader, no matter how badly he has performed, is never something to cheer."

[20] Testimony taken directly from Andrés Izarra. See also "The Media Against Democracy: Venezuela highlights the threat to freedom from corporate control," Naomi Klein, *Guardian* 18 February 2003. See also Venezuelan National Assembly transcripts of special sessions, available online at www.asambleanacional.gov.ve.

CHAPTER 7: AN OFFICE FOR TRANSITIONAL GOVERNMENT

[1] Taken from USAID's own background description of its OTI in a contract between USAID and Development Alternatives, Inc. for $10 million for projects in Venezuela during August 2002–August 2004.

[2] See www.usaid.gov/our_work/cross-cutting_programs/transition_ initiatives

[3] See www.africaspeaks.com/haiti2004

[4] Karenina Velandia Rosales, "EE.UU. invertirá 7 millones en programas para fortalecer la democracia en Venezuela," *El Nacional* 2 March 2003.

[5] See www.usaid.gov/our_work/cross-cutting_programs/ transition_ initiatives

[6] "La Oficina" por Charles S. Shapiro, Embajada de los Estados Unidos, Caracas, Venezuela, Oficina Informative y Cultural, Boletín de Prensa, 2002.

[7] USAID and DAI contract, available at venezuelafoia.

[8] USAID and DAI contract, available at venezuelafoia.

[9] Joel M. Jutkowitz, "Building Confidence out of Discord in Venezuela," DAI News, www.dai.com/dai_news/text_only/ fall_confidence_in_venezuela_text_only.htm

CHAPTER 8: MEDIA CONTROL AND OIL INDUSTRY SABOTAGE

[1] DAI grant, G-3822-101-008, available at venezuelafoia. Please note that USAID and DAI deleted the names of all recipients of the Venezuela project funds. Their stated reason was "fear of persecution" from the Venezuelan government of the groups they were financing.

[2] I provide my own testimony here, and the transcription is

taken from my own footage of the private television channels in Venezuela during December 2002–January 2003, as I was witness to this historical and reprehensible period.

[3] Carlos Rensseler, "Venezuela's Media Mindshock" 20 December 2002, theGully.com. Rensseler is the pseudonym of a Maracaibo businessman whose family immigrated to Venezuela when he was a child. He prefers not to use his own name to protect his family.

[4] President Chávez won the elections in 1998 with more than 57 percent of the vote, defeating six other candidates from the traditional political parties. See also, "How Hate Media Incited the Coup against the President: Venezuela's Press Power," *Le Monde Diplomatique* August 2002.

[5] See Luis Britto Garcia, *Venezuela golpeada. Mediocracia contra democracia* (País Vasco: Editorial Hiro. Colección Sediciones, 2003).

[6] Britto Garcia 216–217.

[7] Britto Garcia, Note 65, citing Roberto Hernández Montoya, "El terrorismo considerado como una de las bellas artes" *La Question* March 2003: 9.

[8] This is all based on my own experience in Venezuela during the December 2002–January 2003 strike. I watched and recorded the private and state-run channels and interviewed numerous Venezuelans about the media war in Venezuela.

[9] See La Ley Orgánica de Protección al Niño y al Adolescente, Artículos 38 (Derecho al Libre Desarrollo de la Personalidad), 32 (Derecho a la Integridad Personal), 35 (Derecho a la libertad de pensamiento, conciencia y religion), 63 (Derecho al Descanso, Recreación, Esparcimiento, Deporte y Juego), 65 (Derecho al Honor, Reputación, Propia Imagen, Vida Privada e Intimidad Familiar), 68 (Derecho a la Información), 71 ("Durante el horario recomendado o destinado a público de niños y adolescentes o a todo público, las emisoras de radio y televisión solo podrán presentar o exhibir programas, publicidad y propagandas que hayan sido consideradas adecuadas para niños y adolescentes, por el órgano competente"), 74 (Envoltura para los Medios que Contengan Informaciones e Imágenes Inadecuadas para Niños y Adolescentes), and Artículo 79 (Prohibiciones para la Protección de los Derechos de Información y a un Entorno Sano).

[10] Rensseler.

[11] Gina María Ramírez, "Powell en Bogotá con golpistas venezolanos," Indymedia Colombia 21 December 2002. See www.colombia.indy-media.org/news/2004/05/12839.php.

[12] www.whitehouse.gov/news/releases/2002/12/20021213.html

[13] www.state.gov/r/pa/prs/dpb/2002/15976.htm

[14] Department of Defense cable, available at venezuelafoia.

CHAPTER 9: ELECTORAL INTERVENTION: THE US'S LAST HOPE

[1] On an interesting note, SAIC had recently taken over the development of security systems and databases for electronic voting machines in the US market.

[2] See USAID documents at venezuelafoia.

[3] See www.sumate.org

[4] Juan O. Tamayo, "US Split Grows Over Chávez Links to Rebels," *Miami Herald* 28 December 2003: 21A.

[5] Martin Arostegui, "Analysis: Venezuela's Islamic Links," United Press International 1 September 2003.

[6] NED and CIPE–CEDICE information available at venezuelafoia.

[7] NED memorandum available at venezuelafoia.

[8] On Friday, 20 August 2004, Roger Noriega, assistant secretary of state for Western Hemisphere affairs, stated, "We have invested a lot of money in the democratic process because we have faith in civil society, which is a pillar of representative democracy. We have given money to similar types of NGOs in Venezuela by means of the State Department and USAID. Civic groups with the mission to defend their democratic institutions and demand basic rights for Venezuelans also represent a good investment."

[9] "US firm embroiled in Venezuela referendum controversy defends its exit poll," Associated Press 19 August 2004.

CHAPTER 10: CLANDESTINE STRATEGIES AND THREATS

[1] House Report: 108-576 to H.R. Bill 4754, NATIONAL ENDOWMENT FOR DEMOCRACY. The language included in this bill was the result of this investigation. The NED requested an extension in late 2004, which was approved by Congress, but they still haven't delivered the report.

[2] "Violence will allow us to remove him. That's the only way we have... [Chávez] must die like a dog, because he deserves it..."

Ex-President Carlos Andrés Pérez interview with Venezuelan newspaper *El Nacional* 26 July 2004.

[3] See "Orlando Urdaneta llama al magnicidio desde Miami," *Temas* 2 November 2004.

[4] See www.comandosf4.org

[5] José de Córdoba, "Miami's Little Havana Finds New Foe in Venezuelan Leader," *Wall Street Journal* 29 January 2003.

GLOSSARY

ACILS (American Center of International Labor Solidarity): An alliance of unions, governments, and corporations in Latin America, fusing three international institutions: the African American Labor Center (AALC), the Asian American K-AAFLI and the AFL-CIO. The American Center for Workers' Solidarity, also known as the Solidarity Center, is headed by John J. Sweeney, the secretary general of the AFL-CIO. The ACILS finances parties and social organizations to overthrow governments that are "enemies" of the United States. For example, in 2001 and 2002, through the mediation of this organization, USAID supplied salaried Cubans working for Washington with electronic communications equipment, books, and other propaganda materials, in addition to cash payments, to create unions "favorable" to the US.

AD (Acción Democrática—Democratic Action Party): This party was founded in Caracas in 1941 by Rómulo Betancourt, with social democratic tendencies. The party has held power on six occasions under Presidents Rómulo Gallegos, Rómulo Betancourt, Raul Leoni, Carlos Andrés Pérez (twice), and Jamie Lusinchi.

AFI (Air Force Intelligence): According to its official description, its mission is espionage, surveillance, and aerial reconnaissance. The planes, which formerly were equipped only with photographic cameras, are now veritable flying fortresses, equipped for electronic warfare. This department is also responsible for the launching of spy satellites.

AI (Army Intelligence): Army Intelligence is officially defined as one of the military espionage corps destined to facilitate strategic information to commando operatives. In truth, it is one of the minor departments within the intelligence community, but it is the most trustworthy whenever the US is involved in armed conflict because its agents collect essential information on the spot.

AIFLD (American Institute for Free Labor Development): Financed by USAID and controlled by the CIA, the AIFLD was created in

February 1962 to control union movements in Latin America. An administrative council made up of powerful businessmen with vested interest in Latin America determines priority activities of the AIFLD. The presidency is in the hands of the general director of the chemical giant, the W. R. Grace Corporation, and the president of the North American chapter of the Order of Malta, J. Peter Grace; the organization promotes the collaboration of classes and bosses, mimicking a model common to fascist corporations.

ALF-CIO (American Federation of Labor and Congress of Industrial Organizations): Founded in 1955 when the two main US unions active in Europe, the AFL (represented by Irving Brown) and the CIO (represented by Victor Reuther), joined forces to create the AFL-CIO with the blessing of Averell Harriman, new administrator of the Marshall Plan, together with his emissary in Europe, Milton Katz. Since its beginnings, the AFL-CIO has directly participated in the destabilization of numerous countries in Europe and Latin America. This organization receives the most funding from USAID.

APF (American Political Foundation): The APF was born in 1979 out of the alliance between the US Republican and Democratic parties, who wished to strengthen the American bipartite system. Its first national president was a Republican, William Brock; a Democrat, Charles Manatt, served as vice president in charge of finances. The APF took on the interchange between the two political parties in order to facilitate alliances with parties in other parts of the world. At the end of the 1970s, when the political climate changed, this organization created the Democratic Project, from which the NED emerged to increase US commitment to the promotion of "democratic" values abroad.

CD (Coordinadora Democrática—Democratic Coordinator): An umbrella organization of a broad spectrum of opposition to Hugo Chávez, including groups from the extreme right (Primero Justicia) and the extreme left (Bandera Roja), the parties that were in power during the period 1959–1999 (the Christian Socialist COPEI and the Democratic Action, the Movement toward Socialism MAS), and others. This organization collected signatures for the referendum to recall the Venezuelan president.

CDN (Coordinadora Democrática Nicaragüense—Nicaraguan Democratic Committee): Anti-Sandinista coalition financed by the United States; it boycotted the 1984 Nicaraguan elections.

CEDICE (Centro de Divulgación del Conocimiento Económico—Center for the Publication of Economic Knowledge): Based in Caracas, it calls itself "a non-profit civilian association whose chief aim is to publicize political and economic philosophies, giving priority to the free actions of individual initiative and the analysis of organizations and conditions that permit the existence of free societies." Actually, it is an investigative center that is funded by CIPE and other American organizations in order to provide incentive for programs favoring the "democratization" of "beneficiary" countries and of incentives in the world economy.

CESAP (Centro al Servicio de la Acción Popular—Center for the Service of Popular Action): Calling itself a center in the service of social projects, CESAP is financed by the United States and its director publicly justified the coup d'état against President Chávez in April 2002.

CEVEU (Consejo de Empresarios Venezuela–Estados Unidos—Council of Venezuelan and US Businessmen): An organization that groups Venezuelan businessmen with commercial, financial, and investment interests from the United States.

CIA (Central Intelligence Agency): The Central Intelligence Agency was created in 1947 under the Nation Security Law. Its responsibilities go beyond the simple collection of information. It is also called upon to intervene in nations where diplomacy has been deemed insufficient and military action would be counter-productive or inconvenient. Its activities include psychological warfare; financing pro-US political parties abroad; provocations; actions against unions, parties, or groups opposed to US foreign policy; supporting and fomenting coups d'état; and training mercenaries and armed groups. Secret special operations increased without limits during the early 1950s. The Iran–Contra scandal (financing the Contras in Nicaragua by illegally selling arms to Iran) and the Bank of Credit and Commerce International (BCCI) scandal (BCCI was the preferred bank of the agency and also of the Medellín drug cartel) placed the CIA in the eye of the hurricane. The CIA was later discredited by revelations made during the

Clinton administration regarding the promulgation of torture techniques to diverse police, military, and intelligence organisms throughout the continent provided through manuals produced by the agency and the atrocities committed by the CIA in Guatemala made public through hard evidence and documents (proof that the Agency utilized and protected torturers). At the end of the Cold War, because of the lack of enemies, the CIA oriented its actions toward the collection of economic information, protecting US interests in emerging markets, and waging war against "terrorism" and drug trafficking. While throughout Latin America amnesty laws that protect the dictators of the past are being questioned and reviewed for legality, the CIA remains unable to escape or accept the past. In August 2000, the agency denied the release of files proving its role in the coup d'état against Salvador Allende in Chile in 1973, at the hand of Augusto Pinochet.

CIPE (Center for International Private Enterprise): Another organization funded by the NED, CIPE acts as an affiliated and tax-free counterpart of the American Chamber of Commerce. This corporation was established in 1983 to support free trade policies and a number of business associations. Also, it is involved in the training of business leaders and their mobilization within political processes. In Eastern Europe, for example, CIPE directs support programs for various business societies and provides them with recommendations and assistance for legislative activities. Hungary, Rumania, Czechoslovakia, and Poland were the recipients of this "advice." The Krakow Industrial Society was formed in Poland in an attempt to publish a national newspaper. This publication was a response to an interest in cultivating and promoting a free enterprise system, in what is known in Western business jargon as "good economic and democratic development." The board of directors is drawn from the business community. Included are William Archey and Richard Lesher of the Chamber of Commerce and representatives of conservative think tanks such as Robert Kruble from the Heritage Foundation and Peter Dougnam from the Hoover Institution. At the present time, it is directed by Thomas J. Donohue, president of the Chamber of Commerce, the "boss of bosses."

Civic Alliance of the Civil Society (Alianza Cívica de la Sociedad Civil): An alliance that unifies several civilian organizations for the defense of "democracy" in Venezuela. This organization signed a document that recognized the legitimacy of the Carmona government, and it was one of the most active in approving the referendum recalling President Chávez.

CNE (Consejo Nacional Electoral—National Electoral Council): The electoral power of the Bolivarian Republic of Venezuela, which organizes and supervises everything related to popular elections by way of universal, direct, and secret voting. It has the ability to organize the elections of unions and of civilian organizations, whenever they so request. Among its functions, it regulates the electoral laws and resolves any doubts or problems resulting from any omissions within these laws; it issues direction in financial and political-electoral matters and applies sanctions whenever laws have not been followed. It is able to declare null and void any election, either totally or partially.

COPEI (Committee of the Independent Political Electoral Organization): The Christian Socialist party founded by Rafael Caldera on January 13, 1946, in Caracas. It also goes by the names, of Christian Socialist Party, Christian Democratic Party, or simply the Christian Democrats.

COSEP (Supreme Council of Private Enterprise): Founded on February 16, 1972, as a civilian non-profit, COSEP pulled together the Nicaraguan private big business sector and was the heart and nerve center of the CDN parties. More than any other social sector of the country, the COSEP always had the closest and most direct ties with the US embassy: it united the class that ruled Nicaragua until 1979 with the US government and with the CDN parties, dominating them completely.

CTV (Confederación de Trabajadores Venezolanos—Confederation of Venezuelan Workers): The CTV is the country's most powerful union organization, with more than a million members; it was one of the main organizers of the strikes and protests in the two months that culminated in the 2002 attempted coup. Then secretary general of this confederation, Carlos Ortega, was closely connected to Carmona.

DAI (Development Alternatives, Inc.): Private consulting firm used by businessmen and governments with headquarters in the US. It was founded in Washington in the 1970s and in recent years has been operating mainly in Afghanistan, Iraq, and Liberia, using

USAID funding. It supports the undercover operations of the US government.

DIA (Defense Intelligence Agency): It coordinates intelligence information obtained by the various branches of the armed services (army, navy, marines, air force, coast guard, and special forces) and administers counter-measures (including the administration of security in the ultra-classified installations of the United States). In short, it is the espionage department of the US Army. Created in 1961, its chief mission is to facilitate intelligence to the commanders of the armed forces.

DCI Strategic Warning Committee: This committee directs the entire protection and advisory warning system of the United States. It is made up of representatives of the CIA, DIA, NSA, State Department/INA, and NIMA.

Department of State: The US department for foreign affairs has its own espionage service, but as in many cases, its agents are not exactly spies, rather analysts and brainy specialists who deliver reports that enable the secretary of state to "hear what must be known, not what would like to be known," as stated in its official description. This department is intertwined with the rest of the intelligence community in order to digest all the information produced, but they do not collect data on the spot—they basically receive the information sent to the department from elsewhere.

Department of the Treasury: This department is also part of the intelligence community, even though it possesses only a small division for the collecting of its own information. It is really fed by the intelligence sent to it by the rest of the agencies related to the international economic policies of the US. It advises the US government when general economic policy decisions are to be made, especially when they relate to international markets.

FBI (Federal Bureau of Investigation): The FBI is the spy agency with powers to execute activities within US territory. It really has the characteristics of a federal police force—it can act in any of the states—but one of its prime missions is to generate intelligence for decisions made on interior polices. It is the oldest of the intelligence agencies. It was founded in 1908, though it was not known by its current name until 1935.

FOIA (Freedom of Information Act): On March 12, 1997, the Committee on Government Reform and Oversight approved and adopted a report entitled "A Citizen's Guide on Using the Freedom of Information Act and the Privacy Act of 1974 to Request Government Records." The Freedom of Information Act establishes the presumption that all persons have access to documents in the possession of the distinct agencies and departments of the US government, if they follow FOIA regulations to request such documents and information. Supposedly, documents in the possession of other entities associated with the federal government are also subject to the FOIA, including private entities that receive government funding. Nevertheless, FOIA also includes a series of exemptions that enable any agency or entity to deny the release or declassification of information in the name of national security, to protect the privacy of individuals or trade secrets, the functioning of the government, or other important interests.

FTAA (Free Trade of the Americas Act): The area of free trade in the Americas, known in Spanish as ALCA. It appeared in 1994 and essentially promotes US economic annexation of Latin America.

FTUI (Free Trade Union Institute): This is the only basic nucleus of the NED—which preceded it—and it is the most complicated. It was created in 1962 as part of the Alliance of Progress initiative developed by President John F. Kennedy. It contained the work that the Free Trade Union Committee (FTUC) carried out with the CIA. This committee had been founded in 1944 to fight the leftist tendencies of European unions. The board of directors is comprised of leaders of the AFL-CIO. The FTUI, a bipartisan group, supported President Ronald Reagan's Central American policies and channeled funds from the NED to the Nicaraguan opposition and to the newspaper *La Prensa*. It was a funnel for the grants that the NED set aside for union groups and for the "independent press" in the Soviet Union and other countries of Eastern Europe. The Department of International Affairs, to which FTUI belongs, is the nerve center of this organization's formation of foreign policy and for its global operations. From its inception, this institute has been strongly linked not only with the US government, but also with the multinational corporations that invest in Latin America. In 1984, the FTUI made headlines because of the transfer of funds made by the NED, using this Institute, to two French groups opposed to the policies of President François Mitterand.

GPS (Global Positioning System): The GPS is a group of satellites—twenty-four to be exact—orbiting the earth, monitoring the location of persons, objects, buildings, et cetera using portable receivers or stations.

Guarimba: Method used by the Venezuelan opposition to boycott government acts, consisting in violent occupation of the streets, destruction of buildings, firing weapons—all intended to incite a repressive governmental reaction. During tense moments, these activities, taking place particularly in areas of Caracas inhabited by the upper class, have resulted in the "enclosure" of residents and thus generated hostility.

IMET (International Military Education and Training): US military education for people from other countries. IMET offers opportunities for the professional development of very carefully selected soldiers and civilian candidates. It grants funds to military and civilian personnel in associated nations so that they may attend professional development courses in US military academies. Many of the graduates advance in their careers until they reach high-ranking levels in the directorships of their respective military and governmental institutions.

INTESA (Information and Technology Enterprise): Enterprise that was composed of Petróleos de Venezuela S.A. (PDVSA) and the US multinational Science Applications International Corporation (SAIC) to control all the information of Venezuela's state-owned oil company, PDVSA. It was a project prompted by the so-called "nomina mayor" of PDVSA and put into the hands of the SAIC, a façade for the CIA, all the information and intelligence of the world's largest petroleum enterprise. Its initial investment was contributed by Venezuela, which had a right to only 40 percent of shares. Such a "business deal" was justified by the fact that this arrangement would drastically lower the costs of computer services—but this did not happen; SAIC charged its partner PDVSA about $80 million annually. INTESA not only controlled all of PDVSA's vital information, but it could also manipulate it and even intervene at will and without scruples. Their servers housed all the financial, technical, budgetary, and business data of the enterprise. During the oil industry strike of 2002–2003, INTESA was the principal participant in the sabotage of the petroleum industry. PDVSA decided not to renew the contract upon expiration and

SAIC sued them for expropriation; this was ratified by OPEC but not accepted by the Venezuelan government.

IRI (International Republican Institute): This Republican Party component of the NED is headed by Senator John McCain.

MAS (Movimiento al Socialismo—Movement toward Socialism): Composed originally of members ousted from the Communist Party or from ultra-radical organizations, it became allied with traditional parties in opposition to President Chávez. It took part in the CD, which demanded a referendum to depose Chávez.

MBR-200 (Movimiento Bolivariano Revolucionario—Revolutionary Bolivian Movement): Organized and led by Chávez, it began on November 17, 1982, following the oath sworn by a small group of fellow soldiers at Saman de Güere, a location that was once an encampment of Simón Bolívar. The "200" in the name marked the 200th anniversary of the birth of Simón Bolívar. In 1997, it was transformed into Movimiento V República.

MCI (Marine Corps Intelligence): The MCI is specialized in rapid military intervention operations, from landings to invasions, using lightning attacks to rescue hostages and so forth. The MCI is little more than a link in the network of espionage departments, especially in naval jurisdictions, but is also related to the air force. Its analysts, above all else, draft plans for all possible scenarios so that once the moment arises to execute a mission, everything is meticulously planned.

MVR (Movimiento V República—Movement Fifth Republic): Founded on October 21, 1997 in Caracas, with Hugo Chávez as its general director. It is the electoral version of the Revolutionary Bolivarian Movement-200, which could not present a candidate in the elections because of legal impediments contained in the Political Parties Act prohibiting the use of the name "Bolivarian." (Since it is of such national importance, Bolívar's name cannot be used for any party affiliations.) For that reason, the name Fifth Republic was adopted, which both hinted at the creation of a new republic and at the same time maintaining the already well-known combination of phonetics and initials—MBR and MVR.

National Intelligence Office for Warning: The mission of this office is to advise and assist the CIA director in all surveillance matters, and also to coordinate activities for national intelligence. Its sources are located outside of the United States. This office is expected to directly alert the president and the National Security Council in the case of danger to national security.

NDI (National Democratic Institute for International Affairs): This institute is headed by Madeleine K. Albright. It is the section of the Democratic Party within the NED and defines itself as "a nonprofit organization for the consolidation and amplification of democracy in the world."

NED (National Endowment for Democracy): Officially created on November 6, 1982, the NED was established by statute as a nonprofit organization, yet its financing is approved by Congress and included in the USAID section of the Department of State budget. In order to maintain the illusion that it is a private organization, the NED also receives very small donations from three associations, which are themselves indirectly financed by federal contracts: the Smith Richardson Foundation, the John M. Olin Foundation, and the Lynde and Harry Bradley Foundation. The majority of the historic figures linked to clandestine CIA actions have at some time been members of the board of directors or the administrative council of the NED, including Otto Reich, John Negroponte, Henry Cisneros, and Elliot Abrams. The present chairman of the NED board of directors is Vin Weber, founder of the ultraconservative organization Empower America, and campaign fundraiser for George W. Bush in 2000. NED's president is Carl Gershman, an ex-Trotskyist gone awry. Once a member of the Social Democrats, USA, Gershman later became one of the neoconservative Reagan-Bush hawks.

NI (Navy Intelligence): The mission of naval intelligence is to provide vital information to the fleet, wherever it may be located. All US naval bases in the world include a division of the Naval Security Group, whose fundamental mission is espionage.

NIMA (National Imagery and Mapping Agency): This used to be known as the National Geospatial-Intelligence Agency, a part of the Department of Defense that developed, among other things, aeronautical map-making. Originally the NIMA was a department within the Air Force Intelligence Agency until it left in 1996 to become a new intelligence agency. From that time on, part of the information obtained from surveillance satellites is later analyzed in this department, which receives the information to draft maps or to locate possible objectives.

NRO (National Reconnaissance Office): This office is responsible for the enormous US satellite operation. It has been in operation since the 1960s, but its existence was not revealed until 1992, when Washington declassified its name. Even though satellite launching depends on the air force, the NRO controls all satellites once they are in orbit. It also directs various other programs such as reconnaissance and surveillance satellites, and those that spy on defense signals or communications.

NSA (National Security Agency): Even though this agency is relatively unknown, it spends nearly one half of the US's annual espionage budget. Founded in 1952 by President Harry Truman, the NSA is responsible for espionage of foreign communications. Its star program, Echelon, has spy stations all over the world that intercept international communications.

NSC (National Security Council): The NSC is a group that designs policy for the army and for the intelligence services of the nation, concerning matters of national and international security. It answers directly to the president. It has a secret committee that directs the "black" or undercover operations and also a sub-committee that directs and controls covert-up policies.

NYPD (New York Police Department): The police department of the city of New York.

OPEC (Organization of Petroleum Exporting Countries): OPEC was founded in Baghdad on September 14, 1960, and has its headquarters in Vienna. Its aims are the unification and coordination of petroleum policies of the member nations, and the defense of their interests as producer countries. It arose as a reply to the decrease of the official price of petroleum, agreed upon unilaterally by the large distributing companies in August of 1960. Initially there were five member countries: Saudi Arabia, Iraq, Iran, Kuwait, and Venezuela; it grew to include another six members: Qatar, Indonesia, Libya, the United Arab Emirates, Algeria, and

Nigeria. Ecuador and Gabon used to be members. The following other important petroleum producing countries are not members of OPEC: Canada, Mexico, Norway, the United States, Russia, and Oman.

OTI (Office of Transition Initiatives): The OTI is an institution that is created in countries where the US faces governments that have not yet acceded to US interests. The webpage of the US embassy in Caracas reads: "The OTIs have arisen to administer assistance programs in the countries of the former Communist Bloc who are in a transition phase toward full democracy and toward a free trade economy." Since 1994, they are established through the initiative of the USAID "to offer a response in countries that are passing through a significant and sometimes rapid political transition, which may or may not be accompanied by a social and/or economic crisis." The OTI "evaluates, designs, and executes programs that are characterized as being expeditious, flexible, innovative, tangible, motivated, catalytic, and openly political and which remove the root causes of crisis." The OTIs have been used in Kosovo, Haiti, Indonesia, Peru, Guatemala, the Philippines, and Colombia, among other nations. Generally speaking, the USAID orients its OTIs to put in place relationships with political organizations, communications media, and non-governmental organizations, and to supply the finances and training necessary to obtain the desired results. In Venezuela, it was created in July of 2002 in the US embassy in Caracas.

PDVSA (Petróleos de Venezuela, SA—Venezuelan Petroleum, South America): Perhaps the most important petroleum enterprise in the world, PDVSA belongs to the Venezuelan government. Founded on January 1, 1976, with the aim of being in charge of the national petroleum industry and all its planning, coordination, and supervision, it concluded the process of returning the hydrocarbon rights worked by the foreign companies on Venezuelan soil. PDVSA produces more than three million barrels per day, refines more than a million barrels daily, and exports more than two and a half million barrels of hydrocarbons on a daily basis.

Plan Bolívar (Bolívar Plan): It was installed in 1999 upon the arrival in power of Hugo Chávez. It is an association of PDVSA with the National Armed Forces to contribute to the improvement of social structures and the standard of living. It seeks to offer complete services to the poorest of the population, to repair and maintain schools, to modernize the public roads system, to provide housing for the homeless, and to bring reasonably priced quality goods to those who need them most.

PP (Polo Patriótico—Patriotic Pole): Political coalition composed of MAS, MVR, and Homeland for All (PPT) parties, all supporters of Chávez's victorious candidacy in the presidential campaign of 1998.

PPT (Patria Para Todos—Homeland for All): Founded on September 26, 1997, during a public ceremony in the Radio City Theatre in Caracas, as a result of a division within the party La Causa R. From inception, the PPT put all its efforts into the struggle against social exclusion and offered a humanist project whose central theme was the integral development of mankind (Declaration of Principles). Some of the members are Aristóbulo Istúriz, José Albornoz, Rafael Uzcátegui, Jacobo Torres, Xiomara Lucena, Rodolfo Sanz, Lelis Páez, and Vladimir Villegas.

POLOFF (Embassy Political Office): The political office in the US embassies throughout the world, headed generally by a CIA or other US intelligence officer.

Punto Fijo Pact: Faced with the proximity of general elections in 1958 and then with two attempted military coups, the presidential candidates of the AD, the Democratic Republican Union (URD), and the Committee of the Independent Political Electoral Organization, Rómulo Betancourt, Jóvito Villalba, and Rafael Caldera, respectively, met on October 31 of that year in Caldera's residence, Punto Fijo Estate in Caracas, to sign a pre-electoral pact that basically agreed to a system of alternating the power. Excluded from the pact, intentionally, was the Communist Party of Venezuela, even though it was part of the Patriotic Junta; likewise left out was the Republican Integration Movement, which had many well-known personalities as members. In November 1958, the URD candidate, Rear Admiral Wolfgang Larrazabal Ugueto, removed himself from the presidency of the government junta in order to dedicate himself to the presidential campaign. Only AD and COPEI stayed in the pact, agreeing to establish a government of "national unity," in which one of the signing pact members would have equal representation in the executive cabinet of the winner of the election.

SEIB (Senior Executive Intelligence Brief): A memorandum for executive officers in the principal US intelligence services. It has fairly broad distribution and generally contains information summarizing intelligence activities. They tend to be careful about protecting sources and the methods used to obtain the information. The originator of this type of report was Richard Clarke, coordinator of antiterrorist activities for the National Security Council (NSC).

VICC (Iniciativa para la Construcción de Confianza—Initiative for the Construction of Confidence): Officially a program of USAID and DAI in Venezuela. It commenced on August 1, 2002, with the goal of "providing opportune and flexible assistance in order to strengthen democracy in Venezuela."

UNO (Unión Nacional Opositora de Nicaragua—ONE, Nicaragua National Opposition Union Party): It was founded on May 29, 1986, composed of CDN members, among whom were former Somoza supporters and ex-communists. Their common ground was an anti-Sandinista point of view.

USAID (United States Agency for International Development): USAID functions as an instrument of CIA penetration into civil society by enabling the "legitimate" funding of millions of dollars to promote US foreign policy abroad and influence internal politics of foreign nations while avoiding congressional scrutiny.

USIA (United States Information Agency): This agency is part of the US Department of State. During Bill Clinton's presidency, starting on October 1, 1999, after 46 years acting as the organization of public diplomacy, the USIA ceased to exist as such; its functions were absorbed within the Department of State.